权威·前沿·原创

皮书系列为

“十二五”“十三五”国家重点图书出版规划项目

智库成果出版与传播平台

中国城市生活质量报告（2020）

REPORT ON THE QUALITY OF LIFE IN CHINESE CITIES (2020)

中国经济实验研究院

张连城　张　平　杨春学
郎丽华　王　钰　张自然／著

图书在版编目（CIP）数据

中国城市生活质量报告. 2020 / 张连城等著. -- 北京：社会科学文献出版社，2021.3

（城市生活质量蓝皮书）

ISBN 978-7-5201-8200-3

Ⅰ.①中… Ⅱ.①张… Ⅲ.①城市-生活质量-指数-研究报告-中国-2020 Ⅳ.① D669.3

中国版本图书馆CIP数据核字（2021）第060924号

城市生活质量蓝皮书

中国城市生活质量报告（2020）

著　　者 / 张连城　张　平　杨春学　郎丽华　王　钰　张自然

出 版 人 / 王利民
组稿编辑 / 恽　薇
责任编辑 / 高　雁
文稿编辑 / 刘　燕

出　　版 / 社会科学文献出版社·经济与管理分社（010）59367226
地址：北京市北三环中路甲29号院华龙大厦　邮编：100029
网址：www.ssap.com.cn
发　　行 / 市场营销中心（010）59367081　59367083
印　　装 / 天津千鹤文化传播有限公司

规　　格 / 开　本：787mm×1092mm　1/16
印　张：21　字　数：283千字
版　　次 / 2021年3月第1版　2021年3月第1次印刷
书　　号 / ISBN 978-7-5201-8200-3
定　　价 / 158.00元

本书如有印装质量问题，请与读者服务中心（010-59367028）联系

本年度报告执笔人

张连城　张　平　杨春学　郎丽华　王　钰

张自然　赵家章　王　银　郝宇彪　郭　毅

殷诗絮

中国经济实验研究院简介

改革开放以来，特别是社会主义市场经济体制建立以来，中国经济发展已经进入一个崭新的阶段。中国已经成为世界第二大经济体，人均国民收入已经达到中等收入国家的水平；同时，中国改革也已经从“浅水区”进入“深水区”，改革所面临的形势更为艰巨和复杂，必须从“摸着石头过河”的“实践试错”向着利用现代手段进行政策模拟和评估的“实验试错”转变。另外，从学科发展的角度看，经济学发展到今天，科学研究正在向协同研究和交叉学科研究的方向发展。这在客观上要求我国的高等院校、研究机构打破学科界限、打破单位界限，整合一切可利用的资源，精诚合作，不断创新，只有这样才有可能应对中国社会所面临的新挑战。在这种背景下，经过长期调研、论证和精心准备，首都经济贸易大学与中国社会科学院经济研究所合作，共同成立了“中国经济实验研究院”。

早在2006年，首都经济贸易大学与中国社会科学院经济研究所就组建了“中国经济增长与周期研究中心”，并联合香港经济导报社，从2007年至2019年，共同成功举办了13届“中国经济增长与周期高峰论坛”。该论坛已经成为国内外研究宏观经济的著名学者进行学术交流的重要平台。2010年，首都经济贸易大学与中国社会科学院经济研究所又组建了“中国城市生活质量研究中心”，经过对城市生活质量指标体系的深入研究和几个月的调研，在2011年举办的第五届“中国经济增长与周期高峰论坛”上，首次发布了中国30个省会城市的生活质量指数，在国内引起了很大的反响，并引起了国际同行和世界银行等国际机构的关注。中国经济实验研究院就是在上述研究机构的基础上，于2012年成立的。

研究院现设有“中国经济增长与周期研究中心”、“中国城市生活质量研究中心”、“数量经济研究中心”和“世界贸易组织研究中心”，并设有经济运行与国际贸易实验室、经济预警实验室、经济数据处理与计算机仿真实验室和数字化调查中心。

中国经济实验研究院成立以后，在对原有机构和实验室进行整合的基础上，拟设如下机构：

1. 中国经济实验研究院专家委员会

2. 中国经济增长与周期研究中心

3. 中国城市生活质量研究中心

4. 数量经济研究中心

5. 研究生指导中心和博士后流动站

6. 中国经济增长与周期论坛

7. 经济运行与经济预警实验室、计算机仿真实验室

中国经济实验研究院成立以后，近期的主要任务如下。

第一，进一步深入开展中国经济增长与经济周期的研究，继续办好中国经济增长与周期高峰论坛，并逐步实现国际化。

第二，进一步扩大生活质量指数研究的覆盖面，使其逐步从省会城市扩展到全国中等城市、从国内扩展到国际，同时实现指数发布的常态化。此外，生活质量只是经济增长质量的一部分内容，研究院将逐步把经济增长质量的研究纳入研究视野，争取取得一批高质量的科研成果。

第三，不断拓展经济实验研究的范围，开展经济改革实验、政策

效应实验、经济增长压力实验等，为中国改革、政府机构及相关部门提供可量化的决策支持，并努力服务社会。

第四，成立具有国际化特色的研究生指导团队，依托首都经济贸易大学经济学院，同时与国外大学紧密合作，共同指导硕士和博士研究生，招收博士后，为首都经济贸易大学的人才队伍建设做出贡献。

第五，中国经济实验研究院 2005 年以来与国际上 20 多所高校建立了紧密的合作关系，将以此为基础，开展广泛的国际合作和国际学术交流，共同进行科学研究，协同创新，构造研究院的国际化特色。

中国经济实验研究院的宗旨是推动经济实验研究，繁荣经济科学，为推进我国的经济体制改革、提高经济增长质量、促进经济发展服务。中国经济实验研究院的定位目标是经过我们的不懈努力，在未来成为这一领域具有国际一流水平的高度开放的研究机构。

主要编撰者简介

张连城 首都经济贸易大学研究生毕业，2004年曾在美国新英格兰大学进修。现为首都经济贸易大学教授、博士生导师、中国经济实验研究院院长。在首都经济贸易大学（北京经济学院）任教30余载。1998~2002年担任首都经济贸易大学经济系副主任，2002~2012年担任首都经济贸易大学经济学院院长，并在2009~2011年兼任研究生部主任。任教期间，于1981~1985年先后兼任中国经济学团体联合会机关报《全国经济学团体通信》和《经济学周报》编辑部主任、记者部主任、研究发展部主任。1985~1987年在国家经济体制改革研究所兼任城市经济体制改革办公室副主任和从事研究工作。目前在多家学会兼任副会长、常务理事。

主要研究领域为经济增长、经济周期与宏观经济政策。在该领域发表了近百篇学术论文和10余部专著、教材、译著，其中5项科研成果获教育部、北京市哲学社会科学优秀科研成果一、二等奖。2011年被国务院批准为享受国务院政府特殊津贴的专家。1986年以来，曾主持多项社科基金课题，目前主持着国家社会科学基金重大项目“正确处理经济平稳较快发展、调整经济结构、管理通胀预期的关系研究”（12&ZD038），担任我国经济理论界“现代外国经济学大系”和“实证中国”丛书的主编。领导着国家级经济学特色专业、国家级经济学国际化人才培养实验区、国家级经济学核心课程教学团队的建设工作。

张　平　1988年加入中国社会科学院经济研究所，曾任宏观经济室副主任、经济增长室主任、经济所所长助理、经济所副所长，现为国家金融与发展实验室副主任。中国社会科学院二级研究员，研究生院教授、博士生导师。主要研究领域：经济增长和中国家庭行为、宏观政策和上市公司。曾经参加和主持世界银行、亚洲开发银行、国际劳工组织等多项国际合作；主持多项国家社科基金重点招标课题、中国社会科学院重大课题和国家交办的课题。合作四次获得孙冶方经济科学奖，合作获得中国社会科学院专著一等奖，独立获得专著二等奖一次，合作获得专著二等奖和三等奖。2009年入选人力资源与社会保障部百千万人才工程国家级候选人。2010年获得国务院政府特殊津贴。

杨春学　首都经济贸易大学、中国社会科学院研究生院教授，博士生导师。曾任职于中国社会科学院经济研究所，曾任《经济学动态》主编。主要研究领域：欧美经济思想史、现实问题的政治经济学。最主要的学术兴趣在于寻求人类本性、个人行为与制度之间的内在关系。主要代表作有《经济人与社会秩序分析》《利他主义经济学的追求》《和谐社会的政治经济学基础》等。

郎丽华　经济学博士，博士生导师，首都经济贸易大学经济学院教授、校学位委员会委员，经济学院学位委员会主任、学术委员会副主任，世界贸易组织研究中心副主任，兼任北京国际经济贸易学会副会长、中国服务贸易协会专家委员会副主任委员等职。主要研究领域：国际贸易理论与政策、国际贸易战略、世界经济。国家级双语示范课和来华留学生英文授课品牌课程“国际商务”的负责人、北京市教学名师、北京市宣传文化系统“四个一批”人才。先后在《人民日报》《经济研究》《世界经济》《管理世界》《经济学动态》《经济管理与研究》等报纸和杂志上发表数十篇学术论文。主持并参与北京市哲学社会科学规划项目、北京市教育委员会社会科学研究计划项目、国家社科基金重大项目等研究工作。

摘　要

本书对 35 个城市的生活质量进行持续跟踪调查，通过调查得到 35 个城市生活质量的满意度情况评价指数。此次满意度调查采用网络调查方法获取相应数据，为了保证调查对象分布的合理性和广泛性，在调查期内调查人员发放了足够多的问卷，调查过程中问卷总访问量为 28050 次，筛选后剩余有效问卷 8824 份。通过对问卷数据进行统计分析，汇总整理了 4 个关于城市生活质量满意度的分指数，包括消费者信心指数、教育质量满意度指数、健康满意度指数和医疗服务满意度指数，对应描述了城市生活质量的一个特定方面。为了便于国际比较，消费者信心指数是依据密歇根消费者信心指数的算法计算的，具体算法是将 1966 年第一季度美国的消费者信心指数确定为 100，如果分值高于 100，则说明消费者信心强于 1966 年第一季度美国的水平。

调查结果表明，2019 年，中国 35 个城市消费者信心指数加权平均值为 138.61，而且每个城市的消费者信心指数都高于 100，2019 年 5 月 17 日美国的密歇根消费者信心指数为 102.4，低于中国 35 个城市消费者信心指数加权平均值。中国 35 个城市居民教育质量满意度指数加权平均值为 67.02，中国 35 个城市居民健康满意度指数加权平均值为 57.26，中国 35 个城市居民医疗服务满意度指数加权平均值为 63.04，以上三个分指数均处在一般（50）和满意（75）之间。

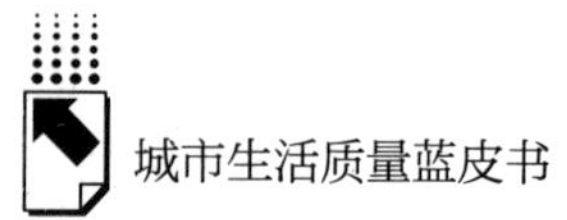

考虑到国际通行做法，同时也便于国际比较，前期城市生活质量客观（社会经济数据）指标部分不再计入指标体系，但是依然会收集反映35个城市生活质量的客观数据，以便于更好地把握35个城市生活质量的实际情况，所需要的客观数据均来自国家权威机构有关35个城市社会经济的数据库，数据来源的权威性和可靠性是有保障的。收集的客观数据还将用在对城市生活质量满意度影响因素的分析中，依据相关理论选取客观数据作为回归变量。

从对35个城市生活质量指数评价的结果看，在我国经济向高质量发展转变的过程中，消费者信心基本稳定；可是从教育、医疗、健康的相关满意度看，短期内满足人民日益增长的美好生活需要和不平衡不充分的发展之间的矛盾依然存在。未来我国政府应继续释放政策和制度红利，使微观经济主体活力得到激发，同时创新和完善宏观调控措施，促进产业结构升级和经济转型；进一步做好“六稳”（稳就业、稳金融、稳外贸、稳外资、稳投资、稳预期）工作，在稳定经济增长的同时不断提高经济增长质量，提高教育、医疗等公共服务水平，为居民获得高质量的生活水平和保持身心健康提供强有力的制度和政策保障。

关键词： 城市生活质量　消费者信心指数　教育质量满意度指数　健康满意度指数　医疗服务满意度指数

目　录

Ⅰ　总报告

Ⅱ　分报告

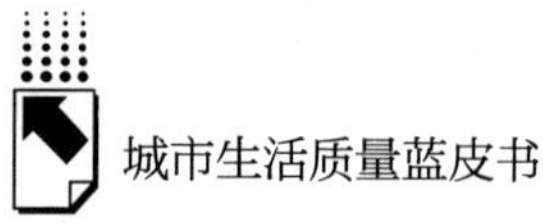

皮书数据库阅读**使用指南**

总 报 告

General Report

B.1 2019年城市生活质量调查报告

中国经济实验研究院中国城市生活质量研究中心课题组*

摘　要：本书对中国35个城市的生活质量进行持续跟踪调查，通过调查得到35个城市生活质量的满意度情况评价指数。调查结果表明：2019年中国35个城市居民的消费者信心指数为138.61，介于临界点（100）和有信心（150）之间，同2018年的消费者信心指数（115.48）相比，消费者信心有所增强；教育质量满意度指数加权平均值为67.02，略低于2018年的水平（69.37）；健康满意度指数加权平均值为57.26，也比2018年的水平（64.48）低；医疗服务满意度指数加权平均值为63.04，同样比2018年的水平（65.31）低，上述三项指数均介于一般（50）和满意（75）之间。从调查的结果看，未来我国政府应继续释放政策和制度红利，同时创新和完善宏观调控措施，使微观经济主体活力得

* 课题组成员：张连城、张平、杨春学、郎丽华、赵家章、张自然、王银、陆明涛、郝宇彪、王钰、郭毅。

到激发，促进产业结构升级和经济转型；进一步做好“六稳”（稳就业、稳金融、稳外贸、稳外资、稳投资、稳预期）工作，在稳定经济增长的同时不断提高经济增长质量，提高教育、医疗等公共服务水平，为居民获得高质量的生活水平和保持身心健康提供强有力的制度和政策保障。

关键词： 消费者信心 教育质量 健康 医疗服务

《中国城市生活质量报告》是一项持续性的研究，也是集体研究的成果。2006 年，首都经济贸易大学和中国社会科学院经济研究所共同组建了“中国经济增长与周期研究中心”，截至 2019 年共同成功举办了 13 届“中国经济增长与周期高峰论坛”。2010 年，又组建了“中国城市生活质量研究中心”，研究中心在 2011 年举办的第五届“中国经济增长与周期论坛”上首次发布了《中国城市生活质量报告》。截至 2019 年，研究中心对城市生活质量的调研已连续进行了 9 年，研究成果产生了较为广泛的影响，使得本课题研究和所产生的成果具有较高的学术价值。自 2012 年开始，研究中心每年将《中国城市生活质量报告》以蓝皮书的形式出版（中英文），截至 2019 年，已经出版了 7 部。《中国城市生活质量报告》在国内学术界产生了积极的影响，不仅为同行学者提供了丰富的数据，还对本领域的研究起到了积极的推动作用。同时，围绕城市生活质量这一主题，参与本项目的研究人员还撰写了多篇研究报告。

中国城市生活质量体系（QLICC）的构建是我国学术界在这一领域的首个尝试。在 QLICC 的设置上，20 多名国内外学者在广泛参考欧盟、美国和其他国家生活质量体系的基础上，结合中国现阶段的经济社会特征，经过一年多的研究和近几年的不断完善，创立了我国评价城市生活质量、指明生活质量持续改进路径和方向的生活质量体系。尽管目前该体系可能还存在一些不尽如人意的地方，但毕竟填补了我国在这一领域的空白，为评价当前城市居民的生活质量、政府决策、城市发展、提高城市居民福利和经济增长质量提供了一个可供参考的坐标和努力的方向，并且这个方向是与党和政府的执政理念相一致的；同时，QLICC 为我国经济工作者深入研究中国居民的生活质量，构建更科学的城市生活质量指标体系奠定了基础。

国外对生活质量的调查，大多停留在满意度调查层面。《中国城市生活质量报告》在最初的 QLICC 的设置上，不仅设立了主观（满意度）指数，也设立了生活质量客观指数，并将两者进行对比。通过对比可以发现某些城市生活质量满意度与客观生活质量的一致性或反差，从而可以为决策者和城市管理者提供更多的信息，有助于其有针对性地改进工作，提高居民生活质量，改善民生。此外，在官方机构发布的众多指标中，遴选哪些指标构建科学的客观生活质量指数，也是本项目组在精心研究的基础上确定的。同时，为了佐证城市居民的生活质量和对生活质量的预期，在 QLICC 之外，项目组还设置了影响生活质量最大因素、房价预期、就业前景等的专项调查。

中国经济实验研究院中国城市生活质量研究中心 2019 年 4~5 月继续对 35 个城市的生活质量进行跟踪调查，本次调查是 2011 年以来的第 9 次年度调查，并通过统计分析和计算得出了评价 2019 年中国 35 个城市生活质量的满意度指数，该指数在 2019 年第十三届“中国经济增长与周期高峰论坛”上发布。本报告是 2019 年度中国 35 个城市生活质量指数的调查结果。

一　对 2019 年中国城市生活质量调查的说明

2019 年度继续采用 2018 年的做法，延续了此前的指标体系和样本选取方法。调查问卷发放的方法如下：为了使调查的空间分布既广泛又合理，先通过 IP 号段对 35 个城市的居民进行甄别，再通过问卷星网络调查平台发放和回收调查问卷。此次调查的问卷总访问量为 28050 次，通过筛选得到 8824 份有效问卷。

（一）往年调查主观指标情况说明

2011 年，中国经济实验研究院创建了中国城市生活质量体系，即 QLICC。该体系包括两个部分：主观（满意度）指标体系（简称“满意度指标体系”）和客观（社会经济数据）指标体系。2012~2016 年，满意度指标体系和客观指标体系基本延续了以往的方法（见表 1）。

表 1　2012~2016 年中国城市生活质量满意度指标体系

指标名称	主观问题	答案赋值				
		100	75	50	25	0
生活水平满意度	收入现状（50%）	很满意	满意	一般	不满意	很不满意
	收入预期（50%）	很乐观	乐观	一般	不乐观	很不乐观
生活成本满意度	生活成本	很低	低	一般	高	很高
人力资本满意度	人力资本	很满意	满意	一般	不满意	很不满意
社会保障满意度	医疗和养老保障（50%）	很满意	满意	一般	不满意	很不满意
	城市安全（50%）	很满意	满意	一般	不满意	很不满意
生活感受满意度	生活节奏（50%）	很慢	慢	一般	快	很快
	生活便利（50%）	很便利	便利	一般	不便利	很不便利

2017 年的调查也基本延续了以往的方法，在采用以往的指标体系、问卷发放办法和样本选取方法的基础上，略做了一些调整。主要

是考虑到我国居民通信习惯已经发生了较大的变化，由原来使用座机转变为以手机为主，因此 2017 年的样本人群选取的方法改用计算机辅助电话调查（CATI）的方法，调查对移动电话用户展开。根据移动电话号码 11 位数的前 3 位代表网络运营商代码，中间 4 位代表地区号，后 4 位代表个人代码，判断用户的地区分布，进而确定 35 个城市的 4 位区号代码段，再通过最后 4 位号码进行随机抽样。通过上述过程就可以建立调查的样本库，这种方法既可以保证样本的空间分布又可以覆盖 35 个被调查的城市，同时可以使每个城市的样本量相对均衡。

2017 年中国城市生活质量体系仍然分为主观（满意度）指标体系和客观（社会经济数据）指标体系，均包含生活水平、生活成本、人力资本、社会保障、生活感受即健康 5 个方面的分指数，5 个分指数各自反映了城市生活质量的某一特定方面。

2017 年满意度指标体系构成有两个变化。第一个变化是社会保障满意度指数内涵的变化。2012~2016 年，社会保障满意度指数是由医疗和养老保障满意度指数、城市安全满意度指数的加权平均值构成的；2017 年的社会保障满意度指数主要针对居民对医疗保险个人负担部分是否满意设计问卷，使问题更有针对性，调查结果更有现实意义。第二个变化是引进健康满意度调查，并以健康满意度指数替代生活感受满意度指数。2012~2016 年，生活感受满意度指数由生活节奏满意度指数和生活便利满意度指数加权得出；2017 年，通过国际通用的 8 条简明量表（SF-8）调查方法得出居民健康满意度指数，替代生活节奏满意度指数和生活便利满意度指数。这样更能真实地反映居民对生活质量的感受，并且可以进行国际比较。健康满意度指数包括身体健康和心理健康两个方面，各占 50% 的权重。赋值区间也是 0~100，用 T-score 的方法处理调查数据，得到最终分值（见表 2）。

表 2　2017 年中国城市生活质量满意度指标体系

指标名称	主观问题	答案赋值				
		100	75	50	25	0
生活水平满意度	收入现状（50%）	很满意	满意	一般	不满意	很不满意
	收入预期（50%）	很乐观	乐观	一般	不乐观	很不乐观
生活成本满意度	生活成本	很低	低	一般	高	很高
人力资本满意度	人力资本	很满意	满意	一般	不满意	很不满意
社会保障满意度	医疗保障	很满意	满意	一般	不满意	很不满意
健康满意度	身体健康（50%）	赋值区间为 0~100，运用 T-score 方法处理调查数据，得到相关赋值				
	心理健康（50%）					

（二）2018年调查的主观指标调整说明

2018 年中国城市生活质量体系仍然分为主观指标体系和客观（社会经济数据）指标体系。2018 年在调查方法、指标体系设置以及样本选取等方面基本延续了以往的做法，但对满意度指标体系做了较大的调整。

根据我国居民通信习惯的进一步变化，2018 年调查采取电话调查和网络调查相结合的方法。电话调查采用计算机辅助电话调查的方法，对移动电话用户进行调查。按照样本分布，首先选取 35 个城市区号代码段，再根据后 4 位号码随机抽样，生成调查使用的样本库。网络调查先根据 IP 号段对 35 个城市进行甄别，在有效调查问卷中随机抽取样本。两者相结合，充分保证了调查空间分布的合理性和广泛性。

为了进一步与国际接轨并进行国际比较，我们对满意度指标体系进行了较大调整，以便更好地反映当前城市居民的生活质量及获得感。2018 年主观指标体系调整为 4 个满意度分指数，分别为消费者信心指数、教育质量满意度指数、健康满意度指数和医疗服务满意度指数，分别反映了城市生活质量的某一特定方面。其中，消费者信心指数采用密歇根消费者信心指数计算方法获得，在国际上具有可比性。问卷开发人员将美国 1966 年第一季度的结果定为 100，如果分值高于 100，则说明消费者信心强于美国 1966 年第一季度。教育质量满意度指数根据教育部发布的《教育部关于推进中小学教育质量综合评价改革的意见》（教基二〔2013〕2 号）[①] 中“建立健全中小学教育质量综合评价体系”的五个指标简化而成。健康满意度指数则利用美国疾病控制与预防中心（CDC）开发使用的健康度量指标，即过去 30 天中身体或心理不够健康的天数。若相加得到天数大于 30 天，则设为 30 天。数值越大，说明身体或心理在过去 30 天越不健康。

（三）2019年调查的指标调整说明

2019 年的中国城市生活质量体系进行了较大的改变，主要是将原有体系中的客观（社会经济数据）指标部分去掉了，新的体系仅包括满意度指标体系，这样做主要是为了更好地与国际接轨以及进行国际比较。2019 年的中国城市生活质量体系在满意度方面与 2018 年相同，即由 4 个满意度分指数构成：消费者信心指数、教育质量满意度指数、健康满意度指数、医疗服务满意度指数。在 4 个分指数中，消费者信心指数参考了美国密歇根消费者信心指数的构建和评价方法，赋值区间为 0~200；而教育质量满意度指数的构建主要是依据我国《教育部关于推进中小学教育质量综合评价改革的意见》（教基二〔2013〕2 号）中“建立健全中小学教育质量综合评价体系”的五个指标；健

① 《教育部关于推进中小学教育质量综合评价改革的意见》（教基二〔2013〕2 号），中华人民共和国教育部网站，2013 年 6 月 3 日，http://old.moe.gov.cn/publicfiles/business/htmlfiles/moe/s7054/201306/153185.html。

康满意度指数利用美国疾病控制与预防中心开发使用的健康评价指标，可以分为身体健康和心理健康两部分；医疗服务满意度指数主要测度居民对医疗机构服务质量和个人承担的医疗保险部分的满意度。后三个指数的取值范围为0~100。

此外，受我国居民通信手段变化的影响，2019年的问卷调查方法与2018年有所不同，2019年全部采用网络调查，通过IP号段对35个城市的空间样本进行识别。

二　2019年中国35个城市生活质量满意度指数

2019年中国城市生活质量的满意度指数分别从消费者信心、教育质量、健康、医疗服务等四个方面进行说明。[①]

（一）消费者信心指数

2019年对中国35个城市居民消费者信心的调查结果如表3所示，从总体上看，中国35个城市消费者信心指数加权平均值为138.61，介于临界值（100）和有信心值（150）之间，这表明消费者对于当前及其未来5年之内的经济前景和经济形势持乐观态度，对于个人收入水平和收入预期趋向满意。与2018年的水平（115.48）相比，消费者信心整体上是有所增强的。与美国相比也是高的，2019年5月17日美国公布的密歇根消费者信心指数为102.4。

从城市个体的表现看，35个城市的消费者信心指数均高于临界值100。从排名的情况看，处于前10位的城市依次是南宁（145.35）、重庆（143.36）、南昌（143.03）、济南（142.10）、青岛（142.01）、

① 下文中的主要调查结果前期已经发布，具体内容见张连城等:《城市居民生活质量“总体稳定、稳中有忧”——2019年中国35个城市生活质量报告》,《经济学动态》2019年第9期，第3~17页。

贵阳（141.87）、长春（141.44）、郑州（141.27）、乌鲁木齐（140.83）、南京（140.40）。其中，东部地区城市 3 个，中部地区城市 3 个，西部地区城市 4 个。排名处于后 10 位的城市分别是呼和浩特（137.50）、福州（137.08）、上海（136.78）、天津（136.64）、沈阳（135.39）、银川（135.34）、北京（135.09）、广州（134.03）、石家庄（130.35）、成都（129.63）。与 2018 年相比，重庆、长春、乌鲁木齐、南京、海口、西安、杭州等 7 个城市居民的消费者信心上升比较显著；上海、沈阳、广州、深圳、兰州、长沙等 6 个城市居民的消费者信心下滑比较明显。

表 3　2019 年中国 35 个城市居民消费者信心指数

排名		城市	2019 年指数	排名		城市	2019 年指数
2019 年	2018 年			2019 年	2018 年		
1	7	南宁	145.35	15	4	长沙	139.68
2	28	重庆	143.36	16	24	大连	139.15
3	5	南昌	143.03	17	17	厦门	139.02
4	2	济南	142.10	18	30	杭州	138.85
5	9	青岛	142.01	19	19	昆明	138.49
6	6	贵阳	141.87	20	15	哈尔滨	138.04
7	29	长春	141.44	21	20	西宁	137.93
8	18	郑州	141.27	22	14	武汉	137.85
9	22	乌鲁木齐	140.83	23	21	宁波	137.85
10	34	南京	140.40	24	11	兰州	137.69
11	33	海口	140.26	25	12	深圳	137.63
12	13	太原	139.96	26	16	呼和浩特	137.50
13	8	合肥	139.77	27	23	福州	137.08
14	35	西安	139.74	28	1	上海	136.78

续表

排名		城市	2019年指数	排名		城市	2019年指数
2019年	2018年			2019年	2018年		
29	26	天津	136.64	33	10	广州	134.03
30	3	沈阳	135.39	34	27	石家庄	130.35
31	32	银川	135.34	35	31	成都	129.63
32	25	北京	135.09			平均值	138.61

在中国城市生活质量体系中，消费者信心指数由个人收入变化、未来收入预期、对未来1~5年国家经济形势的判断、购买耐用消费品时机选择等分指数构成。从细分指数的变化情况看，2019年中国城市居民消费信心基本稳定的主要原因是居民对未来收入水平稳定持乐观态度，同时对我国未来1~5年内经济将保持良好的发展势头具有信心。在当前投资和出口增速放缓，经济下行压力不断增大的情况下，消费者具有较强的消费信心，表明未来1~2年消费需求有可能成为经济增长的稳定器。

再结合被调查者的背景资料看，如表4所示，消费者信心指数受性别、年龄、学历的影响，存在个体差异。首先从性别看，男性消费者信心指数略高于女性。其次从年龄看，消费者信心指数最高的年龄段为20~29岁，消费者信心指数最低的年龄段是40岁及以上。可见，由于不同年龄段的居民承受的生活压力大小不同，其消费信心有所不同。最后从学历看，消费者信心指数与学历水平正相关，消费者信心指数最高的消费者具有研究生及以上的学历，消费者信心指数较低的是具有大学本科以下学历的消费者。这是由于学历的差异导致人们的就业和收入有所不同，进而导致消费者信心的差异。

表 4 不同性别、年龄、学历的消费者信心指数情况

分类标准		消费者信心指数
性别	男	139.44
	女	138.99
年龄	20~29 岁	140.19
	30~39 岁	139.50
	40 岁及以上	134.23
学历	大学本科以下	138.86
	大学本科	139.06
	研究生及以上	140.80

（二）教育质量满意度指数

教育质量满意度指数是用来评价城市居民对学校素质教育情况满意水平的，数值为 100 代表非常满意，数值为 75 代表满意，数值为 50 代表一般，数值为 25 代表不满意，数值为 0 代表非常不满意。表 5 是 2019 年中国 35 个城市居民教育质量满意度指数的调查结果。从调查结果看，2019 年中国 35 个城市居民对教育质量的满意度指数加权平均值为 67.02，处于一般（50）和满意（75）之间，比 2018 年的数值（69.37）略低。教育质量满意度指数本身由 3 个细分指数组成，主要被调查的问题包括“您认为目前普通中小学：1. 是否注重学生的品德发展教育；2. 是否注重学生身体和心理素质的全面发展；3. 是否注重培养学生的兴趣特长”。从调查结果反映出来的这 3 个细分指数的平均值来看，35 个城市的居民认为学校做的最好的是注重学生的品德发展教育，得分为 70.64；其次是注重学生身体和心理素质的全面发展，分值为 65.73；得分最低的是注重培养学生的兴趣特长方面，分值为 64.76。上述 3 个细分指数的得分均介于一般（50）和满意（75）之间。

表 5　2019 年中国 35 个城市居民教育质量满意度指数

排名		城市	2019 年指数	排名		城市	2019 年指数
2019 年	2018 年			2019 年	2018 年		
1	7	厦门	73.02	19	19	南昌	66.73
2	31	青岛	70.99	20	32	合肥	66.67
3	33	海口	70.75	21	15	西宁	66.62
4	13	长沙	70.08	22	18	南京	66.55
5	8	贵阳	69.94	23	21	大连	66.40
6	14	银川	69.17	24	16	重庆	66.27
7	11	深圳	69.00	25	29	北京	66.19
8	35	杭州	68.83	26	30	西安	65.76
9	28	郑州	68.80	27	22	武汉	65.74
10	25	宁波	68.76	28	20	福州	65.55
11	2	乌鲁木齐	67.98	29	34	广州	65.30
12	3	兰州	67.97	30	4	天津	65.17
13	5	南宁	67.96	31	26	哈尔滨	63.49
14	9	太原	67.61	32	23	石家庄	63.45
15	1	济南	67.54	33	27	上海	62.84
16	6	呼和浩特	67.43	34	12	成都	61.86
17	24	长春	66.82	35	17	沈阳	61.70
18	10	昆明	66.75			平均值	67.02

从城市排名情况看，35 个城市居民的教育质量满意度指数排名处于前 10 位的城市依次是厦门（73.02）、青岛（70.99）、海口（70.75）、长沙（70.08）、贵阳（69.94）、银川（69.17）、深圳（69.00）、杭州（68.83）、郑州（68.80）、宁波（68.76）；排在后 10 位的城市分别是西安（65.76）、武汉（65.74）、福州（65.55）、广州（65.30）、天津（65.17）、哈尔滨（63.49）、石家庄（63.45）、上海（62.84）、成都（61.86）、沈阳（61.70）。从经济发达程度看，北京、上海、广州是

经济最发达的城市，也应该是教育最为发达的城市，其教育资源相对优质和集中，居民对教育质量的满意度也应该相对较高，但调查的结果却不是这样。这三个城市居民的教育质量满意度指数排名分别列第25位、第33位和第29位。与2018年比较而言，排名有较大上升的城市包括青岛、海口、杭州、郑州、宁波、合肥等城市，排名有所下降的城市包括天津、成都、沈阳、济南、呼和浩特等城市。

本报告除了对35个城市居民对教育质量的满意度进行调查外，还对居民比较关心的问题进行补充调查，包括以下3问题：子女学业负担、学生或子女进入重点或热门中小学的主要障碍、子女课外教育支出的居民感受。调查的结果如表6、表7和表8所示。

表6为2019年中国35个城市居民对子女学业负担的满意度情况，指数越高代表感觉子女的学业负担越轻。从数值的分布看，数值为100代表非常轻，数值为75代表较轻，数值为50代表一般，数值为25代表较重，数值为0代表非常重。从整体情况看，35个城市该项调查的平均分值为26.17，处于一般和较重之间，并十分接近较重状态。从城市排名情况看，得分最高的是济南（32.02），得分最低的是太原（21.27）。也就是说，35个城市中感觉子女学业负担最轻的是济南居民，感觉子女学业负担最重的是太原居民。实际从得分的数值分布看，35个城市居民均感觉子女学业负担较重。

表6　2019年中国35个城市居民子女学业负担满意度指数

排名		城市	2019年指数	排名		城市	2019年指数
2019年	2018年			2019年	2018年		
1	22	济南	32.02	5	1	青岛	29.13
2	14	贵阳	30.13	6	16	海口	28.81
3	5	深圳	29.88	7	4	乌鲁木齐	28.36
4	3	天津	29.64	8	33	南昌	28.31

续表

排名		城市	2019年指数	排名		城市	2019年指数
2019年	2018年			2019年	2018年		
9	13	北京	28.12	23	35	西安	25.35
10	7	厦门	27.81	24	25	宁波	24.81
11	30	兰州	27.40	25	6	福州	24.74
12	17	长沙	26.88	26	26	大连	24.43
13	11	南宁	26.80	27	10	哈尔滨	24.28
14	21	昆明	26.78	28	20	广州	23.93
15	28	重庆	26.72	29	2	南京	23.61
16	12	郑州	26.59	30	29	杭州	23.55
17	24	呼和浩特	26.55	31	18	长春	23.31
18	31	合肥	26.53	32	19	石家庄	22.78
19	27	西宁	26.31	33	23	沈阳	22.53
20	9	武汉	25.81	34	34	上海	21.70
21	8	成都	25.61	35	32	太原	21.27
22	15	银川	25.40			平均值	26.17

从排名的变化情况看，35个城市居民对子女学业负担满意度比2018年有较大幅度上升的城市包括济南、贵阳、海口、南昌、兰州、重庆、合肥、西安等城市；比2018年满意度有大幅度下降的城市包括南京、福州、哈尔滨、长春、石家庄、成都、武汉等城市。

表7为2019年中国35个城市居民对学生或子女进入重点或热门中小学的主要障碍的认知状况。从整体情况看，选择学生或子女入学的主要障碍在于学区不同的受访者占全国所有受访者的32.60%，有23.30%认为是学生成绩不够，有20.18%的受访者认为择校费用太高，19.05%的受访者认为主要障碍是户口不在本地。此次调查的结果与2018年相比，择校费用和成绩因素占比上升明显，

其中成绩因素上升可以很好地反映出教育公平性的改善，而择校费用太高、学区不同和户口不在本地等因素，是制约教育均衡发展的主要因素。

表7　2019年中国35个城市居民对学生或子女无法进入重点或热门中小学的主要障碍的认知情况

单位：%

序号	城市	占比				
		学区不同	学生成绩不够	择校费用太高	户口不在本地	其他问题
1	北京	39.95	18.56	21.13	19.85	0.52
2	成都	31.33	21.03	27.90	17.60	2.15
3	大连	41.56	22.08	15.15	17.32	3.90
4	福州	34.20	23.38	14.72	22.94	4.76
5	广州	21.02	29.30	21.66	23.89	4.14
6	贵阳	18.39	36.77	12.56	17.94	14.35
7	哈尔滨	31.62	21.79	26.50	14.10	5.98
8	海口	27.19	24.12	15.35	24.56	8.77
9	杭州	32.19	26.18	21.89	15.88	3.86
10	合肥	39.74	23.08	15.38	17.95	3.85
11	呼和浩特	34.20	18.61	20.78	18.61	7.79
12	济南	40.17	20.52	18.78	17.90	2.62
13	昆明	26.43	23.79	24.67	16.74	8.37
14	兰州	30.26	28.07	16.67	14.47	10.53
15	南昌	31.76	23.61	15.88	24.03	4.72
16	南京	43.65	17.92	22.48	13.36	2.61
17	南宁	33.04	19.57	13.48	26.52	7.39
18	宁波	32.16	24.67	14.98	22.91	5.29
19	青岛	41.63	21.46	15.88	14.59	6.44
20	厦门	27.39	23.91	13.48	28.70	6.52

续表

序号	城市	占比				
		学区不同	学生成绩不够	择校费用太高	户口不在本地	其他问题
21	上海	35.75	20.47	18.91	20.98	3.89
22	深圳	24.09	21.45	22.11	28.71	3.63
23	沈阳	47.83	23.04	14.78	13.04	1.30
24	石家庄	30.87	23.91	20.87	22.61	1.74
25	太原	29.69	20.52	23.14	19.65	6.99
26	天津	41.37	19.54	19.87	15.31	3.91
27	乌鲁木齐	35.24	27.75	19.82	11.89	5.29
28	武汉	37.10	19.68	24.52	15.81	2.90
29	西安	28.88	19.83	34.91	13.79	2.59
30	西宁	23.26	26.51	16.74	21.40	12.09
31	银川	22.91	36.12	24.67	11.01	5.29
32	长春	30.30	19.48	25.11	19.05	6.06
33	长沙	29.18	28.33	15.88	22.75	3.86
34	郑州	33.33	18.86	22.81	21.49	3.51
35	重庆	25.96	28.53	26.92	17.63	0.96
2019 年		32.60	23.30	20.18	19.05	4.86
2018 年		33.50	17.10	17.40	19.20	12.80

表 8 是 2019 年中国 35 个城市居民对子女课外教育支出的满意度指数的调查结果，分值分布为 0~100，分值越趋近于 0 表明子女课外教育支出越高，分值越接近 100 表明子女课外教育支出越低，具体层次区分为：0 表示非常高，25 表示较高，50 表示合适，75 表示较低，100 表示非常低。从整体情况看，35 个城市居民的子女课外教育支出满意度指数平均值为 24.92，处于非常高（0）和较高（25）之间，偏向较高。这一结果表明，城市居民家庭支出中子女课外教育支出是比较重要的支出。

表 8　2019 年中国 35 个城市居民子女课外教育支出满意度指数

排名		城市	2019 年指数	排名		城市	2019 年指数
2019 年	2018 年			2019 年	2018 年		
1	9	贵阳	31.33	19	20	呼和浩特	24.90
2	4	厦门	29.60	20	23	北京	24.63
3	7	西宁	28.87	21	26	武汉	24.31
4	12	济南	28.45	22	16	宁波	23.94
5	22	合肥	28.08	23	29	杭州	23.72
6	34	南昌	28.05	24	11	兰州	23.64
7	5	福州	28.03	25	13	郑州	23.28
8	6	海口	27.89	26	28	太原	22.93
9	24	重庆	27.65	27	32	成都	22.77
10	10	昆明	26.73	28	31	西安	22.75
11	21	长沙	26.66	29	19	石家庄	22.31
12	27	深圳	26.50	30	17	南京	21.38
13	2	广州	26.42	31	33	沈阳	20.94
14	15	南宁	26.39	32	25	大连	20.51
15	1	青岛	26.16	33	35	哈尔滨	19.65
16	8	银川	26.09	34	18	长春	18.98
17	14	乌鲁木齐	25.09	35	30	上海	18.58
18	3	天津	24.96			平均值	24.92

整体情况与 2018 年相比，教育质量满意度、子女学业负担满意度和子女课外教育支出满意度都有所下降，这说明我国在教育体制改革、优质教育资源供给和教育资源配置的改善等方面还需要进一步推进。

（三）健康满意度指数

健康状况调查的主要目的是反映城市居民对自己健康水平的感知程度。数值分布为 0~100，对应的满意度水平划分如下：得分为 0 代表差，得分为 25 代表一般，得分为 50 代表好，得分为 75 代表很好，得分为100代表非常好。从整体情况看，本次调查的35个城市居民健康满意度指数加权平均值为57.26，处于好（50）和很好（75）之间，低于2018年的得分（64.48）。表9是2019年中国35个城市居民健康满意度指数的调查结果。

表9　2019年中国35个城市居民健康满意度指数

排名		城市	2019指数	排名		城市	2019指数
2019年	2018年			2019年	2018年		
1	14	郑州	61.50	19	26	沈阳	57.56
2	6	太原	61.04	20	28	武汉	56.92
3	5	深圳	60.82	21	25	宁波	56.79
4	8	北京	60.80	22	2	昆明	56.78
5	35	杭州	60.41	23	15	成都	56.69
6	7	哈尔滨	59.99	24	19	南宁	56.62
7	10	济南	59.95	25	3	合肥	56.21
8	20	厦门	59.27	26	11	天津	55.81
9	4	贵阳	59.01	27	34	银川	55.64
10	13	呼和浩特	58.98	28	12	大连	55.62
11	24	南昌	58.65	29	30	兰州	54.98
12	22	福州	58.51	30	17	上海	54.33
13	31	海口	58.44	31	18	长沙	53.71
14	16	长春	58.44	32	33	广州	53.32
15	27	重庆	58.27	33	32	石家庄	52.72
16	1	青岛	57.89	34	23	乌鲁木齐	52.01
17	21	南京	57.76	35	29	西宁	50.94
18	9	西安	57.70			平均值	57.26

从表9可以看出35个城市居民健康满意度指数的排名情况，排名处于前10位的城市分别是郑州（61.50）、太原（61.04）、深圳（60.82）、北京（60.80）、杭州（60.41）、哈尔滨（59.99）、济南（59.95）、厦门（59.27）、贵阳（59.01）、呼和浩特（58.98）；

排名处于后 10 位的城市分别是天津（55.81）、银川（55.64）、大连（55.62）、兰州（54.98）、上海（54.33）、长沙（53.71）、广州（53.32）、石家庄（52.72）、乌鲁木齐（52.01）、西宁（50.94）。

从排名的变化情况看，35 个城市中比 2018 年排名有较大幅度上升的城市包括郑州、杭州、厦门、南昌、福州、海口、重庆等城市；排名有较大幅度下降的城市包括青岛、昆明、合肥、天津、大连、上海、长沙、乌鲁木齐等城市。

35 个城市居民健康满意度指数是由 2 个细分指数说明的，其问卷主要包括以下两个问题：过去 30 天中身体或心理不够健康的天数；身体或心理健康问题限制日常活动的天数。具体调查结果如表 10、表 11、表 12 和表 13 所示。

在城市居民健康满意度调查中，我们利用了美国疾病控制与预防中心开发使用的指标，即询问受访者过去 30 天中身体或心理不够健康的天数来度量居民的健康状况。依据这一指标，对 35 个城市居民健康情况的调查结果如表 10 所示。

表 10　2019 年中国 35 个城市居民过去 30 天中身体或心理不够健康的天数

单位：天

排名		城市	2019 年天数	排名		城市	2019 年天数
2019 年	2018 年			2019 年	2018 年		
1	1	南京	5.78	11	20	北京	7.10
2	26	武汉	5.88	12	12	南宁	7.45
3	3	深圳	6.08	13	11	郑州	7.56
4	2	福州	6.11	14	5	青岛	7.73
5	4	厦门	6.18	15	23	重庆	7.95
6	6	上海	6.55	16	13	合肥	7.97
7	14	济南	6.70	17	32	长沙	7.98
8	15	广州	6.77	18	27	哈尔滨	8.33
9	9	宁波	6.88	19	30	海口	8.39
10	10	南昌	6.89	20	24	成都	8.64

续表

排名		城市	2019年天数	排名		城市	2019年天数
2019年	2018年			2019年	2018年		
21	8	太原	8.66	29	34	西安	9.62
22	21	大连	8.75	30	7	贵阳	9.73
23	28	天津	8.76	31	19	石家庄	9.80
24	16	杭州	8.85	32	25	呼和浩特	9.82
25	17	昆明	8.85	33	35	长春	9.82
26	33	银川	9.02	34	18	西宁	10.53
27	22	兰州	9.17	35	31	乌鲁木齐	11.14
28	29	沈阳	9.57			平均值	8.14

从表10的调查结果看，2019年全国35个城市居民过去30天中身体或心理不够健康的天数平均值为8.14天，也就是从整体上说35个城市居民在过去30天中平均有8.14天认为自己在身体或心理上处于不健康状态。其中南京和武汉居民身体或心理不健康天数较低，都低于6天，西宁和乌鲁木齐较高，都高于10天。

本次35个城市受访者在过去30天中认为自己身体或心理不健康天数的平均值比2018年的天数（5.5天）高，相对值高出48%。

如果将身体健康和心理健康情况分别显示，表11是2019年中国35个城市居民认为自己过去30天中身体不够健康的天数的调查结果，表12是2019年中国35个城市居民认为自己过去30天中心理不够健康的天数的调查结果。从这两个方面的健康情况比较来看，35个城市居民的身体健康情况要好于心理健康情况，也就是说，主要困扰城市居民的是心理健康。2019年35个城市居民过去30天中身体不够健康的天数平均值为2.87天，2018年为2.53天，两者相差不大；而2019年35个城市居民心理不够健康的天数平均值为5.14天，2018年为3.01天，可见2019年心理不健康的天数比去年有所增加。2018年4月，由中华医学会健康管理学分会牵头，联合国家卫计委科学技术研究所、中国医师协会整合医学分会、北京健康管理协会等机构共同发布了《中国城镇居民心理健康白皮书》，调查结果表明，73.6% 的人处于心理亚健康状态，存在不同程度心理问题的人有 16.1%，而心理健康的人只有 10.3%。[①] 这个结果与我们的调查结果较为一致。这说明我们应当关注居民的心理健康问题。

表 11　2019 年中国 35 个城市居民过去 30 天中身体不够健康的天数

单位：天

排名		城市	2019 年天数	排名		城市	2019 年天数
2019 年	2018 年			2019 年	2018 年		
1	10	宁波	2.25	19	3	贵阳	2.84
2	2	深圳	2.25	20	27	北京	2.85
3	1	南京	2.27	21	17	石家庄	2.92
4	18	成都	2.30	22	32	哈尔滨	3.01
5	6	厦门	2.32	23	13	南宁	3.03
6	9	南昌	2.36	24	20	昆明	3.05
7	11	合肥	2.39	25	21	长沙	3.05
8	5	福州	2.43	26	8	太原	3.07
9	25	武汉	2.47	27	23	兰州	3.30
10	19	济南	2.49	28	28	沈阳	3.31
11	12	杭州	2.52	29	29	海口	3.31
12	4	郑州	2.55	30	30	银川	3.34
13	34	西安	2.63	31	35	长春	3.40
14	14	重庆	2.70	32	22	大连	3.44
15	33	天津	2.72	33	26	呼和浩特	3.51
16	15	广州	2.75	34	31	乌鲁木齐	3.71
17	7	青岛	2.76	35	24	西宁	4.44
18	16	上海	2.79			平均值	2.87

① 《〈中国城镇居民心理健康白皮书〉正式发布》，央视网，2018 年 4 月 30 日，http://jiankang.cctv.com/2018/04/30/ARTIWf496N6d9O0lrIdJM4rG180430.shtml。

表 12　2019 年中国 35 个城市居民过去 30 天中心理不够健康的天数

单位：天

排名		城市	2019 年天数	排名		城市	2019 年天数
2019 年	2018 年			2019 年	2018 年		
1	29	武汉	4.14	19	6	南宁	5.14
2	8	厦门	4.26	20	30	成都	5.21
3	3	福州	4.31	21	23	大连	5.22
4	7	宁波	4.46	22	9	太原	5.24
5	14	广州	4.52	23	28	沈阳	5.29
6	4	济南	4.61	24	24	兰州	5.37
7	1	上海	4.63	25	21	天津	5.43
8	2	南京	4.69	26	15	北京	5.43
9	11	深圳	4.72	27	16	昆明	5.45
10	34	长沙	4.76	28	10	贵阳	5.56
11	19	杭州	4.83	29	35	长春	5.63
12	13	合肥	4.85	30	17	西宁	5.67
13	31	重庆	4.93	31	33	银川	5.73
14	26	海口	4.95	32	20	哈尔滨	5.88
15	12	南昌	5.01	33	25	呼和浩特	5.91
16	5	青岛	5.03	34	22	石家庄	5.95
17	18	郑州	5.04	35	27	乌鲁木齐	6.86
18	32	西安	5.14			平均值	5.14

为了深入研究居民身心健康状况与日常生活的关系，我们进一步对居民身体或心理健康限制日常活动的天数进行了问卷调查，2019 年 35 个城市居民过去 30 天中因为身体或心理健康问题限制日常活动的天数如表 13 所示。从整体情况看，35 个城市的居民因为身体或心理健康问题限制日常活动的天数的平均值为 3.22 天，而 2018 年为 2.19 天。从城市个体情况看，因为身体或心理健康问题限制日常活动的天数最少的是深圳（2.24 天），因为身体或心理健康问题限制日常活动的天数最多的是贵阳（5.78 天）。

表 13　2019 年中国 35 个城市居民过去 30 天中因为身体或心理健康问题限制日常活动的天数

单位：天

排名		城市	2019 年天数	排名		城市	2019 年天数
2019 年	2018 年			2019 年	2018 年		
1	4	深圳	2.24	19	24	南昌	3.24
2	8	南京	2.26	20	7	长沙	3.27
3	5	厦门	2.27	21	19	哈尔滨	3.30
4	1	福州	2.41	22	18	呼和浩特	3.43
5	12	北京	2.42	23	27	大连	3.44
6	2	上海	2.43	24	16	合肥	3.51
7	10	广州	2.43	25	33	沈阳	3.52
8	13	杭州	2.61	26	29	海口	3.57
9	23	济南	2.66	27	15	昆明	3.58
10	3	武汉	2.72	28	35	银川	3.59
11	31	重庆	2.81	29	21	西宁	3.63
12	22	天津	2.88	30	11	石家庄	3.71
13	9	青岛	2.99	31	26	西安	3.78
14	14	太原	2.99	32	28	兰州	3.86
15	6	宁波	3.03	33	17	成都	3.94
16	20	南宁	3.16	34	32	乌鲁木齐	4.64
17	30	郑州	3.21	35	25	贵阳	5.78
18	34	长春	3.22			平均值	3.22

从被调查的居民的个体差异情况看，表 14 反映了性别、年龄、学历对居民健康状况满意度的影响。从性别看，男性的健康满意度略高于女性；从学历看，学历与健康满意度成正比；从年龄看，对自己总体健康的满意度最高的受访者处于 20~29 岁，同时处于这一年龄段的受访者还认为自己身体或心理健康限制日常活动的天数是最多的。

表 14 不同性别、年龄、学历的居民的健康满意度情况

分类标准		总体健康指数 *	“身体 + 心理”不健康天数（天）	身体或心理健康限制日常活动的天数（天）
性别	男	59.54	7.39	3.03
	女	56.68	8.36	3.10
年龄	20~29 岁	59.51	8.08	3.25
	30~39 岁	57.22	7.44	2.76
	40 岁及以上	52.14	8.51	2.96
学历	大学本科以下	57.53	8.48	3.51
	大学本科	57.67	7.88	3.01
	研究生及以上	60.04	7.85	2.97

注：总体健康指数是根据受访者对问卷“您觉得您的健康情形如何？”的答案及答案赋值获得的。

（四）医疗服务满意度指数

医疗服务满意度用于衡量城市居民对医疗机构服务质量和医疗保险个人负担部分的满意程度，其数值分布为 0~100，其中数值越接近 0 代表越不满意，越接近 100 代表满意度越高，具体满意程度划分如下：数值为 0 是非常不满意，数值为 25 是不满意，数值为 50 是一般，数值为 75 是满意，数值为 100 是非常满意。

2019 年中国 35 个城市居民医疗服务满意度指数的调查结果如表 15 所示。表 15 中的结果是表 16 和表 17 中数据的加权平均值。

表 15 2019 年中国 35 个城市居民医疗服务满意度指数

排名		城市	2019 年指数	排名		城市	2019 年指数
2019 年	2018 年			2019 年	2018 年		
1	1	北京	66.79	4	25	南昌	65.54
2	33	南京	66.31	5	3	宁波	65.27
3	15	杭州	65.92	6	20	合肥	65.12

续表

排名		城市	2019 年指数	排名		城市	2019 年指数
2019 年	2018 年			2019 年	2018 年		
7	21	西安	65.03	22	7	成都	62.45
8	4	济南	64.94	23	34	贵阳	62.19
9	6	郑州	64.94	24	26	兰州	61.99
10	9	沈阳	64.70	25	35	海口	61.91
11	23	广州	64.37	26	14	武汉	61.87
12	11	乌鲁木齐	63.93	27	32	西宁	61.62
13	18	石家庄	63.73	28	27	深圳	61.55
14	8	青岛	63.54	29	19	银川	61.40
15	16	天津	63.47	30	28	太原	60.53
16	2	南宁	63.40	31	30	昆明	60.28
17	5	厦门	63.05	32	13	大连	60.16
18	10	呼和浩特	62.99	33	22	福州	60.08
19	31	上海	62.87	34	29	哈尔滨	60.00
20	17	重庆	62.71	35	12	长春	59.16
21	24	长沙	62.46	平均值			63.04

从调查结果看，2019 年中国 35 个城市居民医疗服务满意度指数加权平均值为 63.04，处于一般（50）和满意（75）之间，比 2018 年的得分（65.31）较低。从 35 个城市居民的医疗服务满意度排名的情况看，排在前 10 位的城市分别是北京（66.79）、南京（66.31）、杭州（65.92）、南昌（65.54）、宁波（65.27）、合肥（65.12）、西安（65.03）、济南（64.94）、郑州（64.94）、沈阳（64.70）；排在后 10 位的城市分别是武汉（61.87）、西宁（61.62）、深圳（61.55）、银川（61.40）、太原（60.53）、昆明（60.28）、大连（60.16）、福州（60.08）、哈尔滨（60.00）、长春（59.16）。

从 35 个城市居民医疗服务满意度排名的变化情况看，与 2018 年相比，2019年南京和南昌的排名有较大幅度上升，分别上升了31位和21位；长春和大连排名有较大幅度下降，分别下降了23位和19位。4个特大城市北京、上海、广州、深圳中，北京（第1位）和深圳（第28位）排名比较稳定，而上海和广州的排位有较大幅度的上升。

35个城市居民医疗服务满意度指数包含了两个细分指数，分别是表16的居民对医疗机构服务质量（包含诊疗水平、服务态度、就诊环境）的满意度指数和表17的居民对医疗保险个人负担部分的满意度指数。从两个细分指数的情况看，35个城市居民对医疗机构服务质量的满意度（64.91）比医疗保险个人负担部分的满意度（61.16）高。

表16　居民对医疗机构服务质量（包含诊疗水平、服务态度、就诊环境）的满意度指数

排名		城市	2019年指数	排名		城市	2019年指数
2019年	2018年			2019年	2018年		
1	3	北京	69.35	14	13	合肥	66.35
2	34	南京	68.82	15	5	宁波	66.34
3	19	杭州	68.69	16	2	南宁	65.86
4	27	广州	67.45	17	1	厦门	64.66
5	9	郑州	67.27	18	12	上海	64.42
6	23	南昌	67.26	19	21	呼和浩特	64.42
7	6	济南	66.81	20	25	长沙	64.34
8	11	西安	66.78	21	10	武汉	64.31
9	7	石家庄	66.64	22	18	深圳	64.22
10	4	天津	66.58	23	30	兰州	64.01
11	16	成都	66.48	24	17	重庆	63.99
12	8	沈阳	66.42	25	20	乌鲁木齐	63.89
13	14	青岛	66.40	26	35	海口	63.79

续表

排名		城市	2019 年指数	排名		城市	2019 年指数
2019 年	2018 年			2019 年	2018 年		
27	28	大连	63.77	32	31	昆明	61.26
28	26	太原	62.97	33	24	福州	61.11
29	29	银川	62.37	34	33	贵阳	60.39
30	32	西宁	62.30	35	15	长春	60.17
31	22	哈尔滨	61.98			平均值	64.91

表 17　居民对医疗保险个人负担部分的满意度指数

排名		城市	2019 年指数	排名		城市	2019 年指数
2019 年	2018 年			2019 年	2018 年		
1	2	北京	64.24	19	30	西宁	60.94
2	1	宁波	64.19	20	20	石家庄	60.82
3	31	贵阳	63.99	21	9	青岛	60.67
4	12	乌鲁木齐	63.98	22	25	长沙	60.57
5	17	合肥	63.89	23	10	银川	60.44
6	29	南昌	63.81	24	24	天津	60.37
7	33	南京	63.80	25	34	海口	60.02
8	26	西安	63.29	26	16	兰州	59.98
9	18	杭州	63.16	27	13	武汉	59.42
10	8	济南	63.08	28	23	昆明	59.31
11	21	沈阳	62.97	29	19	福州	59.04
12	3	郑州	62.62	30	32	深圳	58.89
13	6	呼和浩特	61.56	31	5	成都	58.43
14	7	厦门	61.43	32	15	长春	58.14
15	11	重庆	61.43	33	28	太原	58.10
16	35	上海	61.32	34	27	哈尔滨	58.01
17	22	广州	61.29	35	14	大连	56.55
18	4	南宁	60.94			平均值	61.16

再结合被调查者的个体情况看，表 18 反映了包括性别、年龄、学历对居民医疗服务满意度的影响。从性别看，女性对医疗服务的满意度略低于男性；从年龄看，医疗服务满意度最高的是 20~29 岁的受访者；从学历看，学历与医疗服务满意度成正比，但是差异程度并不大。

表 18　不同性别、年龄、学历的居民的医疗服务满意度情况

分类标准		医疗服务满意度指数
性别	男	64.32
	女	63.53
年龄	20~29 岁	65.16
	30~39 岁	63.08
	40 岁及以上	59.95
学历	大学本科以下	61.93
	大学本科	63.94
	研究生及以上	65.68

为了更好地分析城市居民的健康感受，我们进一步调查了 35 个城市居民在过去一年中去过医院或诊所就诊的人数比例。表 19 是对 35 个城市过去一年中受访居民因为自己的健康问题或陪同亲友去过医院或诊所就诊比例的调查结果。

表 19　在过去一年中因为自己的健康问题或陪同亲友去过医院或诊所就诊的比例

单位：%

序号	城市	未去就诊	社区医院 / 诊所	综合医院	专科医院	其他医疗机构
1	海口	37.72	20.61	32.02	6.14	3.51
2	乌鲁木齐	34.80	22.03	36.12	5.29	1.76
3	呼和浩特	34.20	18.61	33.77	11.26	2.16
4	兰州	32.46	19.74	33.33	12.72	1.75

续表

序号	城市	未去就诊	社区医院 / 诊所	综合医院	专科医院	其他医疗机构
5	银川	32.16	12.33	36.56	15.86	3.08
6	太原	31.88	27.07	28.38	11.79	0.87
7	青岛	30.04	15.45	46.35	7.30	0.86
8	厦门	29.57	27.39	31.74	10.43	0.87
9	贵阳	29.15	29.15	28.70	8.97	4.04
10	长春	26.84	20.35	39.39	12.12	1.30
11	南昌	26.61	22.75	38.63	9.87	2.15
12	哈尔滨	25.64	23.08	40.60	7.69	2.99
13	西宁	25.58	20.47	35.35	13.95	4.65
14	大连	24.68	19.05	44.59	9.96	1.73
15	长沙	24.03	30.90	34.33	8.58	2.15
16	南京	22.80	24.43	46.25	4.23	2.28
17	深圳	22.77	37.29	34.65	4.62	0.66
18	福州	22.08	31.17	37.66	6.06	3.03
19	沈阳	21.74	22.17	44.35	10.87	0.87
20	昆明	21.59	22.91	42.73	8.81	3.96
21	西安	21.12	32.33	37.93	7.76	0.86
22	石家庄	20.00	33.91	38.70	6.52	0.87
23	重庆	19.87	28.85	40.06	9.94	1.28
24	宁波	19.82	25.99	41.85	10.57	1.76
25	广州	18.79	33.12	40.45	7.01	0.64
26	天津	18.57	20.85	52.44	6.84	1.30
27	郑州	18.42	32.46	40.35	8.77	0.00
28	上海	18.13	16.06	55.96	9.59	0.26
29	合肥	17.52	28.21	43.59	7.69	2.99
30	武汉	17.10	31.61	43.87	6.45	0.97
31	杭州	15.88	27.47	47.21	8.15	1.29
32	北京	15.46	25.77	52.32	5.93	0.52
33	成都	15.45	25.75	47.64	9.87	1.29
34	济南	14.41	33.62	41.92	10.04	0.00

续表

序号	城市	未去就诊	社区医院 / 诊所	综合医院	专科医院	其他医疗机构
35	南宁	13.48	27.39	47.39	9.57	2.17
2019 年均值		23.44	25.44	40.49	8.89	1.74
2018 年均值		36.00	25.10	27.40	9.00	2.60

从调查的结果看，2019 年中国 35 个城市居民受访者过去一年没去过医疗机构的人数占比的平均值为 23.44%，比 2018 年的整体水平低 12.56 个百分点，也就是说 2019 年 35 个城市居民去过医疗机构的人数占比比上一年度增长了 12.56 个百分点。在去过医疗机构的受访者中，去综合医院就诊的比例为 40.49%，比 2018 年高出 13.09 个百分点；去社区医院 / 诊所就诊的比例变化不大。上述调查结果表明，我国还需要进一步推进分级诊疗制度。

从 35 个城市的排名看，没去过医疗机构就诊的比例排前 10 位的城市分别为海口（37.72%）、乌鲁木齐（34.80%）、呼和浩特（34.20%）、兰州（32.46%）、银川（32.16%）、太原（31.88%）、青岛（30.04%）、厦门（29.57%）、贵阳（29.15%）、长春（26.84%）；排名居于后 10 位的城市分别为天津（18.57%）、郑州（18.42%）、上海（18.13%）、合肥（17.52%）、武汉（17.10%）、杭州（15.88%）、北京（15.46%）、成都（15.45%）、济南（14.41%）、南宁（13.48%）。

三　2019 年中国 35 个城市生活质量一级指标雷达图

图 1 为 2019 年中国 35 个城市生活质量一级指标雷达图（按一级指标中的消费者信心由大到小排列）。雷达图显示 35 个城市生活质量一级指标整体的共同特征是消费者信心比较高，健康满意度较低。

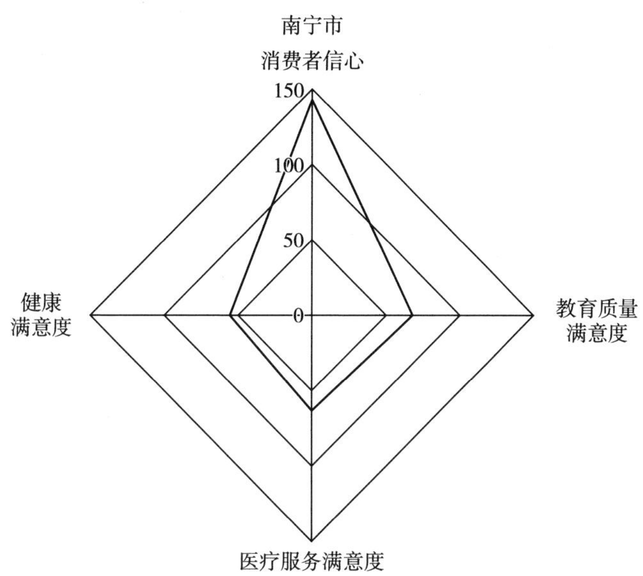
南宁市
消费者信心
150
100
50
0
健康
满意度
教育质量
满意度
医疗服务满意度

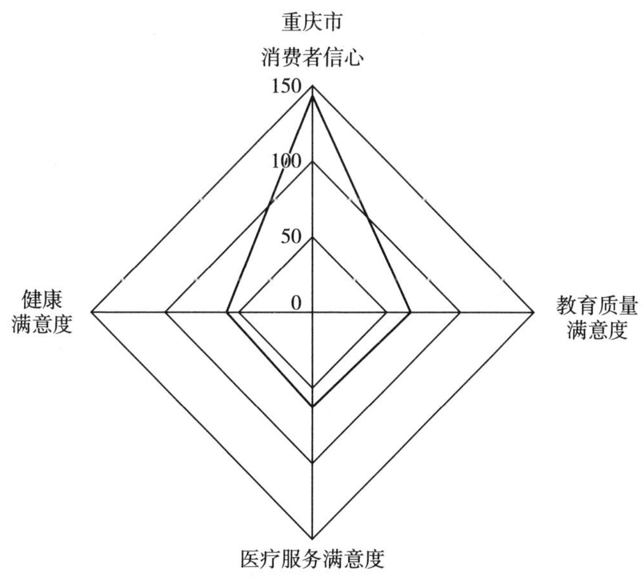
重庆市
消费者信心
150
100
50
0
健康
满意度
教育质量
满意度
医疗服务满意度

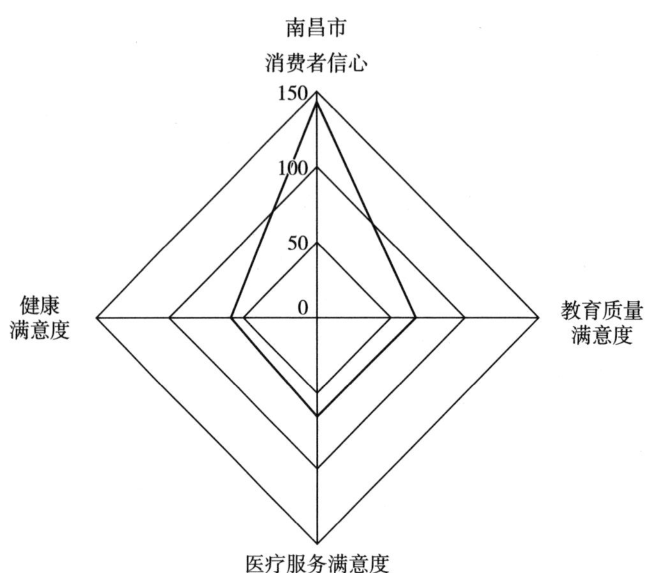
南昌市
消费者信心
150
100
50
0
健康
满意度
教育质量
满意度
医疗服务满意度

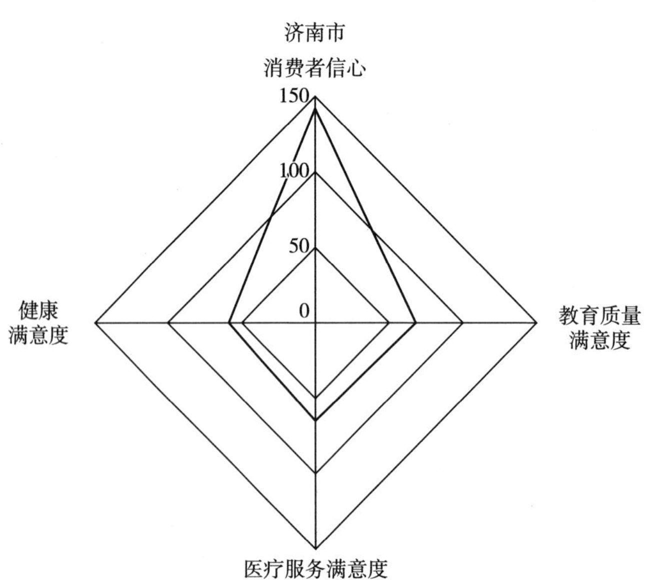
济南市
消费者信心
150
100
50
0
健康
满意度
教育质量
满意度
医疗服务满意度

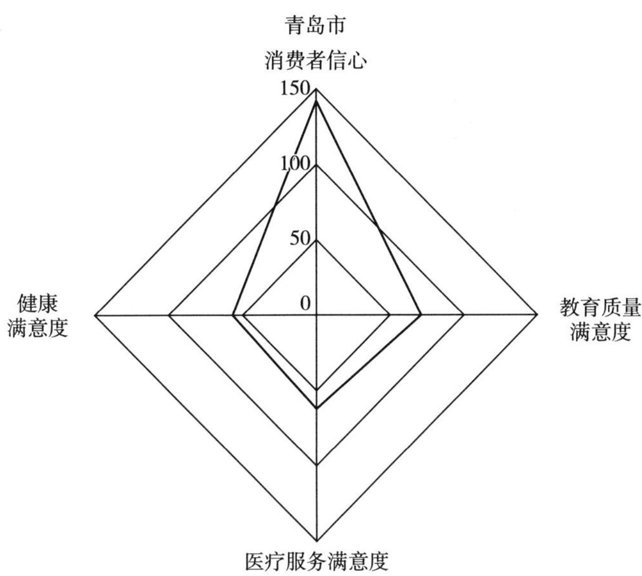
青岛市
消费者信心
150
100
50
0
健康
满意度
教育质量
满意度
医疗服务满意度

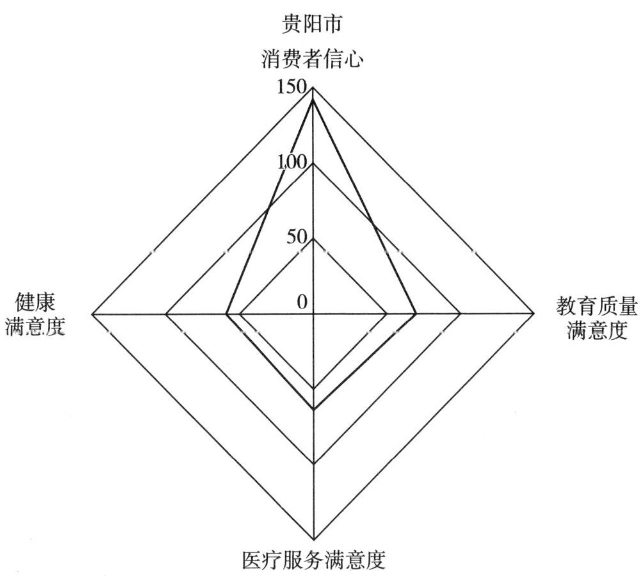
贵阳市
消费者信心
150
100
50
0
健康
满意度
教育质量
满意度
医疗服务满意度

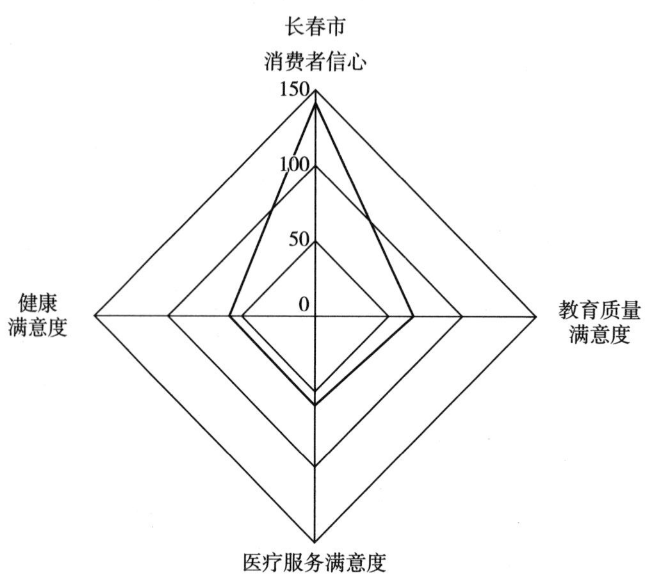
长春市
消费者信心
150
100
50
0
健康
满意度
教育质量
满意度
医疗服务满意度

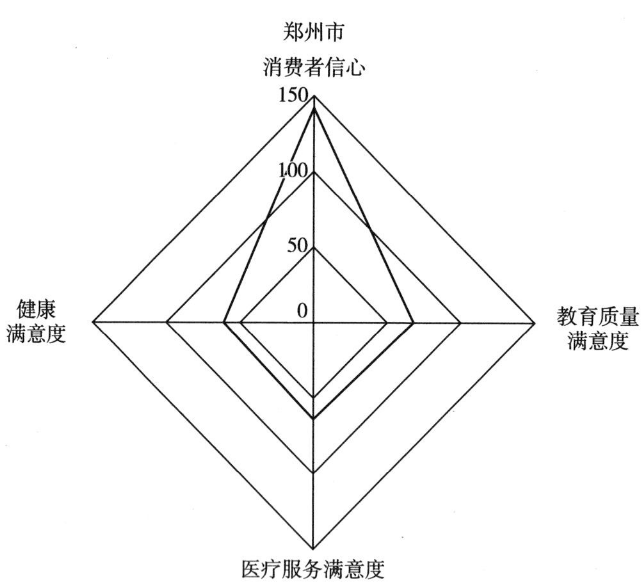
郑州市
消费者信心
150
100
50
0
健康
满意度
教育质量
满意度
医疗服务满意度

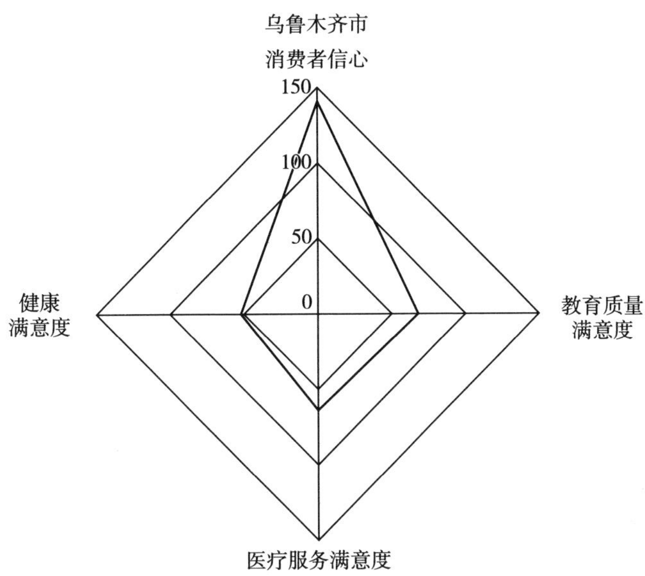

乌鲁木齐市
消费者信心
150
100
50
0
健康
满意度
教育质量
满意度
医疗服务满意度

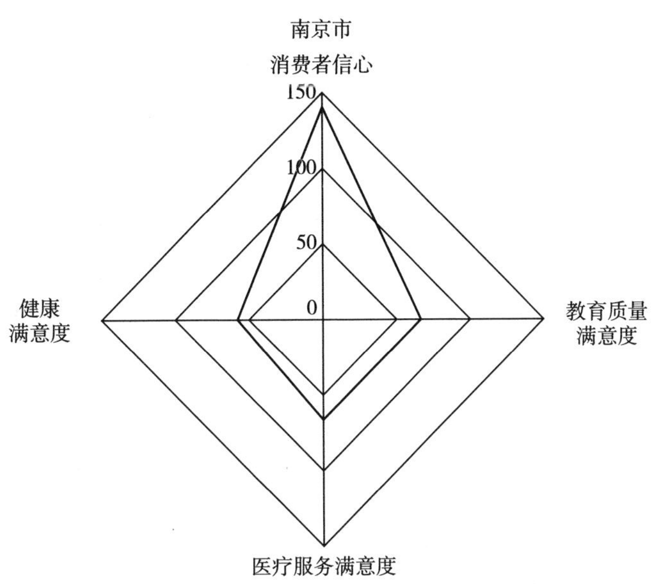

南京市
消费者信心
150
100
50
0
健康
满意度
教育质量
满意度
医疗服务满意度

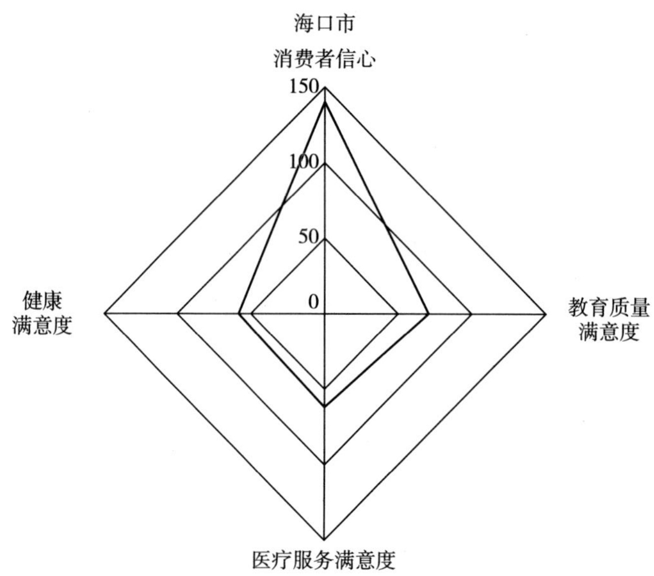
海口市
消费者信心
150
100
50
0
健康
满意度
教育质量
满意度
医疗服务满意度

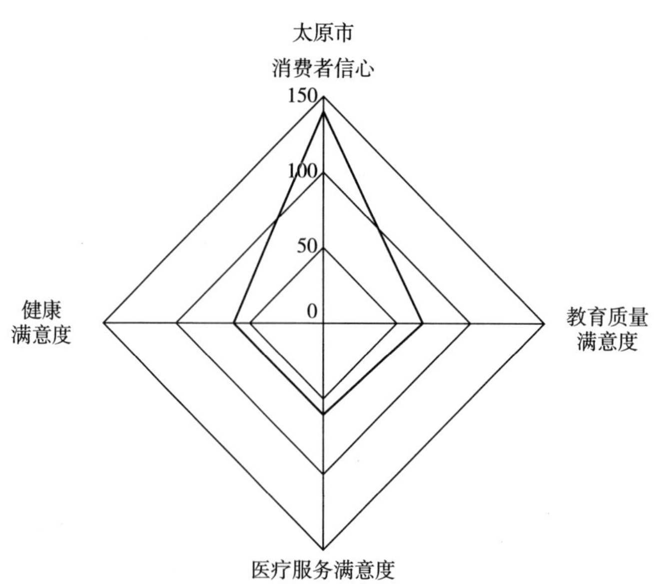
太原市
消费者信心
150
100
50
0
健康
满意度
教育质量
满意度
医疗服务满意度

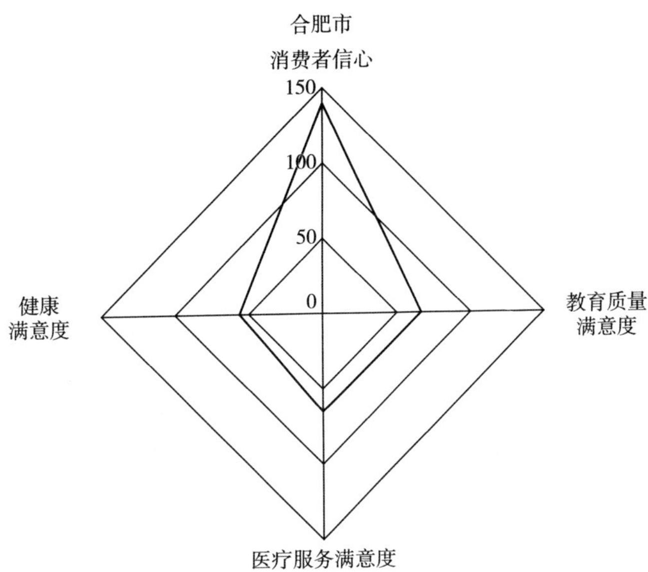
合肥市
消费者信心
150
100
50
0
教育质量
满意度
医疗服务满意度
健康
满意度

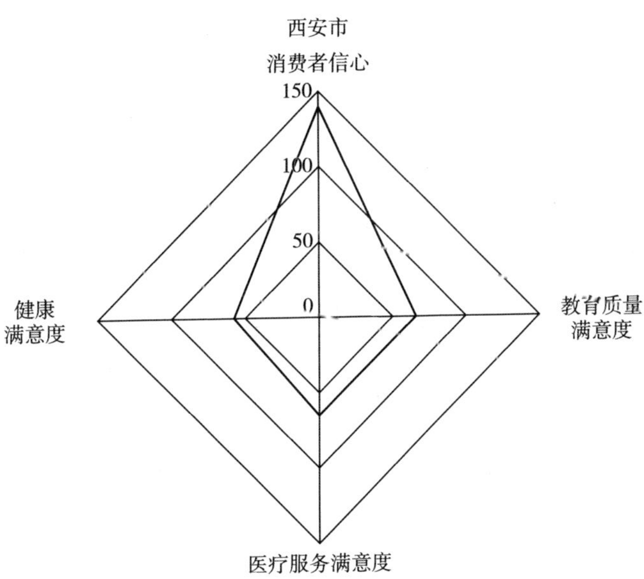
西安市
消费者信心
150
100
50
0
教育质量
满意度
医疗服务满意度
健康
满意度

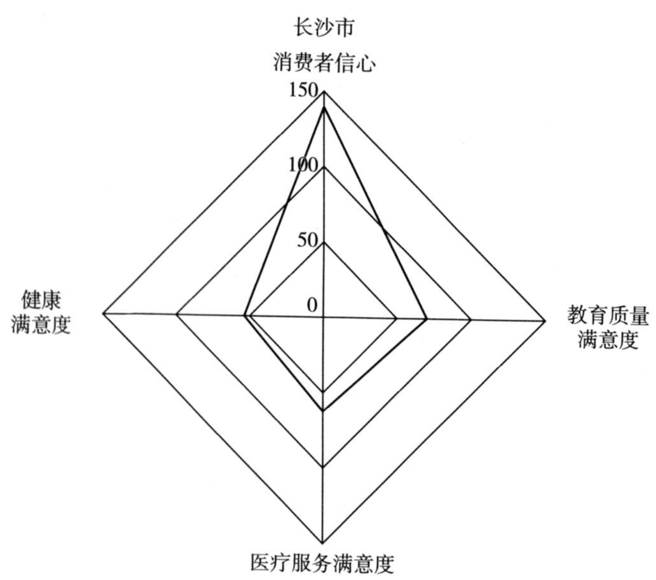
长沙市
消费者信心
150
100
50
0
健康
满意度
教育质量
满意度
医疗服务满意度

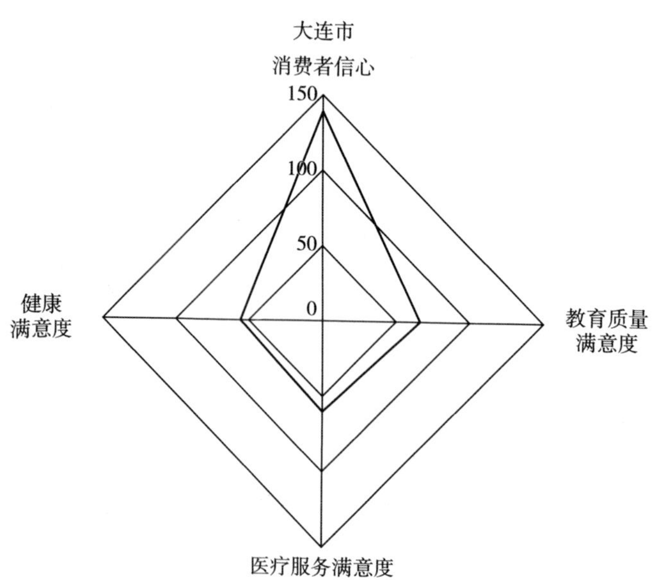
大连市
消费者信心
150
100
50
0
健康
满意度
教育质量
满意度
医疗服务满意度

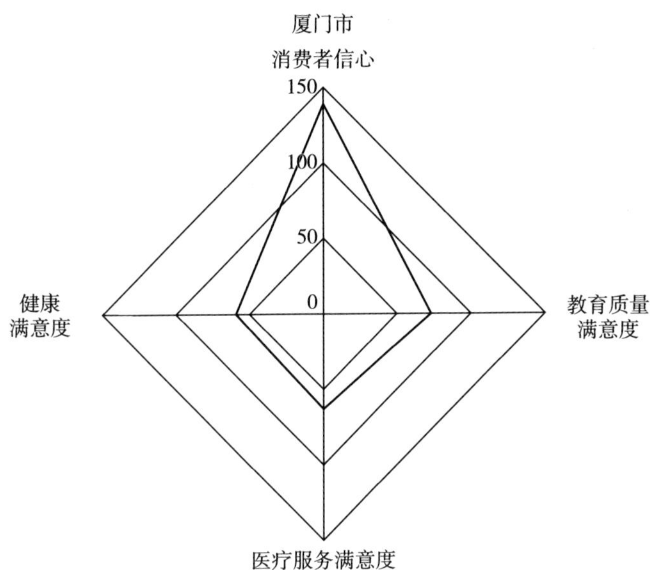
厦门市
消费者信心
150
100
50
0
健康
满意度
教育质量
满意度
医疗服务满意度

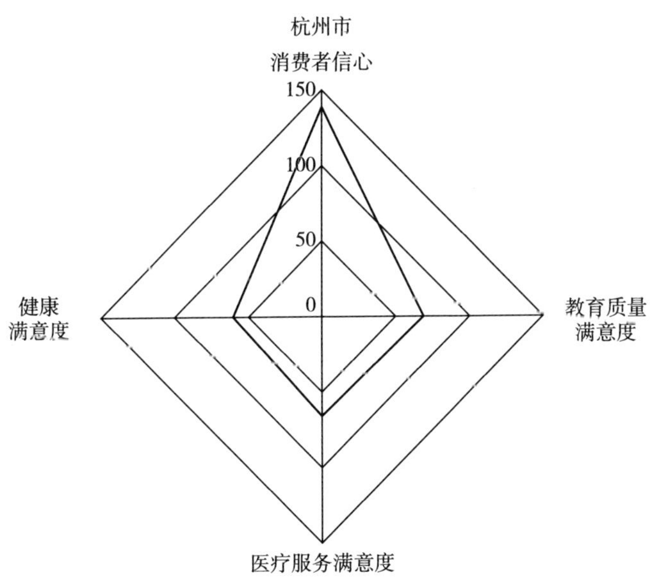
杭州市
消费者信心
150
100
50
0
健康
满意度
教育质量
满意度
医疗服务满意度

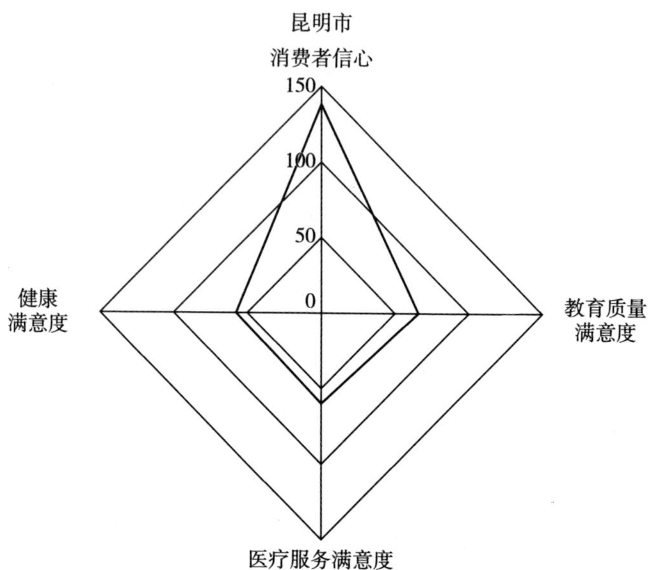
昆明市
消费者信心
150
100
50
0
健康
满意度
教育质量
满意度
医疗服务满意度

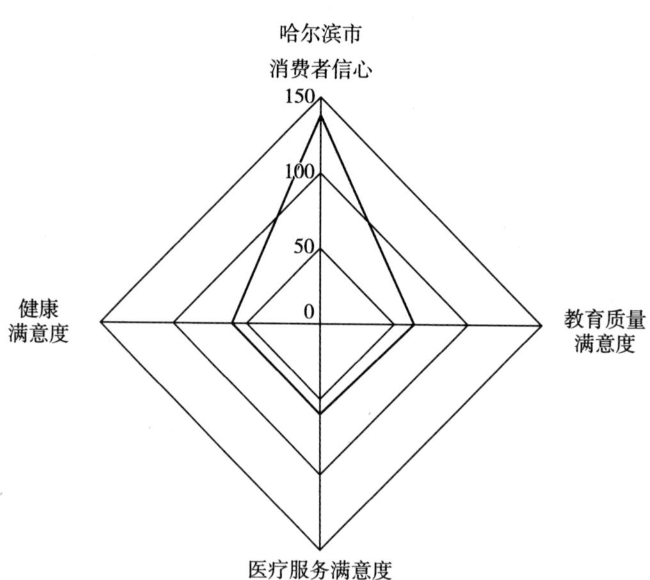
哈尔滨市
消费者信心
150
100
50
0
健康
满意度
教育质量
满意度
医疗服务满意度

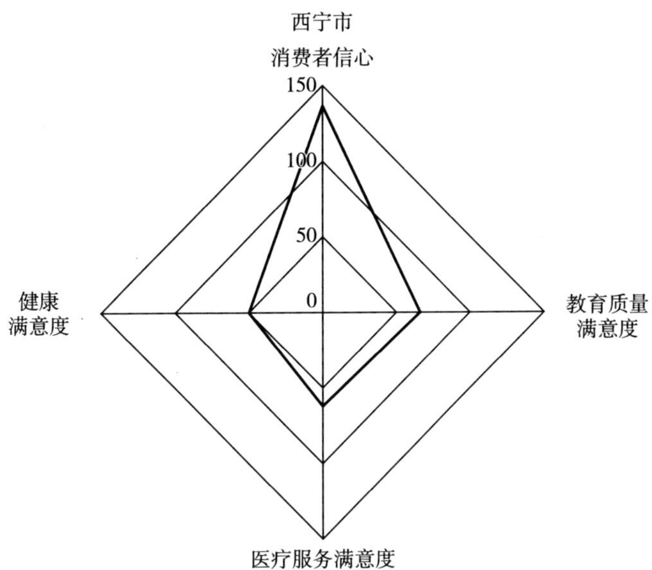
西宁市
消费者信心
150
100
50
0
健康
满意度
教育质量
满意度
医疗服务满意度

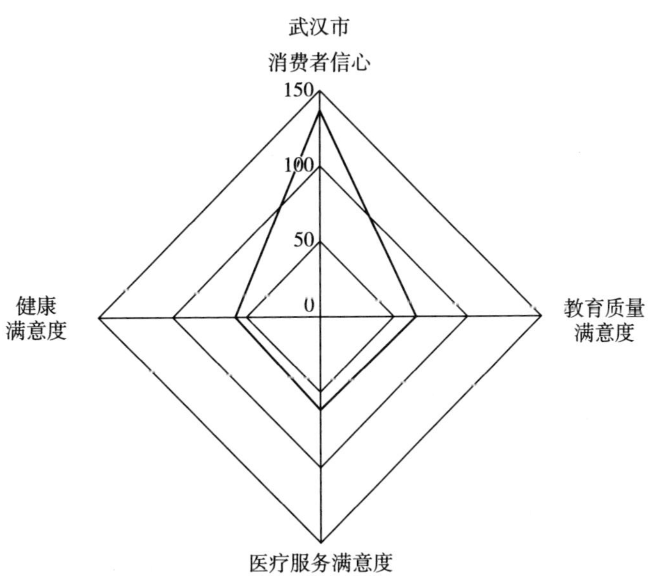
武汉市
消费者信心
150
100
50
0
健康
满意度
教育质量
满意度
医疗服务满意度

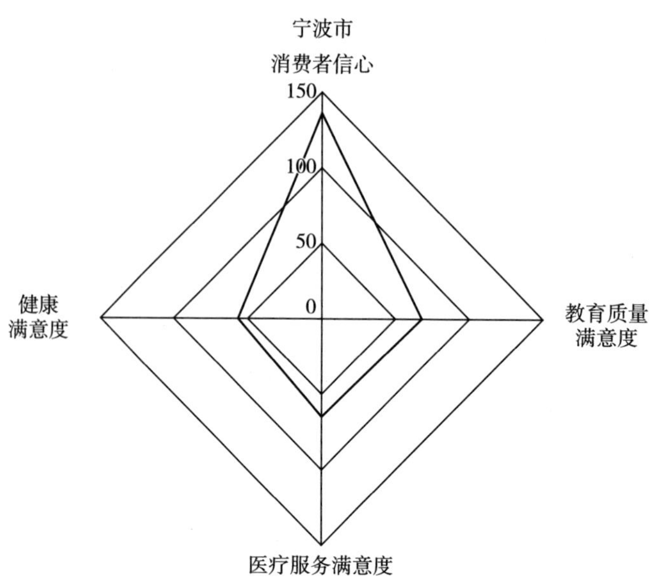
宁波市
消费者信心
150
100
50
0
健康
满意度
教育质量
满意度
医疗服务满意度

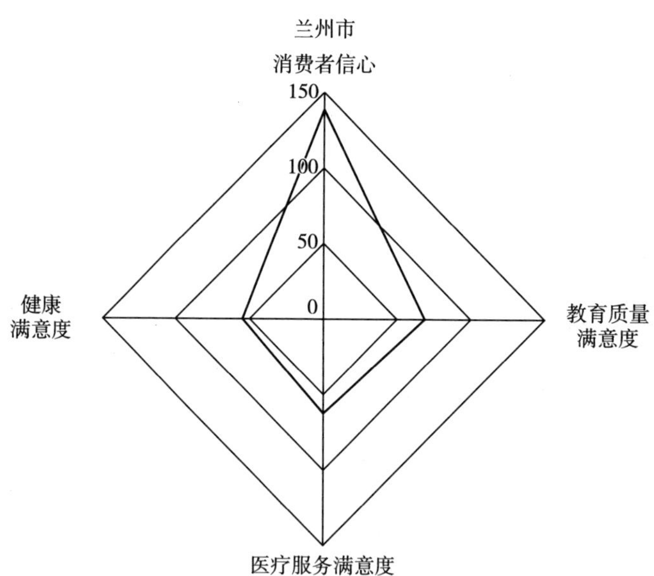
兰州市
消费者信心
150
100
50
0
健康
满意度
教育质量
满意度
医疗服务满意度

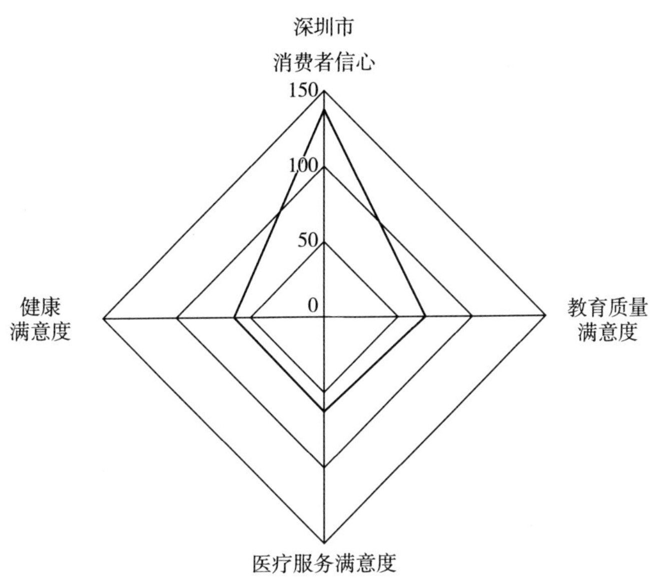
深圳市
消费者信心
150
100
50
0
教育质量
满意度
医疗服务满意度
健康
满意度

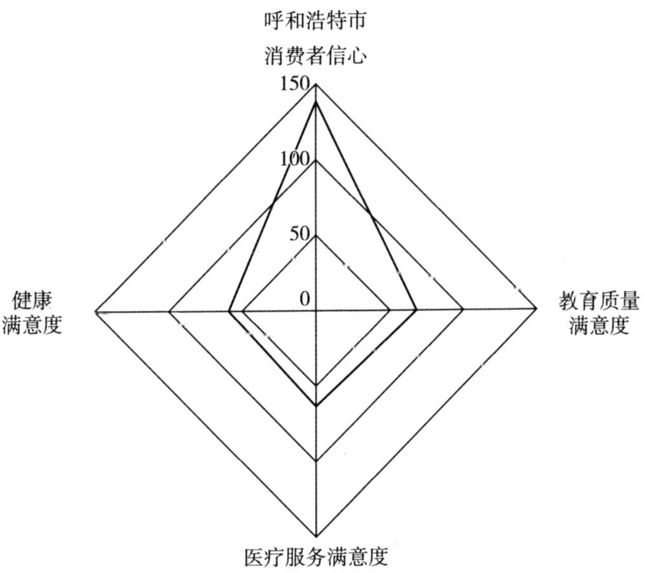
呼和浩特市
消费者信心
150
100
50
0
教育质量
满意度
医疗服务满意度
健康
满意度

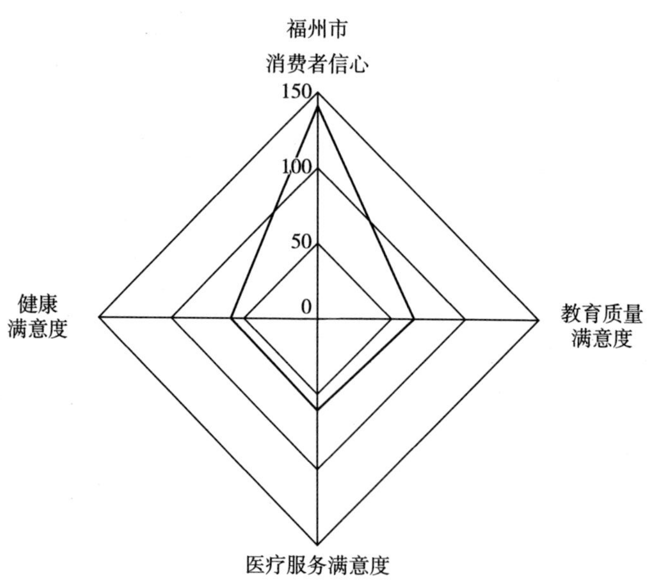
福州市
消费者信心
150
100
50
0
教育质量
满意度
医疗服务满意度
健康
满意度

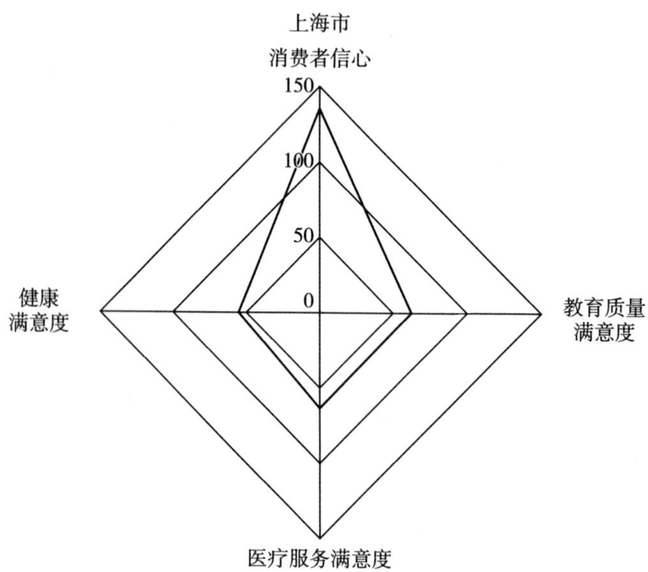
上海市
消费者信心
150
100
50
0
教育质量
满意度
医疗服务满意度
健康
满意度

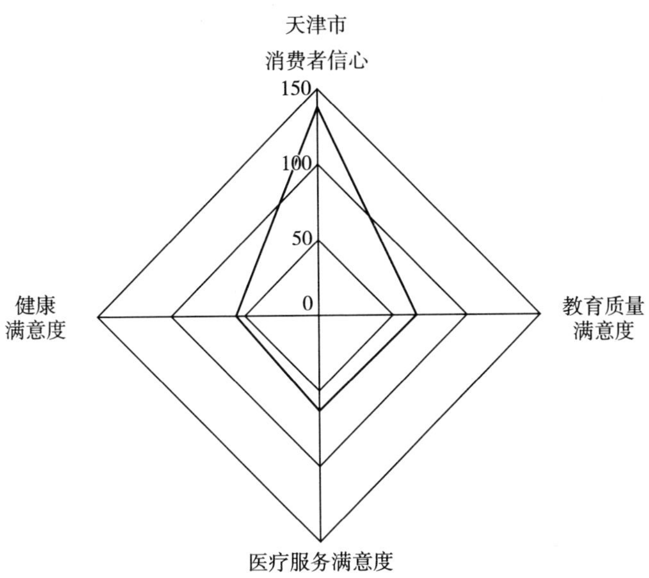
天津市
消费者信心
150
100
50
0
教育质量
满意度
医疗服务满意度
健康
满意度

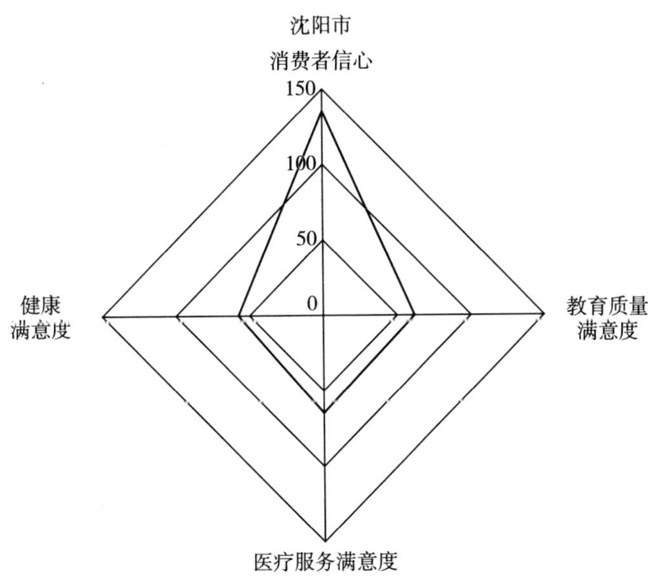
沈阳市
消费者信心
150
100
50
0
教育质量
满意度
医疗服务满意度
健康
满意度

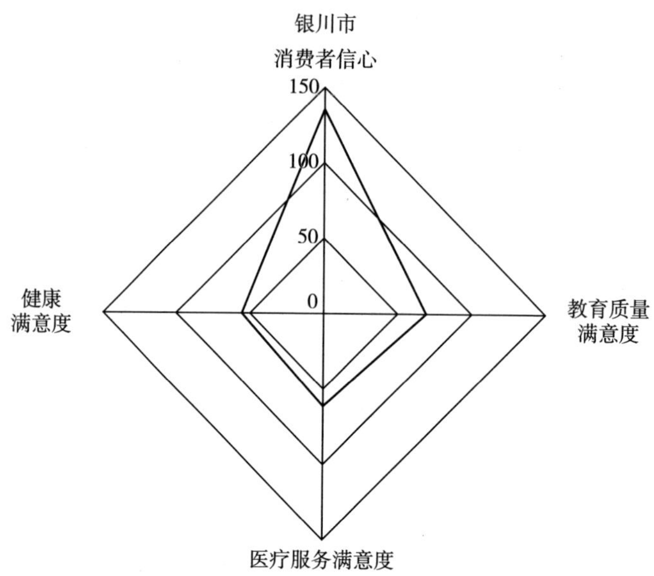
银川市
消费者信心
150
100
50
0
健康
满意度
教育质量
满意度
医疗服务满意度

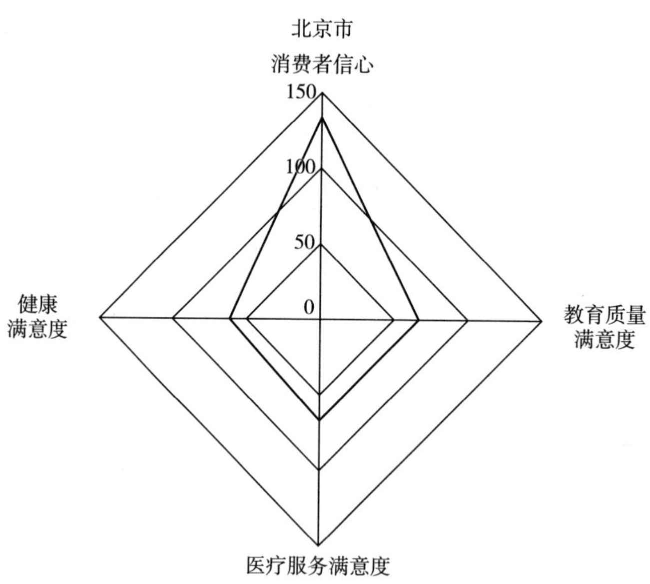
北京市
消费者信心
150
100
50
0
健康
满意度
教育质量
满意度
医疗服务满意度

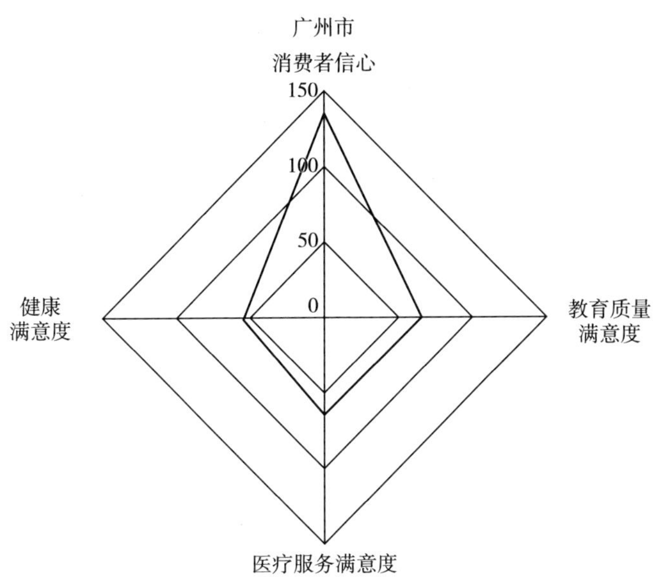
广州市
消费者信心
150
100
50
0
教育质量满意度
医疗服务满意度
健康满意度

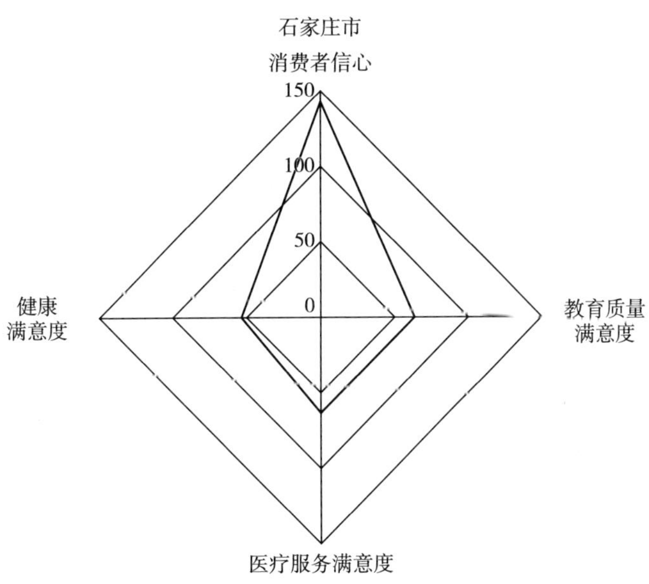
石家庄市
消费者信心
150
100
50
0
教育质量满意度
医疗服务满意度
健康满意度

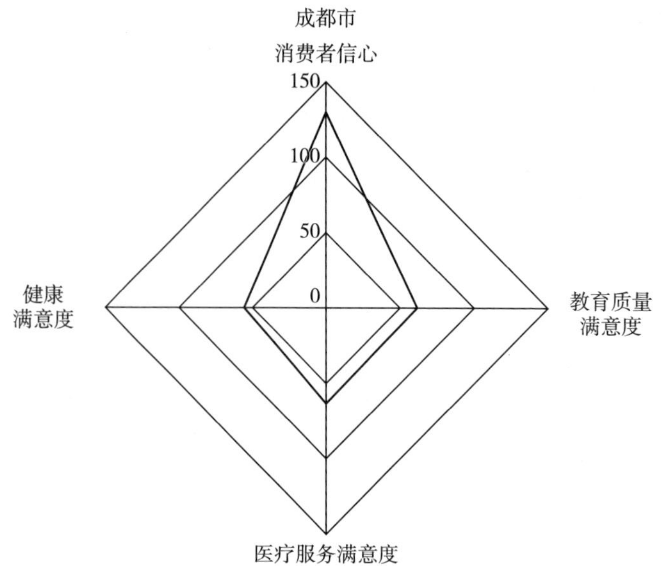

图 1 2019 年中国 35 个城市生活质量一级指标雷达图

四 结论与建议

次贷危机后，中国经济发展的外部环境发生了深刻变化，经济全球化遭遇波折，多边主义遭受冲击，中美经贸摩擦对中国的经济增长带来较大压力。然而，根据 35 个城市居民生活质量各项指数的调查结果，总体而言，消费者信心基本稳定。在当前经济增速、投资增速、出口增速下行压力较大的情况下，稳定的消费者信心表明，未来一两年消费需求有可能成为我国经济增长的稳定器。但要实现这一点，稳增长、稳就业以及居民收入水平不下降、财富不缩水应是必要条件。

从教育质量、医疗服务、健康等各项满意度指数来看，许多指数的数值不尽如人意。消费者信心指数虽然稳中有升，但并不是很明显。所有这些均表明，解决满足人民日益增长的美好生活需要和不平衡不充分的发展之间的矛盾依然任重道远。

调查结果表明，未来我国政府应进一步释放制度红利和政策红利，激发微观经济主体活力，加快经济转型和产业结构升级，创新和完善宏观调控措施；进一步稳就业、稳金融、稳外贸、稳外资、稳投资、稳预期，进而稳定经济增长，并在此基础上不断提高经济增长质量，不断提高教育、医疗等公共服务水平，为居民身心健康和生活质量水平的提高奠定坚实的经济基础，并提供强有力的制度保障和政策保障。

参考文献

张自然等:《中国经济发展中的两个反差——中国30个城市生活质量调查报告》,《经济学动态》2011年第7期。

张连城等:《高生活成本拖累城市生活质量满意度提高——中国35个城市生活质量调查报告（2012）》,《经济学动态》2012年第7期。

张连城等:《生活质量：指数平稳，挑战严峻——中国35个城市生活质量调查报告（2013）》,《经济学动态》2013年第8期。

张连城等:《生活质量指数趋升　空气质量食品安全堪忧——2014中国35个城市生活质量报告》,《经济学动态》2014年第8期。

张连城等:《经济承压，生活质量满意度稳中有升——2015年中国35个城市生活质量报告》,《经济学动态》2015年第9期。

赵家章等:《预期稳定挑战犹存——2016年中国35个城市生活质量报告》,《经济学动态》2016年第8期。

中国经济实验研究院:《中国城市生活质量报告（2012）》，社会科学文献出版社，2013。

中国经济实验研究院:《中国城市生活质量报告（2013）》，社会科学文献出版社，2014。

中国经济实验研究院：《中国城市生活质量报告（2014）》，社会科学文献出版社，2014。

张连城等主编《中国城市生活质量报告（2015）》，社会科学文献出版社，2015。

中国经济实验研究院：《中国城市生活质量报告（2016）》，社会科学文献出版社，2017。

张连城等：《中国城市生活质量报告（2017）》，社会科学文献出版社，2017。

张连城等：《中国城市生活质量报告（2018）》，社会科学文献出版社，2019。

分 报 告

Topical Reports

B.2
中国35个城市居民消费者信心指数报告

王 钰*

摘 要： 本次通过问卷调查了中国35个城市居民的消费者信心指数，结果显示，2019年中国35个城市居民消费者信心指数加权平均值为138.61，35个城市居民的消费者信心指数全部超过100，全部高于2018年的水平，这表明中国经济未来向消费驱动转型具有良好的基础。分地区比较的结果表明，中部和西部地区的城市居民的消费者信心指数略高于东北和东部地区城市居民的消费者信心指数，不同地区间的消费者信心指数的变化方向是一致的，变化幅度也较为一致。通过相关性分析发现，消费者信心指数的变化与通货膨胀率指数和消费率指数的变化具有高度正相关性，说明消费者信心的增强，会导致通货膨胀

* 王钰，首都经济贸易大学经济学院教授，主要研究方向为经济增长与经济周期。

水平增高，同时也会使居民的消费率有所提高。回归分析影响消费者信心变化的主要因素，结果表明人均可支配收入、基本医疗保险覆盖率和失业保险覆盖率的提高对消费者信心指数具有很强的正向作用，而人均财富水平和社会保险覆盖率对消费者信心的影响并不是正向的。据此，稳定消费者信心的关键在于稳定居民的收入和就业，此外还要稳定和扩大社会保障的覆盖范围，并不断发展和完善金融市场。

关键词：消费者信心指数　通货膨胀率　消费率　人均财富水平

一　引言

通过高速经济增长阶段，中国已经成为上中等收入国家，随着人均收入水平的提高，消费者消费受硬预算约束性得到了缓解。在这种情况下，消费者信心对于消费者消费需求的影响力将逐步增强。同时由于中国地域辽阔，地域之间的经济发展水平差异较大，在中国经济由投资驱动向消费驱动转型的情况下，对中国居民消费者信心指数的变化进行调查和测算对于稳定经济增长和促进经济转型是很有必要的。

消费者信心指数（Index of Consumer Sentiment, ICS; Consumer Confidence Index，CCI）最早起源于美国，是由美国密歇根大学的调查研究中心（Survey Research Center）的乔治·卡通纳（George Katona）于20世纪40年代提出的，他认为消费者需求是收入的函数，也是消费者意愿（欲望）的函数，消费者的心理决定了消费的意愿，包括消费动机和消费态度，一般可以用消费者信心指数、消费者满意指数描述消费者意愿。消费者信心指数是综合反映消费者信心强弱的指标，量化了消费者对当前收入水平、对未来收入水平预期、消费状态心理的主观感受，是反映当前和未来经济运行状态和趋势的先行指标，主要用于对经济周期和波动的预测。

从 20 世纪 40 年代以来，美国密歇根大学一直在测算和发布 ICS 的季度指数，该指数至少可以提前九个月预报经济转折点的到来，也可以提前预测失业水平的变化。但研究也发现美国密歇根大学的消费者信心指数存在偏差，该指数与美国的经济景气水平存在偏差，并可以使用缩放和平移等方法进行调整。[①] 20世纪60年代后，美国联邦储备局也认识到这一指数的重要性，开展了消费者信心指数的编制和测算工作，此后其他国家也相继开展了这一指数的编测工作，包括澳大利亚、日本、加拿大等共计 40 多个国家。从 1998 年开始，中国官方和各大财经高校逐步开始编制该指数，并定期对全国和分地区的消费者信心指数进行监测和发布，定期监测和发布消费者信心指数的财经高校包括首都经济贸易大学（CUEB）、上海财经大学（SUFE）和西南财经大学（SWUFE）。

二　对 35 个城市居民消费者信心指数的分析

消费者信心指数采用美国密歇根消费者信心指数计算方法，由问卷第 1 题至第 5 题计算得到，分数越高，消费者信心越强。其赋值范围为 0~200，问卷开发人员将美国 1966 年第一季度的消费者信心指数定为 100。问卷的内容和相应的五级评价标准如下：

1、您认为您（和您居住在一起的家人）的收入比一年前更好还是更差？

① 许永洪、朱建平:《消费者信心指数的偏差和修正研究》,《数理统计与管理》2018 年第 5 期。

○好很多　○好一些　○没什么变化　○差一些　○差很多

2、展望未来，您认为在未来一年里，您（和您居住在一起的家人）的收入会更好、更差、还是没什么变化？

○会好很多　○会好一些　○会没什么变化　○会差一些　○会差很多

3、纵观整个国家的经济形势，您对未来一年我国经济保持良好发展是否有信心？

○很有信心　○有信心　○不确定　○没信心　○很没信心

4、纵观整个国家的经济形势，您对未来5年我国经济保持良好发展是否有信心？

○很有信心　○有信心　○不确定　○没信心　○很没信心

5、您认为现在是不是购买耐用消费品（例如购买汽车，房屋装修）的好时机？

○好时机　○不确定　○不好时机

（一）描述性统计

2018年35个城市居民消费者信心指数平均值为115.48，2019年的消费者信心指数平均值为138.61，2018年和2019年35个城市居民消费者信心指数的描述性统计如表1所示。总体上看，2019年消费者信心指数分布在129.63到145.35，平均值（138.61）处于临界点（100）和有信心（150）的区间，或者说趋向于有信心；2018年消费者信心指数分布于104.44到122.84，其平均值为115.48，与2018年相比，2019年消费者信心有所增强，整体平均上升20%。如表1所示，2019年的消费者信心指数方差为10.94，标准差为3.31，而2018年的消费者信心指数方差为16.33，标准差为4.04。与2018

年相比，2019 年 35 个城市居民消费者信心指数离散程度缩小，相似性提高。这表明 2019 年消费者信心的提升是全国范围内普遍意义上的。

表 1　2018 年和 2019 年中国 35 个城市居民消费者信心指数描述性统计

年份	极小值	极大值	均值	方差	标准差	偏度	峰度
2018	104.44	122.84	115.48	16.33	4.04	−0.39	0.38
2019	129.63	145.35	138.61	10.94	3.31	−0.72	1.27

2018 年和 2019 年 35 个城市居民消费者信心指数的分布状况如图 1 所示，可以更为清楚地看出 2019 年 35 个城市居民消费者信心指数分布更为相近，大部分集中于 135~145 的范围内，少数分布于 129~130，分布左偏。2018 年 35 个城市居民消费者信心指数分布虽然也呈左偏，但比较接近于正态。

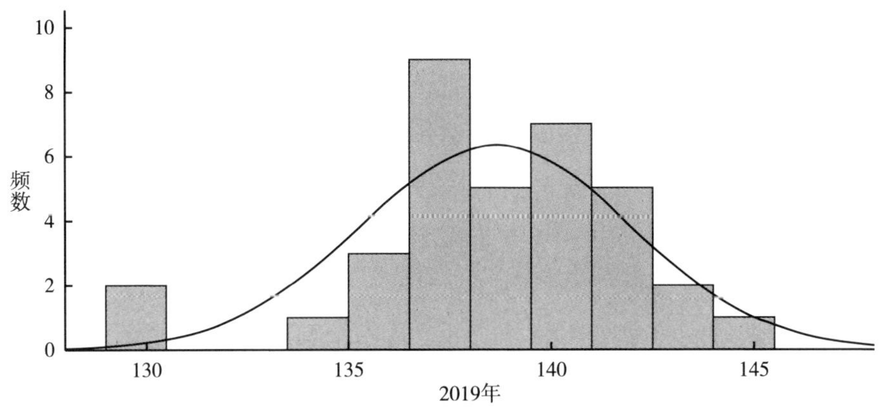

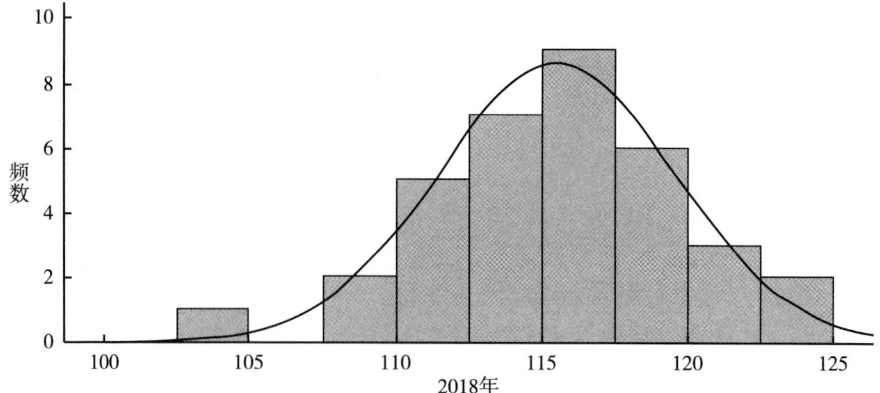

图 1　2018 年和 2019 年 35 个城市居民消费者信心指数直方图

将此次调查的结果与美国同期相比，2018 年 4 月底 5 月初美国的密歇根消费者信心指数为 98.8，2019 年 6 月初，美国的密歇根消费者信心指数为 97.9，2019 年美国的密歇根消费者信心指数比 2018 年下降了近 1%。这表明，和 2018 年相比，2019 年中国的消费者信心有所上升，且上升幅度较大；而美国的消费者信心有所下降，下降幅度不大。

（二）不同城市和地区比较

2018 年和 2019 年 35 个城市居民消费者信心指数各自变化的情况如图 2 所示，从整体的变化趋势来看，虽然变化幅度略有差异，但整体变化一致性较高，消费者信心指数均有不同程度的提高。在当前经济增速、投资增速、出口增速面临下行压力的情况下，未来 1~2 年消费需求有可能成为经济增长的稳定器。

如果按空间区域进行划分，可以将中国划分为四大地区，即东北地区、东部地区、中部地区和西部地区，还可以按八大综合经济区域进行划分，分别按上述两种划分方法将调查的 35 个城市进行空间分组，相应的划分结果如表 2 和表 3 所示。

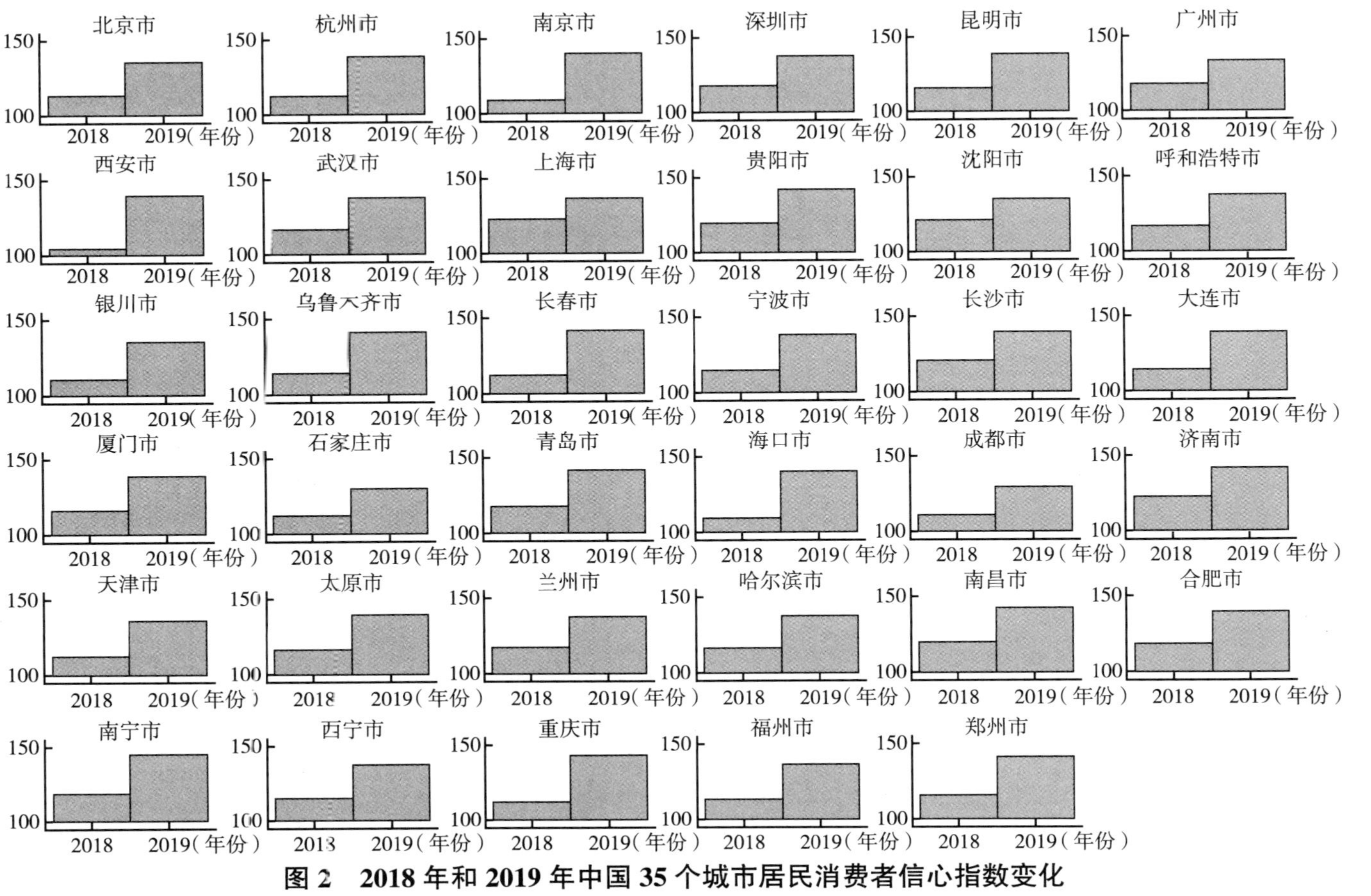

图 2　2018 年和 2019 年中国 35 个城市居民消费者信心指数变化

表 2　中国 35 个城市四大地区空间划分

序号	地区	包括城市
1	东北（4）	沈阳、长春、哈尔滨、大连
2	东部（14）	北京、天津、石家庄、上海、南京、杭州、宁波、福州、厦门、济南、青岛、广州、深圳、海口
3	中部（6）	太原、合肥、南昌、郑州、武汉、长沙
4	西部（11）	呼和浩特、南宁、重庆、成都、贵阳、昆明、西安、兰州、西宁、银川、乌鲁木齐

表 3　中国 35 个城市八大综合经济区域空间划分

序号	地区	包含省、自治区和直辖市
1	东北（4）	沈阳、长春、哈尔滨、大连
2	北部沿海（5）	北京、天津、石家庄、济南、青岛
3	东部沿海（4）	上海、南京、杭州、宁波
4	黄河中游（4）	西安、太原、郑州、呼和浩特
5	长江中游（4）	武汉、长沙、南昌、合肥
6	南部沿海（5）	福州、厦门、广州、深圳、海口
7	大西南（5）	昆明、贵阳、重庆、成都、南宁
8	大西北（4）	兰州、西宁、银川、乌鲁木齐

依据 35 个城市按四大地区的空间分布计算 2018 年和 2019 年消费者信心指数的平均值，并进行相应的比较，结果如表 4 和图 3 所示。

表 4　2018 年和 2019 年中国 35 个城市居民消费者信心指数四大地区平均值比较

2018 年排名	地区	平均值	2019 年排名	地区	平均值
1	中部	118.2	1	中部	140.3
2	东北	116.0	2	西部	138.9
3	东部	115.2	3	东北	138.5
4	西部	114.2	4	东部	137.7

从表 4 的结果看，2018 年消费者信心指数最高的地区是中部地区，平均值为 118.2，其次是东北地区，平均值为 116.0，东部地区较低，平均值为 115.2，西部地区最低，平均值为 114.2；2019 年四大地区的消费者信心指数有所提高，增长速度比较接近，排序基本稳定，最高的还是中部地区，其次是西部地区，与 2018 年略有不同的是，东部地区的消费者信心指数最低，西部地区上升到第二位。

从图 3 可以看出，四大地区的消费者信心指数比较接近，均由 2018 年的近 120 上升至 2019 年的 140 左右，可见 2018 年和 2019 年消费者信心指数的地区间差异比较微小，变动趋势也较为一致。

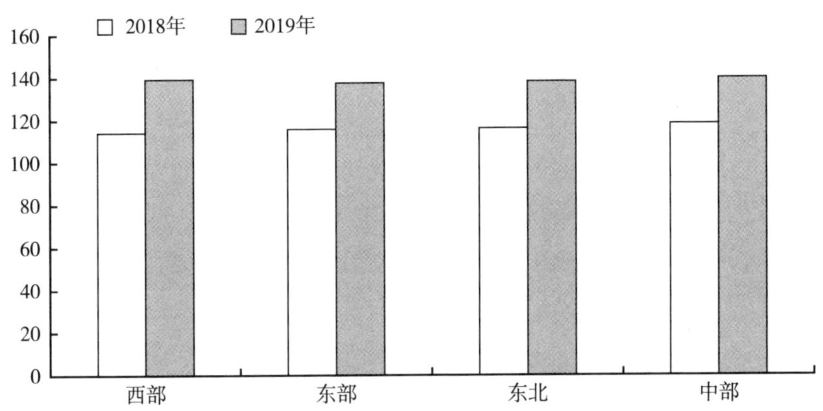

图 3　2018 年和 2019 年中国 35 个城市居民消费者信心指数四大地区间的比较

如表 5 所示，如果从八大综合经济区域角度进行比较，2018 年消费者信心指数排第一位的是长江中游地区（119.1），其次依次是东北地区（116.0）、北部沿海地区（115.8）、大西南地区（115.6）、南部沿海地区（115.0）、东部沿海地区（114.6）、大西北地区（114.5）和黄河中游地区（113.4），而 2019 年八大综合经济区域的消费者信心指数排名有明显的变化，排名最高的依然是长江中游地区（140.1），其次依次是大西南地区（139.7）、黄河中游地区（139.6）、东北地区（138.5）、东部沿海地区（138.5）、大西北地区（138.0）、南部沿海地区（137.6）和北部沿海地区（137.2）。

表 5　2018 年和 2019 年中国 35 个城市居民消费者信心指数八大综合经济区域平均值比较

2018 年排名	地区	平均值	2019 年排名	地区	平均值
1	长江中游	119.1	1	长江中游	140.1
2	东北	116.0	2	大西南	139.7
3	北部沿海	115.8	3	黄河中游	139.6
4	大西南	115.6	4	东北	138.5
5	南部沿海	115.0	5	东部沿海	138.5
6	东部沿海	114.6	6	大西北	138.0
7	大西北	114.5	7	南部沿海	137.6
8	黄河中游	113.4	8	北部沿海	137.2

从八大综合经济区域的整体变化形势来看，如图 4 所示，与 2018 年相比，2019 年消费者信心指数均明显上升，上升幅度没有显著差异。

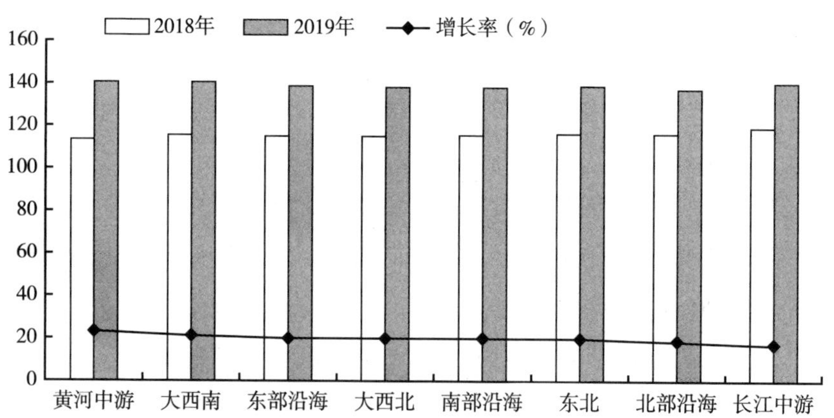

图 4　2018 年和 2019 年中国 35 个城市居民消费者信心指数八大综合经济区域间的比较

通过对 2018 年和 2019 年四大地区和八大综合经济区域消费者信心指数的比较，可以看出全国整体的消费者信心增强，并且没有显著的空间差异。这表明虽然现在经济下行压力较大，但中央明确提出了向高质量发展转变，稳定楼市，积极有效地预防和化解金融风险，各地也都在发力向新经济转型，积极改革，关注民生，增强环境保护，采取了增强群众的获得感等诸多举措，已经切实起到了重要的作用，这将有利于稳定消费需求。

三　消费者信心指数与客观经济因素的关系

消费者信心指数的作用在于可以从主观层面分析判断和预测客观经济运行的状态，包括预测物价水平的变化，可以分析消费需求的变化。据此，可以分析 35 个城市居民消费者信心指数与通货膨胀率指数和消费率指数的相关性。

（一）消费者信心指数与通货膨胀率指数的关系

2019 年中国 35 个城市的通货膨胀率指数和消费率指数排序结果如表 6 所示，2019 年通货膨胀率指数最高的是兰州（1.021），其余排前 5 位的城市分别是成都（1.008）、福州（1.007）、贵阳（1.005）和昆明（1.005），通货膨胀率指数排最后 5 位的城市依次是西宁（0.995）、深圳（0.994）、沈阳（0.992）、大连（0.992）、上海（0.987）。2019 年 35 个城市的通货膨胀率指数和消费者信心指数的相关关系如图 5 所示，其中变异较大的是兰州、成都和石家庄，虽然兰州消费者信心指数与通货膨胀率指数正相关，但是相对于其他城市而言，通货膨胀水平过高，而成都和石家庄这两个城市的消费者信心指数低，而通货膨胀率指数则较高。其余 32 个城市整体上表现为消费者信心指数与通货膨胀率指数正相关，即消费者信心指数高则通货膨胀率指数高，消费者信心指数低则通货膨胀率指数相应较低。

表 6　2019 年中国 35 个城市通货膨胀率指数和消费率指数排名

排名	城市	通货膨胀率指数	排名	城市	消费率指数
1	兰州	1.021	1	西安	1.207
2	成都	1.008	2	深圳	1.151
3	福州	1.007	3	贵阳	1.139
4	贵阳	1.005	4	天津	1.132
5	昆明	1.005	5	长春	1.124
6	太原	1.004	6	兰州	1.091
7	厦门	1.004	7	乌鲁木齐	1.073
8	武汉	1.003	8	沈阳	1.069
9	西安	1.003	9	大连	1.062
10	天津	1.002	10	长沙	1.058
11	长春	1.002	11	哈尔滨	1.057
12	合肥	1.002	12	银川	1.047
13	长沙	1.002	13	广州	1.028
14	重庆	1.002	14	重庆	1.012
15	呼和浩特	1.001	15	西宁	1.008
16	青岛	1.001	16	海口	0.995
17	银川	1.000	17	杭州	0.994
18	乌鲁木齐	1.000	18	上海	0.988
19	宁波	1.000	19	郑州	0.983
20	石家庄	0.999	20	福州	0.981
21	杭州	0.999	21	南昌	0.964
22	南昌	0.999	22	武汉	0.963
23	南京	0.998	23	济南	0.961
24	郑州	0.998	24	南宁	0.958
25	广州	0.998	25	成都	0.947
26	海口	0.998	26	青岛	0.946

续表

排名	城市	通货膨胀率指数	排名	城市	消费率指数
27	北京	0.997	27	北京	0.943
28	哈尔滨	0.997	28	呼和浩特	0.941
29	南宁	0.997	29	厦门	0.938
30	济南	0.996	30	昆明	0.907
31	西宁	0.995	31	宁波	0.892
32	深圳	0.994	32	石家庄	0.888
33	沈阳	0.992	33	太原	0.864
34	大连	0.992	34	合肥	0.862
35	上海	0.987	35	南京	0.826

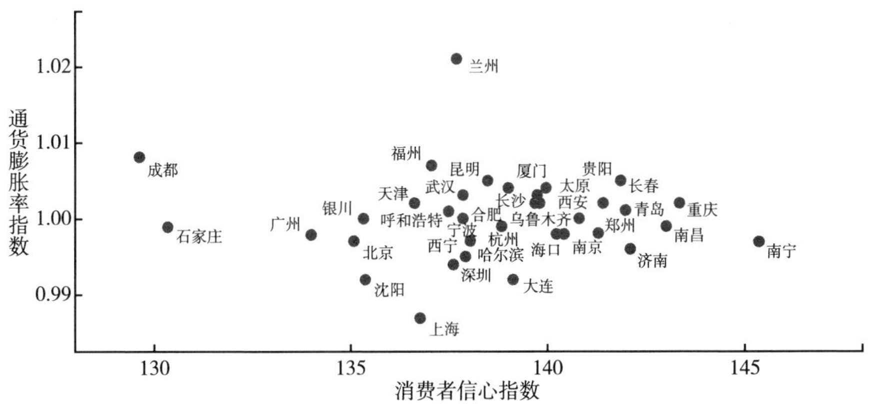

图5　2019年中国35个城市居民消费者信心指数与通货膨胀率指数相关性分析

（二）消费者信心指数与消费率指数的关系

2019年中国35个城市居民消费者信心指数与消费率指数成正相关，即当消费者信心指数较高时，消费率指数也较高，这也较好地说明了当人均收入水平不断提高后，人们的消费会越来越多地受主观因素的影响。如图6所示，35个城市中变异较大的城市是西安、成都、石家庄，其中成都和石家庄的消费者信心指数和消费率指数都相对较低，西安的消费者信心指数和消费率指数都处于较高水平。相较于图 5 的分析结果可以发现，与其他城市相比，成都和石家庄的消费者信心指数比较低，因而消费率指数也较低，而通货膨胀率指数则较高，这可能主要受农产品价格上涨的影响。

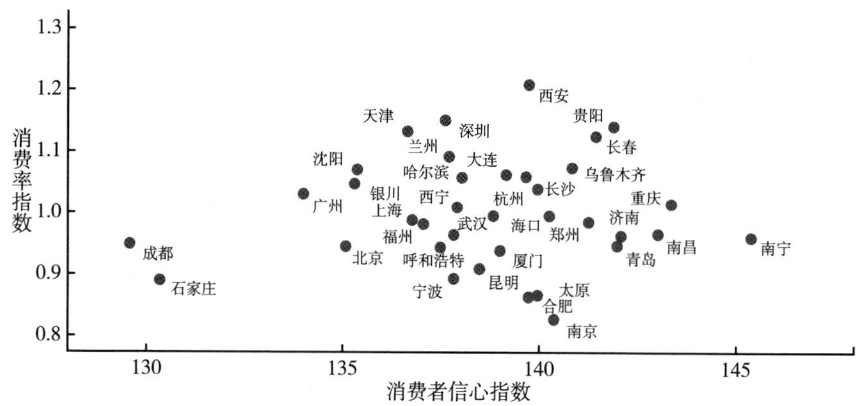

图 6　2019 年中国 35 个城市居民消费者信心指数与消费率指数相关性分析

四　影响因素分析

虽然消费者信心指数主要是反映消费者的主观感受的，但由于主观感受主要来源于客观经济环境，因此还应该从消费的角度来分析消费者信心的影响因素，并识别主要影响因素，以便于从稳定宏观经济的角度对消费者信心进行有效的干预和管理。

从消费的角度分析，消费者的消费除了偏好之外，应当主要受到收入水平、财富水平、社会保障水平的影响。当实际收入水平以及对收入的预期较高时，消费者的消费信心才会得到增强；同时财富水平越高，消费者消费能力越强，则消费信心越充分；社会保障水平不断完善和提高，消费者消费没有后顾之忧，不用过于节俭进行储蓄，则消费信心也应较高。基于上述原因，可以对 35 个城市居民消费者信心的影响因素进行回归分析。

由于消费者信心指数反映的是消费者的主观心理感受，是一种集体社会心理的表现[①]，因此一般需要通过发放调查问卷收集样本并进行测算。消费者信心指数会如同一个镜像一样反照出消费者通过主观感受觉察到的经济变化情况[②]。解释消费者消费行为的传统理论一般是依据莫迪利安尼（Franco Modigliani）的生命周期理论（Life-cycle Theory）和弗里德曼（Milton Friedman）的持久性收入理论（Permanent Income Hypothesis，PIH），而 McIntyre 则持不同的观点，其认为消费不能仅从长期的收入水平角度进行解释，消费者的信心具有短期变化，消费者消费水平的变化对于消费者信心具有敏感性，为此可以月度或季度为时间分隔对消费者的信心变化进行调查，这样就可以提前预知总消费需求的变化情况。[③]实际上消费者信心指数对于消费需求的先导性很早就被发现了，Fuhrer、Carroll 等、Bram 和 Ludvigson 的研究都得出了相关的结论，因此认为消费者信心指数与消费支出正相关。[④]

---

① G.Katona, "Psychology and Consumer Economics," *Journal of Consumer Research* 1（1974）:1–8.

② M.W.Roos, "Willingness to Consume and Ability to Consume," *Journal of Economic Behavior and Organization* 66（2008）:387–402.

③ K.H. McIntyre, "Reconciling Consumer Confidence and Permanent Income Consumption," *Eastern Economic Journal* 2（2007）: 257–275.

④ J.C.Fuhrer, "On the Information Content of Consumer Surrey Expectations," *Review Economics and Statistics* 1（1988）:140–144; C.D.Carroll, J.C.Fuhrer, D.W.Wilcox, "Does Consumer Sentiment Forecast Household Spending? If So, Why?" *The American Economic Review* 84（1994）; J.Bram, S.Ludvigson, "Does Consumer Confidence Forecast Household Expenditure?A Sentiment Index Horse Race," *Economic Policy Review* 4（1998）.

另外，消费者信心指数作为行为经济学的一个应用，其也可以应用于金融领域。Saul 和 Katona 都认为耐用消费品消费者信心指数可以反映消费者对金融稳定性的感受，也可以很好地反映金融危机的概率。① 由于耐用消费品属于非流动性资产，因此如果消费者感到经济不景气或是金融不稳定，消费者购买耐用消费品的意愿就会下降，在这种情况下消费者更会倾向于持有流动性更高的资产。消费经济学的学者们正在更为深入地研究消费者信心指数对消费者其他决策的影响，如 Aneta 研究认为，消费者的消费信心对家庭的金融行为具有影响，消费者信心指数对股市和外汇市场也具有较大的影响。② 一般认为，消费者信心指数走强代表消费者具有强烈的消费意愿，经济有扩张趋势，股市未来也将向好；而当消费者信心指数上升时，消费扩张，经济走强，意味着中央银行未来可能会加息以应对经济过热；在开放的经济条件下，意味着该国货币将走强。例如美联储加息，则意味着美元升值。

国内的学者们也认同消费者信心指数是消费需求的先行指标，并且消费者信心指数对 CPI 具有预测能力③，会影响消费者的消费需求④，因此，消费者信心指数作为消费者对客观经济运行现状和未来

① Saul H. Hymans，"Consumer Durable Spending: Ex Planation and Prediction，" *Brookings Papers on Economic Activity* 2（1970）:173-199; G.Katona，"Consumer Durable Spending，" *Brookings Papers on Economic Activity* 1（1971）：234-239; Frederic S. Mishkin, "Illiquidity, Comumer Durable Expediture and Monetary Policy，" *American Economic Review* 66（1976）:642-654.

② Aneta Maria Klopcka, "Does Consumer Confidence Forecast Honsehold Saving and Borrowing, Behavior? Evidence for Poland," *Social Indicators Research* 133（2017）: 693-717.

③ 张英奎、张帅:《消费者信心指数与居民消费价格指数波动相关性分析》，《价格理论与实践》2014 年第 12 期，第 66~68 页；徐国祥、刘璐:《中国消费者信心指数与居民消费价格指数的关系研究》，《统计与决策》2018 年第 23 期，第 5~10 页。

④ 郑璋鑫:《消费者信心指数与消费需求关系研究——以南京居民消费需求为例》，《统计与信息论坛》2011 年第 10 期，第 58~63 页。

主观判断的反映，将通过消费者的行为决策而影响消费需求，最终影响宏观经济的运行。消费者的消费者信心指数存在地区差异和个体差异。[①] 褚春阳对比了洛阳市的城乡居民消费者信心状况，认为消费者信心提升且农村居民的消费者信心高于城镇居民的消费信心，主要是由就业和预期的不同导致的，进而使城乡居民对未来的消费、储蓄方面的信心存在差距。[②] 2009 年中国银联和新华社第一次发布了“新华 · 银联”中国银行卡消费者信心指数（Bankcard Consumer Confidence Index，BCCI），调查结果显示，虽然在国际金融危机后消费者信心指数出现一定幅度的振荡，但中国的城市居民消费者信心仍处于较高水平。

（一）回归模型

将消费者信心指数作为被解释变量，记作 *Confidence*，解释变量包括人均可支配收入，记作 *Income*；人均财富水平，记作 *Wealth*；社会保险覆盖率，记作 *Socialins*；基本医疗保险覆盖率，记作 *Medicalins*；失业保险覆盖率，记作 *Unemploymentins*，回归方程可以表示如下：

$$Confidence=\alpha+\beta_1 Income+\beta_2 Wealth+\beta_3 Socialins+\beta_4 Medicalins+\beta_5 Unemploymentins+\varepsilon$$

通过上述回归方程主要可以观测到客观经济环境对消费者信心的影响程度和结果。

① 纪宏、任韬、阮敬：《中国消费者信心分析——源自海峡两岸消费者信心指数》，《经济学动态》2010 年第 1 期，第 53~55 页。

② 褚春阳：《洛阳市消费者信心指数调查报告》，《市场研究》2012 年第 2 期，第 40~41 页。

（二）变量分析

回归方程中使用的客观数据包括 35 个城市的人均可支配收入、人均财富水平、社会保险覆盖率、基本医疗保险覆盖率和失业保险覆盖率数据来自《中国城市统计年鉴》、《中国经济与社会发展统计数据库》和《中国劳动和社会保障年鉴》，为了分析和使用方便，上述数据均进行了标准化处理，得到相应的指数化数据，2019 年 35 个城市的人均可支配收入、人均财富水平、社会保险覆盖率、基本医疗保险覆盖率和失业保险覆盖率数值及其排名如表 7 所示。

2019 年 35 个城市的人均可支配收入排前五位的城市分别为上海（1.52）、北京（1.46）、杭州（1.36）、宁波（1.34）和广州（1.34），排在后五位的城市分别是贵阳（0.78）、兰州（0.78）、重庆（0.78）、太原（0.75）和西宁（0.72）。

2019 年 35 个城市的人均财富水平排前五位的城市分别为北京（2.68）、上海（2.54）、深圳（2.40）、杭州（2.30）和南京（1.58），排在后五位的城市分别是兰州（0.47）、银川（0.46）、南宁（0.45）、西宁（0.34）和昆明（0.32）。

2019 年 35 个城市的社会保险覆盖率排前五位的城市分别为深圳（2.23）、杭州（2.10）、沈阳（2.05）、厦门（1.84）和北京（1.77），排在后五位的城市分别是兰州（0.56）、太原（0.48）、南昌（0.46）、呼和浩特（0.41）和哈尔滨（0.39）。

2019 年 35 个城市的基本医疗保险覆盖率排前五位的城市分别为杭州（2.26）、深圳（2.11）、厦门（2.07）、北京（1.76）和大连（1.71），排在后五位的城市分别是重庆（0.51）、南昌（0.50）、郑州（0.47）、石家庄（0.38）和西宁（0.29）。

2019 年 35 个城市的失业保险覆盖率排前五位的城市分别为深圳（3.64）、北京（2.31）、厦门（2.30）、杭州（1.80）和广州（1.65），排在后五位的城市分别是长春（0.44）、南宁（0.41）、哈尔滨（0.38）、石家庄（0.37）和西宁（0.30）。

表 7　2019 年 35 个城市的模型解释变量数值及排名

	城市	人均可支配收入		人均财富水平		社会保险覆盖率		基本医疗保险覆盖率		失业保险覆盖率	
		数值	排名	数值	排名	数值	排名	数值	排名	数值	排名
1	北京	1.46	2	2.68	1	1.77	5	1.76	4	2.31	2
2	天津	0.95	18	1.23	9	1.40	7	1.66	6	0.87	15
3	石家庄	0.79	28	0.70	21	0.60	28	0.38	34	0.37	34
4	太原	0.75	34	0.59	26	0.48	32	1.26	11	0.93	13
5	呼和浩特	1.04	13	0.58	27	0.41	34	1.03	16	0.78	20
6	沈阳	0.98	15	0.69	22	2.05	3	0.94	20	0.73	21
7	长春	0.79	29	0.64	24	0.73	24	1.59	7	0.44	31
8	哈尔滨	0.84	25	0.52	30	0.39	35	0.69	24	0.38	33
9	上海	1.52	1	2.54	2	1.67	6	1.46	8	1.49	6
10	南京	1.32	6	1.58	5	0.97	14	1.19	13	1.44	7
11	杭州	1.36	3	2.30	4	2.10	2	2.26	1	1.80	4
12	合肥	0.93	20	0.98	14	0.78	21	0.58	27	0.83	18
13	福州	0.99	14	0.86	15	0.80	18	0.51	30	0.67	25
14	南昌	0.88	22	0.60	25	0.46	33	0.50	32	0.48	30
15	济南	1.12	10	1.13	11	1.15	10	0.75	22	0.89	14
16	郑州	0.87	24	0.72	20	0.88	15	0.47	33	0.50	29
17	武汉	1.06	12	0.98	13	0.77	22	0.96	19	0.87	16
18	长沙	1.13	9	0.76	18	0.72	25	0.66	25	0.80	19
19	广州	1.34	5	1.38	7	1.35	8	1.26	10	1.65	5
20	南宁	0.79	30	0.45	33	0.57	30	1.43	9	0.41	32
21	海口	0.81	26	1.21	10	0.64	26	0.55	28	0.68	23
22	重庆	0.78	33	0.64	23	0.79	20	0.51	31	0.67	24
23	成都	0.94	19	0.98	12	1.13	11	1.21	12	0.86	17
24	贵阳	0.78	31	0.82	16	0.82	17	0.70	23	0.59	28
25	昆明	0.96	17	0.32	35	0.62	27	0.55	29	0.65	26
26	西安	0.88	23	0.81	17	1.09	12	1.11	14	0.72	22
27	兰州	0.78	32	0.47	31	0.56	31	0.61	26	0.64	27
28	西宁	0.72	35	0.34	34	0.58	29	0.29	35	0.30	35

续表

	城市	人均可支配收入		人均财富水平		社会保险覆盖率		基本医疗保险覆盖率		失业保险覆盖率	
		数值	排名	数值	排名	数值	排名	数值	排名	数值	排名
29	银川	0.79	27	0.46	32	0.88	16	1.00	17	0.98	11
30	乌鲁木齐	0.89	21	0.53	29	0.98	13	0.98	18	1.07	9
31	大连	0.97	16	0.56	28	0.80	19	1.71	5	0.96	12
32	宁波	1.34	4	1.49	6	1.25	9	1.09	15	1.34	8
33	厦门	1.21	7	1.28	8	1.84	4	2.07	3	2.30	3
34	青岛	1.13	8	0.76	19	0.75	23	0.91	21	1.00	10
35	深圳	1.09	11	2.40	3	2.23	1	2.11	2	3.64	1

从上述35个城市的人均可支配收入、人均财富水平、社会保险覆盖率、基本医疗保险覆盖率和失业保险覆盖率指数排名的情况看，上述指数排前几位的城市基本是北京、上海、广州、深圳、厦门和杭州，而排后几位的城市主要有兰州、重庆、西宁、南宁、太原、哈尔滨。

据此，回归过程中使用的变量及其描述性统计如表8所示。

表8　模型回归变量及其描述性统计

变量类别	变量	英文缩写	均值	标准差	最小值	最大值
被解释变量	消费者信心指数	*Confidence*	138.61	3.31	129.63	145.35
解释变量	人均可支配收入	*Income*	1.00	0.22	0.72	1.52
	人均财富水平	*Wealth*	1.00	0.63	0.32	2.68
	社会保险覆盖率	*Socialins*	1.00	0.39	0.51	2.23
	基本医疗保险覆盖率	*Medicalins*	1.65	0.53	0.29	2.26
	失业保险覆盖率	*Unemploymentins*	1.00	0.68	0.30	3.64

（三）结果讨论

将表 7 中的变量分为两类，其中人均可支配收入和人均财富水平是消费者的硬预算约束，人均可支配收入和人均财富水平较高相当于提高消费者的购买能力，而社会保险覆盖率、基本医疗保险覆盖率和失业保险覆盖率的提高，将有助于减轻消费者消费负担，由此可以将这两类变量进行分别回归，最终再将这两个方面的因素放在一起回归。因此，模型一的变量选取人均可支配收入（*Income*）和人均财富水平（*Wealth*）；模型二的变量选取社会保险覆盖率（*Socialins*）、基本医疗保险覆盖率（*Medicalins*）和失业保险覆盖率（*Unemploymentins*）；模型三将考虑全部变量对消费者信心的影响。各方程的回归结果如表 9 所示。

模型一的回归结果表明人均可支配收入与消费者信心指数具有正向影响，人均可支配收入提高 1%，消费者信心指数可以提高 0.047%，人均财富水平与消费者信心指数成反向变动关系，人均财富水平提高 1%，消费者信心下降 0.531%。

模型二的回归结果表明基本医疗保险覆盖率和失业保险覆盖率与消费者信心指数正相关，其中基本医疗保险覆盖率提高 1%，消费者信心指数将提高 0.799%；失业保险覆盖率提高 1%，消费者信心指数将提高 0.021%。社会保险覆盖率与消费者信心指数为负相关关系。

模型三的回归结果得到的结论与模型一和模型二基本一致，即人均可支配收入、基本医疗保险覆盖率、失业保险覆盖率与消费者信心指数正相关，而人均财富水平、社会保险覆盖率与消费者信心指数负相关，只是两种因素汇合在一起时，人均可支配收入和失业保险覆盖率对消费者信心的正向作用有所提高，基本医疗保险覆盖率的正向作用减弱，人均财富水平和社会保险覆盖率对消费者信心的负向作用有所减弱。

表 9　模型回归结果

变量	模型一		模型二		模型三	
	系数	P 值	系数	P 值	系数	P 值
Income	0.047	0.394			0.052	0.689
Wealth	–0.531	0.151			–0.037	0.491
Socialins			–0.418	0.150	–0.386	0.232
Medicalins			0.799	0.263	0.206	0.277
Unemploymentins			0.021	0.490	0.033	0.406
R^2	0.514		0.317		0.321	

综合上述三个模型的回归结果可见，35 个城市居民消费者信心受到人均可支配收入、人均财富水平、社会保险覆盖率、基本医疗保险覆盖率和失业保险覆盖率的影响，其中已经发挥正向影响力且作用效果较大的是基本医疗保险覆盖率和人均可支配收入，而人均财富水平和社会保险覆盖率对消费者信心的影响还有待改善。

五　结论与启示

（一）结论

消费者信心指数主要刻画消费者对经济环境中客观因素的主观感受，是消费者消费动机的影响因素之一，因此会影响消费者的消费行为，同时由于消费和储蓄共同构成收入，在收入水平既定的情况下，也就会影响消费者的金融行为。当人均收入水平不断提高时，消费者在消费和金融资产的选择和配置过程中将越来越多地受到本身主观因素的影响。在中国经济向消费驱动方式转变的情况下，关注和追踪消费者信心的变化是必需的。同时，由于消费者信心先导于物价水平，通过观测消费者信心的变化，也可以提前预判物价水平的变化，为宏观经济政策的取向提供参考。

从消费者个体的角度看，不同年龄、性别和学历的消费者的消费者信心有所不同,35 个城市中越年轻的消费者的消费者信心指数越高，年龄较大的消费者则消费信心较低，受访者中的男性消费者比女性消费者的信心高，学历水平越高的消费者消费信心越高，学历低的消费者则信心略低。上述调查结果的个体差异性说明年轻消费者对自己未来的收入预期和前景比较乐观，男性比女性更为理性且乐观，学历高的消费者对自己未来的发展比较自信。

从消费者信心大小的地区分布看，调查结果表明与 2018 年相比，2019 年 35 个城市居民消费者信心都有所增强，增强的幅度相近。2019 年中部地区消费者信心最强劲，而东部地区则较弱，中部地区的长江中游地区的消费者信心指数排名最高，黄河中游地区消费者信心指数排名第三，略低于大西南地区。这与经济增长水平较为相符，中部地区有崛起之势，而东部地区发展正在放缓。

由于消费者信心最终会影响消费者的消费行为，消费者的集体意志最终会表现在物价水平上，消费者信心会影响消费率和通货膨胀率。通过相关性分析发现，除少数城市外，消费者信心指数的变化对于消费率指数和通货膨胀率指数均有正向影响，即消费者信心指数越高，消费率指数越高，则物价水平有上涨趋势。

消费者信心作为消费者的主观反映，主要来自对客观经济环境的认知，已有的研究结果表明可能的客观影响因素来自两个方面：一是硬预算约束；二是社会保障水平。硬预算约束主要选取两个变量：人均可支配收入和人均财富水平。社会保障水平选取三个变量：社会保险覆盖率、基本医疗保险覆盖率和失业保险覆盖率。模型回归的结果表明人均可支配收入、基本医疗保险覆盖率和失业保险覆盖率对消费者信心提高具有正向作用，而现阶段人均财富水平和社会保险覆盖率没有对消费者信心提高起到应有的正向作用。

（二）启示

通过对35个城市居民消费者信心指数的研究可见，中国经济虽然面临下行压力，但从消费者层面看承受下行压力的微观基础较好。消费者信心对于消费者实际的消费行为和通货膨胀均具有一定的影响力，同时消费者信心的影响因素也较好地发挥了作用。这在一定程度上为未来干预和管理消费者信心提供了一定的理论支持。由此得到的启示包括以下三个方面。

第一，从现有分析结论看，增强消费者信心主要还是从稳定就业和稳定人均收入水平着手。只有当收入水平稳定且对未来的预期较为理想时，消费者才有较高的信心，并且有能力维持并超过现在的消费水平。

第二，不断扩大社会保障的覆盖范围，特别是应保障经济发展水平落后地区的社会保障覆盖率。经济发展水平较高的地区收入水平较高，社会保障制度也较为健全，社会保障制度不会成为制约消费的主要障碍，而经济越落后的地区微观自我保障能力越是相对较弱，对社会保障的需求越大，社会保障覆盖水平对消费者信心的影响就越大。

第三，随着收入水平的不断提高，人均财富水平对消费者信心的影响力将不断提高。为此，中国未来应不断发展和完善金融市场，使居民的财富水平不断提高，使财富保值和增值的途径多样化，降低金融风险，而不仅是将财富保存在房地产上，应通过金融市场实现财富流动配置，使人均财富水平发挥对消费的正向影响。

参考文献

张蕾：《中国银行卡消费者信心指数显示我国城市居民消费稳中有升》，《金融博览》2009年第5期。

李成:《消费者信心能预测产出波动吗——来自中国的经验数据》,《经济学动态》2016年第12期。

B.Dosroches, M.A.Grosselin, "Evaluating Threshold Effects in Consumer Sentiment," *Southern Economic Journal* 4 (2004).

S.C.Ludvigson, "Consumer Confidence and Consumer Spending," *Journal of Economic Perspectives* 2 (2004).

M.Malgarini, P. Margani, "Psychology, Consumer Sentiment and Household Expenditures:A Disaggregated Analysis ," *Applied Economics* 13 (2007).

J.G.Matsusaka, A.M. Sbordone, "Consumer Confidence and Economic Fluctuations," *Economic Inquiry* 2 (1995).

T.Proietti, C.Frale, "New Proposals for the Quantification of Qualitative Survey Data," *Journal of Forecasting* 4 (2011).

D.Acecmoglu, A.Scott, "Consumer Confidence and Rational Expectations: Are Agents' Beliefs Consistent with the Theory?" *Economic Journal* 104(1994).

R.Batchelor, P.Dua, "Improving Macro-economic Forecasts: The Role of Consumer Confidence," *International Journal of Forecasting* 1 (1998).

Eva Mueller, "Ten Years of Consumer Attitude Surveys: Their Forecasting Record," *Journal of the American Statistical Association* 58 (1963).

F. Thomas Juster, Paul Wachtel, "Inflation and the Consumer," *Brookings Papers on Economic Activity* 3 (1972).

F. Thomas Juster, Paul Wachtel, "Anticipatory and Objective Models of Durable Goods Demand," *American Economic Review* 62 (1972).

Frederic Mishkin, "What Depressed the Consumer? The Household Balance Sheet and the 1973-75 Recession," *Brookings Papers on Economic Activity* 1 (1977).

F. Thomas Juster, Paul Wachtel, "Uncertainty Expectations, and Durable Goods Demand Models," in Burkhard Strumpel, Lames N. Morgan, and Ernest Zahn, eds., *Human Behavior in Economic Affairs: Essays in Honor of George Katona* (1972).

Saul Hymans, "Consumer Durables Spending: Explaration and Prediction," *Brookings Papers on Economic Activity* 2 (1970).

B.3
中国35个城市居民教育质量满意度指数报告

张自然*

摘 要： 实际上，新中国成立以来，党和政府就高度重视教育事业的发展，统计结果显示，居民对教育质量的关注度一直是民生问题的最大热点。本报告通过问卷对中国35个城市居民的教育质量满意度进行了调查，调查显示，2019年，中国35个城市居民教育质量满意度指数加权平均值为67.02，介于一般（50）和满意（75）之间，略低于2018年的69.37。但学业负担（26.17）、课外教育支出（24.92）两项调查结果均处于不满意或非常不满意区间，并且均低于去年的指数（分别为29.94和28.77），说明我们在教育体制改革方面还有很长的路要走。通过对影响居民教育质量满意度的因素分析发现，教育提供能力（万人拥有的学校数和万人拥有的教师数）、人均可支配收入和教育文化娱乐消费比对提高居民教育质量满意度均有正向作用。因此建议继续贯彻“教育优先发展战略”，保持和稳定财政性教育经费支出水平，优化财政性教育经费投入的结构，同时加强教师队伍建设，加强教育制度改革力度和步伐，促进教育资源的公平配置，特别是运用好优质教育资源。

* 张自然，中国社会科学院经济所研究员，经济增长理论研究室主任，主要研究方向为城市化、技术进步与经济增长。

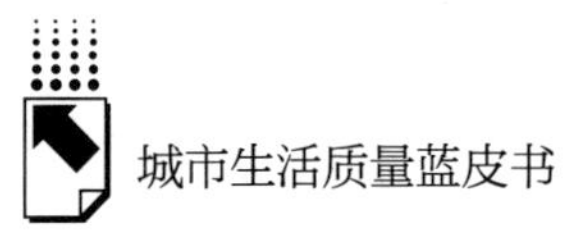

关键词：　教育质量满意度　学业负担　课外教育支出　优质教育资源供给

一　引言

百年大计，教育为本。党的十八大以来，党中央就明确地提出将教育放在优先发展的位置，新时代优先发展教育事业具有重要战略意义。习近平总书记指出："教育是提高人民综合素质、促进人的全面发展的重要途径，是民族振兴、社会进步的重要基石，是对中华民族伟大复兴具有决定性意义的事业。加快教育现代化，办好人民满意的教育。"① 为实现中华民族的伟大复兴，实现"两个一百年"奋斗目标，优先发展教育事业具有重要的战略意义。为全面建成小康社会，办好人民满意的教育，党的十九大以来，结合中国实际情况和中国社会主义初级阶段的主要社会矛盾，十九大报告对如何办好人民满意的教育进行了重大布置，政府实行了一系列教育惠民举措，提出建成小康社会的一个经得起历史检验的标准是看教育的体系结构、质量水平、师资力量和制度建设是否得到新的提升，人民满意度是否得到了提高。

新中国成立以来，党和政府一直重视对教育的投入，大力发展教育事业，在庆祝中华人民共和国成立70周年的新闻发布会上，教育部部长陈宝生指出，"70年来，经过几代人的不懈努力和艰苦拼搏，中国的教育发生了翻天覆地的变化。回顾70年来我们走过的路，可以说教育走过的历程波澜壮阔，教育事业发展取得的成就和我们每一个家庭是那样的紧密相连，也与我们每一个人的成长是那样的息息相

① 《深入学习贯彻党的十九大精神　全面开创教育改革发展新局面》，人民网，2018年3月15日，http://theory.people.com.cn/n1/2018/0315/c40531-29869921.html。

关”[①]。近年来，国家财政在公共财政支出方面优先保障教育，自2012年起中国的财政性教育支出占GDP的比重已经连续七年达到4%的水平。中国已经拥有世界上最大规模的教育体系，2019年拥有各级各类学校51.9万所，在校生人数达到2.76亿人，专任教师有1670万人。教育质量处于世界中上等水平，教育结构适宜，功能完善，为中国经济建设源源不断地输送专业人才，进行人力资本积累，2019年新增劳动力的平均受教育年限已经达到13.6年。

1978年以来，中国经济经过高速增长后，经济结构已经发生了明显的变化，其中人口结构的变化最为显著。中国人口的出生率和死亡率都有所下降，人口增长率放缓，人口结构先是出现了老龄化，后出现了少子化的趋势。为此，国家已经全面放开了二胎生育，鼓励生育二孩。放开二胎生育政策并没有使生育出现峰值，学者们研究认为家庭生育意愿与生活满意度有密切关系，其中包括公共教育对生育意愿的影响。

本报告的研究将调查收集到的主观数据作为被解释变量，以教育发展的客观数据作为解释变量，通过定量关系的研究识别影响教育质量满意度的因素，再根据定量分析的结果提出相应的对策建议，以提高人民对教育质量的满意度，提高公众对公共教育服务的获得感。

所谓教育质量本质上是对教育水平和教育效果的评价，是衡量教育结果的尺度。从学校的角度而言，教育质量是各级各类学校按一定的培养目标或教育目的对教育对象进行培养的结果。一般从内源的角度进行评价，教育质量往往受教育本身的影响，包括教育的制度、手段、计划、方法，也受教师和学生素质的影响。但是如果从社会公众的角度讲，教育质量会涉及教育的家庭支出、教育的公平、家长的精

① 《国庆70周年活动新闻中心第二场新闻发布会》，人民网，2019年9月26日，http://live01.people.com.cn/zhibo/Myapp/Html/Member/html/201909/100738_968_5d8b077702119_quan.html。

力负担、教育内容的广度和深度等。考虑到教育的层次包括基础教育和高等教育，对居民教育质量满意度的调查会分为基础教育质量满意度和高等教育质量满意度，而基础教育是国家义务教育覆盖范畴，因此一般主要针对基础教育满意度展开调查。

二　对35个城市居民教育质量满意度指数的分析

对35个城市居民教育质量满意度的调查问题的设计依据为《教育部关于推进中小学教育质量综合评价改革的意见》(教基二〔2013〕2号)中“建立健全中小学教育质量综合评价体系”的五个指标，具体问题如下。

> 7、您是否有子女正在接受普通中小学教育（小学、初中或普通高中）？（多子女请选年长子女）
>
> 8、您认为目前普通中小学（或您子女所在中小学）是否注重学生的品德发展教育（例如行为习惯、公民素养、人格品质、理想信念等方面）？
>
> 9、您认为目前普通中小学（或您子女所在中小学）是否注重学生身体和心理素质的全面发展（例如身体形态与机能、健康生活方式、审美修养、情绪行为调控、人际沟通等方面）？
>
> 10、您认为目前普通中小学（或您子女所在中小学）是否注重培养学生的兴趣特长（例如学习的主动性、积极性、好奇心求知欲、个人爱好、潜能发展等方面）？

对问题8~10的答案进行加权平均，得到反映各城市的教育质量满意度（注重程度）指数，赋值范围为0~100。

（一）描述性统计

如表 1 所示，2019 年中国 35 个城市居民教育质量满意度指数的极小值为 61.70，极大值为 73.02，均值为 67.02。总体上看，居民对教育质量的满意程度在满意和不满意的临界点（50）之上，35 个城市的平均值为 67.02，处于临界点和满意（75）区间。2018 年 35 个城市的居民教育质量满意度指数极小值为 64.20，极大值为 74.60，均值为 69.37。可见 2019 年居民对教育质量的整体满意度与 2018 年相比是有所下降的，下降幅度为 3.5%。2019 年 35 个城市居民教育质量满意度的方差为6.36，标准差为2.52，而2018年方差为6.43，标准差为2.53，相比较而言,2019 年居民教育质量满意度的离散程度略有缩小的趋势。

表 1　2018 年和 2019 年中国 35 个城市居民教育质量满意度指数描述性统计

年份	极小值	极大值	均值	方差	标准差	偏度	峰度
2018	64.20	74.60	69.37	6.43	2.53	−0.046	−0.279
2019	61.70	73.02	67.02	6.36	2.52	−0.097	−0.278

2018 年和 2019 年 35 个城市居民教育质量满意度指数分布的直方图如图 1 所示，2019 年与 2018 年相比，峰度的值均为负数，说明整体分布比较平坦，但 2019 年的峰度绝对值比 2018 年的略低，说明 2019 年居民对教育质量的满意程度均比较接近平均值，而 2018 年的评价则较为分散。从分布的情况看，2018 年和 2019 年居民教育质量满意度指数均略有左偏倾向，说明居民教育质量满意度低于平均值的较多。

（二）不同城市和地区间比较

2018 年和 2019 年 35 个城市居民教育质量满意度指数的变化如图 2 所示，可以看出不同城市居民教育质量满意度的变化趋势并不是一致的，大多数城市的满意度是下降的，满意度明显有所上升的城市包括杭州（7.18%）、广州（1.17%）、宁波（0.56%）、厦门（2.02%）、青岛（6.33%）、海口（8.17%）和郑州（2.22%），与2018年基本持平略微上升的城市有长沙（0.11%）和合肥（0.26%）。从上升的幅度看，海口居民对教育质量的满意度提升最大，满意度提高了8.17%，其次是杭州提高了7.18%。居民对教育质量的满意度下降最大的城市是成都，下降幅度为11.63%，其次是天津，居民对教育质量的满意度下降了10.61%。

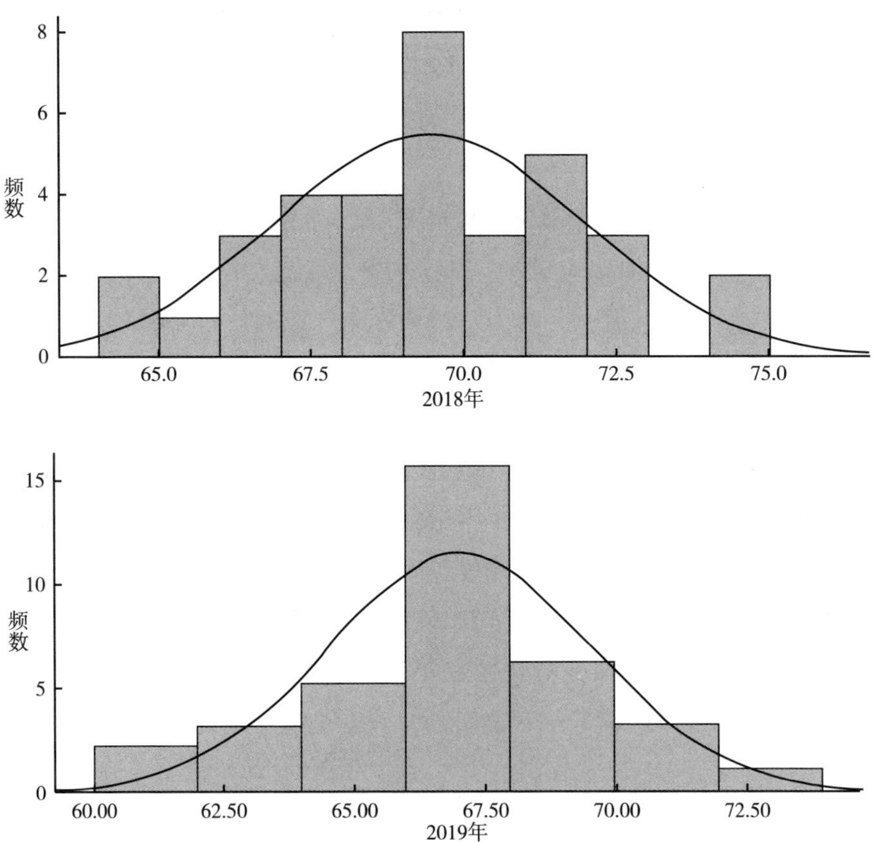

图1　2018年和2019年中国35个城市居民教育质量满意度指数直方图

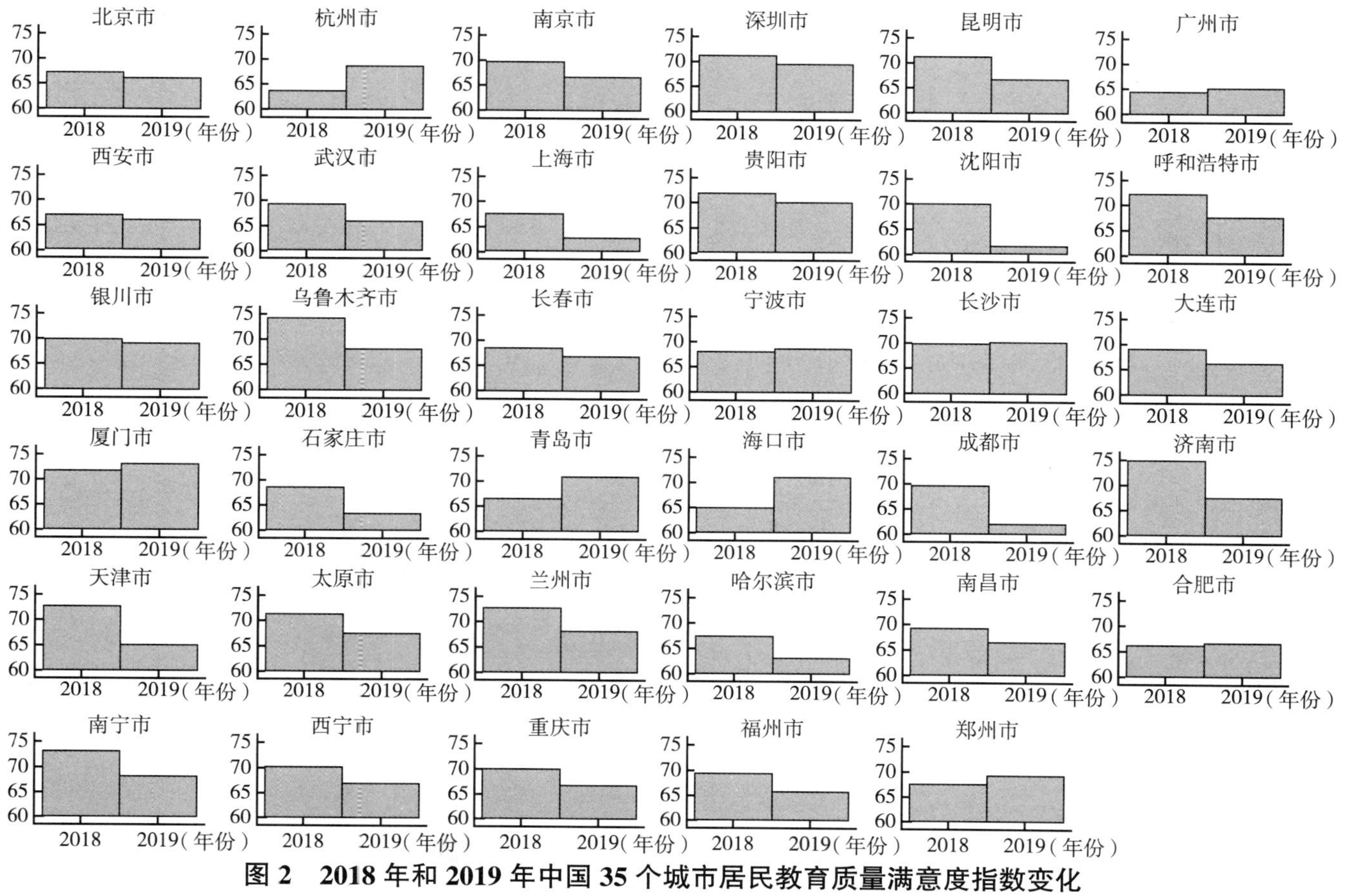

图 2 2018 年和 2019 年中国 35 个城市居民教育质量满意度指数变化

分四大地区进行比较，如表2所示，2018年四个地区中城市居民教育质量满意度指数排名第一的为西部地区（71.0），排名第二的是中部地区（68.9），排名第三的是东北地区（68.8），排名第四的为东部地区（68.7）；2019年排名第一的是中部地区（67.6），排名第二的是东部地区（67.4），西部地区（67.1）排第三位，东北地区（64.6）排第四位。如果以满意度分值达到75分为满意，只有2018年西部地区较为接近满意，且经济发展水平较低的地区，居民对教育质量的满意度略高，而经济发展水平高的地区，居民对教育质量的预期较高，满意度会相对低一些。

表2　2018年和2019年中国35个城市居民教育质量满意度指数四个地区平均值比较

2018年排名	地区	平均值	2019年排名	地区	平均值
1	西部	71.0	1	中部	67.6
2	中部	68.9	2	东部	67.4
3	东北	68.8	3	西部	67.1
4	东部	68.7	4	东北	64.6

为了进一步分析居民教育质量满意度相对较低的原因，研究中心还设计了深入研究的问题：

11、您认为目前普通中小学学生（或您的在读子女）的学业负担状况如何（例如学习时间、课业质量、课业难度、学习压力等方面）?

○非常重　○较重　○一般　○较轻　○非常轻

12、您认为目前普通中小学学生（或您的子女）无法进入重点或热门中小学的最主要障碍是：

○户口不在本地　○学区不同　○择校费用太高　○学生成绩不够　○其他问题

13、您认为目前普通中小学学生（或您的子女）课外教育的支出情况是：

○非常高　○较高　○合适　○较低　○非常低

统计发现2019年学业负担最重的地区为东北地区（23.6），其次是中部地区（25.9）和东部地区（26.5），最轻的是西部地区（26.9）；学生课外教育支出负担最重的地区也是东北地区（20.0），其次是东部地区（25.2）和中部地区（25.6），负担最轻的还是西部地区（26.0）。由此可以看出，居民对教育质量的满意度与学生的学业负担和课外教育的支出是高度相关的，学业负担重和课外教育支出较高是居民对教育质量不满意的主要原因。此外，对中小学生无法进入重点或热门中小学的最主要障碍的调研结果显示，有最高48%最低20%的城市居民认为学区不同是主要障碍，约有最低14%最高35%的城市居民认为择校费用太高是另一个较大的障碍。

从调查结果来看，学业负担（26.17）、课外教育支出（24.92）均处于不满意或非常不满意区间，并且均低于去年的指数（分别为29.94和28.77）。说明我们在教育体制改革方面还有很长的路要走。

从整体情况看，四个地区的城市居民对教育质量的满意度有不同程度的下降，如图3所示，下降最多的是东北地区，其次是西部地区，相对变化较小的是中部地区和东部地区。

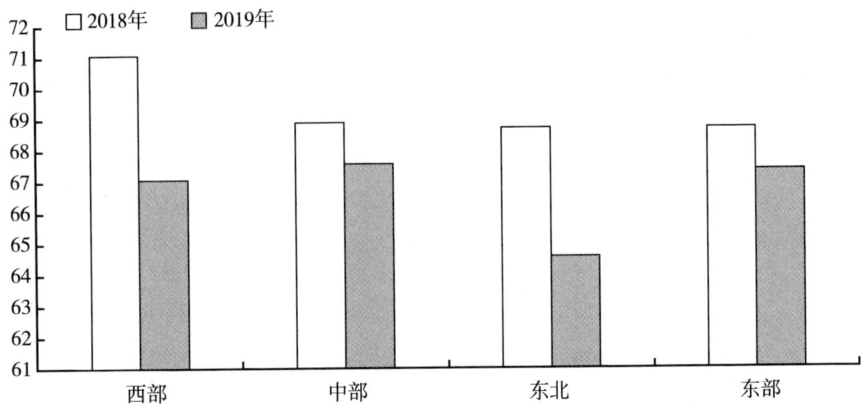

图 3　2018 年和 2019 年中国 35 个城市分四个地区居民教育质量满意度指数变化

分八大综合经济区域对 35 个城市的居民教育质量满意度进行比较，结果如表 3 所示，2018 年城市居民教育质量满意度最高的地区是大西北地区（71.7），其后依次是大西南地区（71.0）、北部沿海地区（70.0）、黄河中游地区（69.4）、东北地区（68.8）、长江中游地区（68.7）和南部沿海地区（68.3），东部沿海地区（67.4）最低。而 2019 年满意度最高的是南部沿海地区（68.7），其后依次是大西北地区（67.9）、黄河中游地区（67.4）、长江中游地区（67.3）、东部沿海地区（66.7）、北部沿海地区（66.7）、大西南地区（66.6），最低的是东北地区（64.6）。

从地区排名看，满意度提高幅度较大的地区主要是南部沿海地区和东部沿海地区，这可能与政府加大教育投入力度，大力引进优秀人才，提高教师队伍的力量有一定关系，而东北地区城市居民教育质量满意度下降幅度较大，这可能与东北地区的人才流失有较大关系。

表3　2018年和2019年中国35个城市居民教育质量满意度指数八大综合经济区域平均值比较

2018年排名	地区	平均值	2019年排名	地区	平均值
1	大西北	71.7	1	南部沿海	68.7
2	大西南	71.0	2	大西北	67.9
3	北部沿海	70.0	3	黄河中游	67.4
4	黄河中游	69.4	4	长江中游	67.3
5	东北	68.8	5	东部沿海	66.7
6	长江中游	68.7	6	北部沿海	66.7
7	南部沿海	68.3	7	大西南	66.6
8	东部沿海	67.4	8	东北	64.6

如图4所示，除南部沿海地区外，2019年八大综合经济区域居民教育质量满意度相对于2018年均有不同程度的下降，下降幅度最大的是东北地区，满意度下降了6%，南部沿海地区城市居民教育质量满意度提高了0.6%。

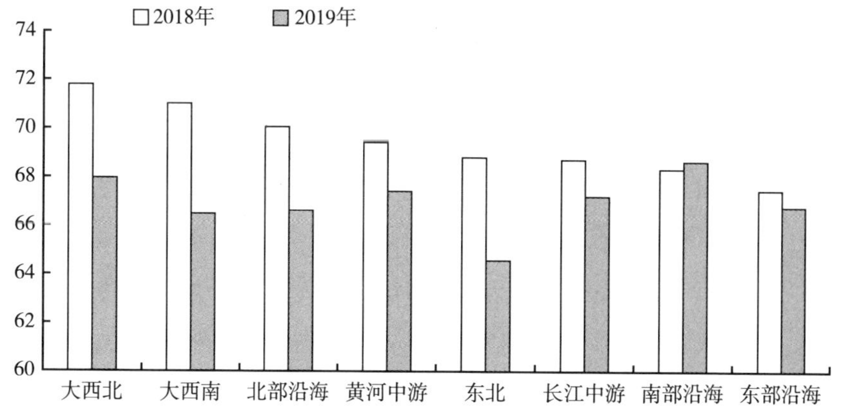

图4　2018年和2019年中国35个城市分八大综合经济区域居民教育质量满意度指数变化

在未来深度城市化阶段，人才的争夺将会更加激烈，在人口流动性不断提高的情况下，居民对教育质量的满意度可能会导致人口的净流入和净流出，也会直接和更为长远地影响地区经济发展的潜力。

三　影响因素分析

为了深入剖析影响教育质量满意度的决定因素，下面将结合影响城市居民教育质量满意度的因素进行定量分析。

义务教育是社会和公众关注的重点和焦点。早在 2012 年中国社会科学院财经战略研究院在发布的《中国公共财政建设报告 2007—2012》（全国版）中就指出，在 9 项公共服务（市政建设、公共基础设施、政府部门公共服务、义务教育、环境保护、治安和司法、高等教育和科研、社会保障、医疗卫生）中公众对义务教育的关注度最高，公众对义务教育的满意度连续五年最高。李志峰、赵承福认为，义务教育作为公共产品，具有很强的公益性，家长和学生是教育的主要消费者，因此也应以消费者满意度为导向对其服务水平进行评价，运用结构方程（SEM）方法构建评价体系，并对山东省义务教育质量进行了评价。[①] 胡平和秦惠民则针对北京的义务教育展开调查和分析，通过分析发现家长对义务教育的满意度主要受家长的收入水平和受教育程度影响，高收入和高学历的家长对义务教育的满意度较低，而低收入和低学历的家长则对义务教育的满意度较高。[②] 从最新的研究成果看，郑方辉和胡晓月对广东省进行抽样调查，公众对 10 项民生领域的问题关注度较高，其中满意度较高的是教育，

① 李志峰、赵承福:《基于 SEM 的义务教育满意度研究——以山东省为例》,《中国人民大学教育学刊》2013 年第 1 期，第 102~111 页。

② 胡平、秦惠民:《政府在义务教育服务中的绩效分析——基于北京义务教育满意度的调查》,《中国人民大学教育学刊》2011 年第 4 期，第 90~100 页。

通过交互分析发现，经济发展水平的差异对教育满意度影响不大，但相对收入低和非本省户籍的居民对教育的满意度偏低。① 崔紫芸、齐文娥和林晓璇选取广州农民工对子女教育的满意度进行调查，实地发放问卷主要询问了家长和学生对过程教育质量和结果教育质量的满意度情况，总体教育质量的满意度与过程教育质量和结果教育质量正相关，广州农民工对子女基础教育的满意度较高。② 魏炜等运用中国综合社会调查（CGSS 2015）数据，分析了居民在生育二孩时受主观幸福感和公共教育满意度影响的程度，研究结果表明，两者对居民生育二孩具有显著正向影响，其中公共教育满意度促进了农村家庭生育二孩的意愿。③

教育针对的对象是学生，保证教育质量，不断提高学生满意度是教育的主要目标，特别是在高等教育阶段。中国教育研究院 2016~2018 年针对全国 31 个省区市的高等教育学生满意度进行了专项调查，张男星等运用 PLS 结构方程对上述调查结果进行了满意度分析，结果表明本科教育的满意度不断向好，满意度指数趋于上升，学生的满意度结构比较稳定，影响学生满意度的因素主要包括学生学习的努力程度、老师和学生对学校满意度的认知程度等。④

通过上述分析可见，教育是十分重要的民生项目，政府和社会公众的关注度较高，现有的研究一般是针对比较发达的城市进行的，如北京、广州等城市，本报告则主要针对中国 35 个城市居民对教育质

---

① 郑方辉、胡晓月:《积极的财政教育政策应着力提升公众教育满意度》,《中国行政管理》2019 年第 6 期，第 111~116 页。

② 崔紫芸、齐文娥、林晓璇:《城市农民工子女教育质量感与学生满意度研究——基于广州市农民工子女的实证调查》,《文教资料》2019 年第 9 期，第 166~168 页。

③ 魏炜等:《主观幸福感、公共教育满意度对居民二孩生育意愿的影响——基于 CGSS 实证分析》,《社会发展研究》2019 年第 3 期，第 120~134 页。

④ 张男星等:《大学师生双重视角下的本科教育多维评价——基于全国高等教育满意度调查的实证分析》,《中国高教研究》2019 年第 7 期，第 70~103 页。

量的满意度进行调查，并分析影响因素，进而提出相应的建议。

考虑到影响居民对教育质量的评价因素包括家长的收入水平，首先将选取人均可支配收入作为自变量，再选取教育文化娱乐消费比、教育提供指数（包含万人拥有的学校数和万人拥有的教师数）作为自变量，通过回归分析研究影响教育质量的因素。

（一）回归模型

将城市居民教育质量满意度作为被解释变量，记作 *Edusatisfaction*，解释变量包括人均可支配收入，记作 *Income*；教育文化娱乐消费比，记作 *Educonsumption*；教育提供指数，记作 *Edusupply*。回归方程如下：

$$Edusatisfaction=\alpha+\beta_1\ Income+\beta_2\ Educonsumption+\beta_3\ Edsupply+\varepsilon$$

通过上述回归方程可以分析居民的人均可支配收入、教育提供指数和教育文化娱乐消费比对教育质量满意度的影响。

（二）变量分析

回归方程中使用的客观数据包括 35 个城市的人均可支配收入、万人拥有的学校数、万人拥有的教师数、教育文化娱乐消费比，数据来自《中国城市统计年鉴》和 CEIC 数据库，为了分析和使用方便，上述数据均进行了标准化处理，得到相应的可比数据。其中教育提供指数是用万人拥有的学校数和万人拥有的教师数按平权进行计算后得到的指数值。

回归方程中的自变量 2019 年的数值以及 35 个城市对应指数的排名如表 4 所示。2019 年中国 35 个城市的教育提供指数排前 5 位的城市依次是昆明（1.77）、兰州（1.58）、南宁（1.49）、贵阳（1.34）、长春（1.32），排后 5 位的城市分别是北京（0.76）、乌鲁木齐（0.71）、沈阳（0.68）、上海（0.63）和深圳（0.53），其余排第6~30位的城市依次是南昌（1.27）、西安（1.25）、海口（1.20）、长沙（1.19）、太原（1.10）、济南（1.07）、福州（1.06）、广州（1.05）、郑州（1.04）、石家庄（1.02）、哈尔滨（1.01）、青岛（0.97）、西宁（0.93）、重庆（0.90）、呼和浩特（0.87）、南京（0.87）、大连（0.85）、天津（0.85）、武汉（0.85）、银川（0.85）、合肥（0.84）、杭州（0.81）、厦门（0.80）、成都（0.78）和宁波（0.77）。

2019年35个城市教育文化娱乐消费比排前5位的城市分别是贵阳（1.89）、南京（1.88）、武汉（1.82）、北京（1.42）和杭州（1.31），排后5位的城市分别是海口（0.60）、兰州（0.53）、重庆（0.50）、厦门（0.46）、西宁（0.39），排第6~30位的城市依次是石家庄（1.29）、西安（1.29）、上海（1.28）、昆明（1.26）、广州（1.22）、太原（1.20）、银川（1.12）、大连（1.11）、长春（1.07）、呼和浩特（1.05）、沈阳（0.99）、深圳（0.97）、济南（0.92）、合肥（0.88）、天津（0.87）、福州（0.84）、南宁（0.80）、宁波（0.80）、长沙（0.78）、哈尔滨（0.78）、成都（0.78）、乌鲁木齐（0.77）、南昌（0.73）、青岛（0.73）、郑州（0.66）。

表4　回归方程式解释变量2019年数值及35个城市对应指数的排名

	城市	人均可支配收入		教育提供指数		教育文化娱乐消费比	
		数值	排名	数值	排名	数值	排名
1	北京	1.46	2	0.76	31	1.42	4
2	天津	0.95	18	0.85	23	0.87	20
3	石家庄	0.79	28	1.02	15	1.29	6
4	太原	0.75	34	1.10	10	1.20	11
5	呼和浩特	1.04	13	0.87	20	1.05	15
6	沈阳	0.98	15	0.68	33	0.99	16
7	长春	0.79	29	1.32	5	1.07	14
8	哈尔滨	0.84	25	1.01	16	0.78	25

续表

	城市	人均可支配收入		教育提供指数		教育文化娱乐消费比	
		数值	排名	数值	排名	数值	排名
9	上海	1.52	1	0.63	34	1.28	8
10	南京	1.32	6	0.87	21	1.88	2
11	杭州	1.36	3	0.81	27	1.31	5
12	合肥	0.93	20	0.84	26	0.88	19
13	福州	0.99	14	1.06	12	0.84	21
14	南昌	0.88	22	1.27	6	0.73	28
15	济南	1.12	10	1.07	11	0.92	18
16	郑州	0.87	24	1.04	14	0.66	30
17	武汉	1.06	12	0.85	24	1.82	3
18	长沙	1.13	9	1.19	9	0.78	24
19	广州	1.34	5	1.05	13	1.22	10
20	南宁	0.79	30	1.49	3	0.80	22
21	海口	0.81	26	1.20	8	0.60	31
22	重庆	0.78	33	0.90	19	0.50	33
23	成都	0.94	19	0.78	29	0.78	26
24	贵阳	0.78	31	1.34	4	1.89	1
25	昆明	0.96	17	1.77	1	1.26	9
26	西安	0.88	23	1.25	7	1.29	7
27	兰州	0.78	32	1.58	2	0.53	32
28	西宁	0.72	35	0.93	18	0.39	35
29	银川	0.79	27	0.85	25	1.12	12
30	乌鲁木齐	0.89	21	0.71	32	0.77	27
31	大连	0.97	16	0.85	22	1.11	13
32	宁波	1.34	4	0.77	30	0.80	23
33	厦门	1.21	7	0.80	28	0.46	34
34	青岛	1.13	8	0.97	17	0.73	29
35	深圳	1.09	11	0.53	35	0.97	17

通过上述35个城市的教育提供指数和教育文化娱乐消费比的比较可以看出，经济发达地区由于人口较多，教育资源是相对紧张的，而经济欠发达地区的教育资源则相对充裕，而教育文化娱乐消费支出

则主要受经济发展水平和文化底蕴的影响。上述变量的描述性统计分析如表 5 所示。

表 5　模型回归变量及其描述性统计

变量类别	变量	英文缩写	均值	标准差	最小值	最大值
被解释变量	教育质量满意度	*Edusatisfaction*	67.02	2.52	61.70	73.02
解释变量	人均可支配收入	*Income*	1.00	0.22	0.72	1.52
	教育提供指数	*Edusupply*	1.00	0.27	0.53	1.77
	教育文化娱乐消费比	*Educonsumption*	1.00	0.38	0.39	1.89

（三）结果讨论

表 5 中的变量主要涉及居民的教育支出和城市对公共教育的提供能力，如果仅考虑城市居民的人均可支配收入和教育提供指数，则可以形成模型一，因此模型一的自变量选取人均可支配收入（*Income*）和教育提供指数（*Edusupply*）；在此基础上模型二加入教育文化娱乐消费比作为支出结构数据，模型二的自变量选取在前两个变量的基础上，再加上教育文化娱乐消费比（*Educonsumption*）。模型一和模型二的回归结果如表 6 所示。

模型一的回归结果表明城市居民教育质量满意度与人均可支配收入和教育提供指数正相关，人均可支配收入每提高 1%，居民的教育质量满意度将提高 0.214%，教育提供指数每提高 1%，居民的教育质量满意度会相应提高 0.551%，其中教育提供指数与教育质量满意度表现为显著相关。

模型二的回归结果表明居民的人均可支配收入、教育提供指数和教育文化娱乐消费比与教育质量满意度正相关，其中教育提供指数和教育文化娱乐消费比与教育质量满意度显著正相关。加入教育文化娱乐消费比变量后，人均可支配收入对教育质量满意度的作用显著下降，人均可支配收入提高 1% 会使教育质量满意度提高 0.097%，而教育提供指数每提高 1%，教育质量满意度则将提高 0.505%，教育文化娱乐消费比每提高 1%，教育质量满意度会提高 0.313%。

表 6　模型回归结果

变量	模型一		模型二	
	系数	P 值	系数	P 值
Income	0.214	0.223	0.097	0.584
Edusupply	0.551	0.03	0.505	0.005
Educonsumption			0.313	0.054
R^2	0.492		0.573	

上述回归结果说明人均可支配收入提高以及教育文化娱乐消费比对教育质量提高虽然较为重要，但是更重要的是政府对教育的投入水平，不断提高教育的提供能力，才是提高教育水平的根本举措。

四　结语

教育质量是党、政府和人民都普遍关注的重要问题，随着中国经济发展水平不断提高，人民生活水平不断提高，这个问题变得越来越重要。通过前述分析可知，提高教育质量最重要的是提高教育提供能力和水平，为此政府应持续保证教育的财政支持水平并不断提高教育资源的质量，不断进行制度改革，改善教育资源分配不均的状态。

第一，贯彻“教育优先发展战略”，保持和稳定财政性教育经费支出水平的同时，优化财政性教育经费投入的结构。新中国成立以来，中国财政性教育经费投入的绝对数额是不断增加的，1952年为11.62亿元，2018年公共财政教育经费支出达到32446亿元，按1952年不变价格计算，2018年的支出规模是1952年的329.1倍。但相较于发达国家的人均教育经费投入而言，中国还是存在一定的差距的，即使与金砖国家相比，中国的人均教育经费投入也仅高于印度。杨蓉、刘婷婷研究指出，中国的教育经费来源主要是公共财政，非财政性经费来源比重较低，教育经费的使用中，用于学前教育和高中教育阶段的经费较低，用于人员的经费比重较高，但与OECD国家相比还是较低的。① 柳倩、黄嘉琪的研究也表明中国对学前教育的投入与OECD国家相比也是很不足的。② 王培石研究认为，财政对基础教育投入对居民收入提高作用最大，过高比重的生均投入会降低经济的产出效率。③

2012年以来，中国的财政性教育经费投入进入“4%时代”，在经济增长下行压力不断增大的情况下，财政性教育经费的投入应相对保持稳定，对于地方政府而言保持财政性教育经费投入绝对额的稳定或增长是比较困难的事情。对于经济贫困地区而言，提高教育质量是帮助地区提高经济发展水平的重要推动力，因此就需要地方政府保证对公共教育资源的投入和建设，避免地方异质性偏好导致的投入不均，不断改善落后地区的教育供给能力，调整地区间教育资源配置失衡的问题，特别是要保障农村地区义务教育经费的充足性，提高教育均等化的水平。

---

① 杨蓉、刘婷婷:《中国教育经费配置结构分析——基于历史趋势和国际视野的双重探讨》,《全球教育展望》2019年第6期。

② 柳倩、黄嘉琪:《中国与OECD国家学前教育投入水平的比较研究》,《教育经济评论》2019年第3期。

③ 王培石:《政府教育投入对民众可支配收入提升的关系研究——基于我国1999至2017年的省际实证分析》,《国家教育行政学院学报》2019年第4期。

第二，加强教师队伍建设，提高教育教学质量。教师是教育的实施者，稳定和高素质的教师队伍是高质量教育的保障，特别是农村中小学教师队伍的稳定，是保证农村义务教育质量的基础。在保证农村基础教育硬件投入的基础上，应不断提高教师待遇，并动员城市师资去乡村支教。其次，要加强师德教育和约束。学校教育的实施主要由教师来完成，学校应拥有一支师德高尚、学识渊博、业务精干的教师队伍，其中师德建设必不可少。

第三，加大教育制度改革的力度和步伐，促进教育资源的公平配置。十九大报告指出，推进教育公平，努力让每个孩子都能享有公平而有质量的教育。随着经济的发展，人均收入水平的不断提高，未来社会的主要矛盾将表现为优质教育资源的供求紧张，因此在未来较长一段时间内，政府要努力解决优质教育资源短缺和配置不公平的问题。为此，政府应进一步进行改革和机制创新，加强顶层制度设计，提高社会参与度，鼓励社会资本投入，拓宽办学渠道；同时应减轻学生学业压力，由升学为主向育人为主转变。

B.4
中国 35 个城市居民健康满意度指数报告

张自然*

摘　要：国民健康是一个国家综合国力和社会进步的标志，只有具有健康的体魄才能幸福生活，国家才能有更长远的发展潜力。本报告通过问卷调查了 35 个城市居民的健康满意度，调查显示，2019 年中国 35 个城市居民健康满意度指数加权平均值为 57.26，介于好（50）和很好（75）之间，低于 2018 年 64.48 的水平。从身体健康和心理健康的调查结果来看，2019 年 35 个城市每月居民不健康的天数平均为 8.14 天，高于 2018 年的 5.5 天。其中心理不健康的天数由 3.01 天增加到 5.14 天，身体不健康的天数由 2.53 天增加到 2.87。因为健康原因影响日常生活工作的天数为 3.22，高于 2018 年的 2.19 天。居民健康满意度指数下降可能有多方面的原因，回归结果显示对城市居民健康满意度具有正向影响的因素包括人均可支配收入、人均绿地面积和空气质量，具有负向影响的因素包括基尼系数、房屋销售价格、房价收入比和交通提供能力。因此，建议不断提高居民的人均可支配收入，改善城市绿化和交通环境条件，并稳定房价，多途径向市民提供住房。

* 张自然，中国社会科学院经济所研究员，经济增长理论研究室主任，主要研究方向为城市化、技术进步与经济增长。

关键词： 健康满意度 身体健康 心理健康 适应性调节能力

一 引言

随着中国经济的高速发展，工作、生活等各方面的诸多压力，使国民对健康的关注度不断提高，健康压力甚至超过了经济压力。随着市场化水平的提高和市场化改革的深入，竞争压力与日俱增，医学研究结果表明，学习、工作、生活或家庭压力不断增大，可能会提高心脏病等心脑血管疾病发病率，人也比较容易抑郁，而当人从学习、生活、工作中得到快乐时，则有益于身体健康。2007~2009 年《小康》杂志社会同新浪网等有关机构和专家对中国的生命小康指数进行调查，其中的分指数就包括居民健康满意度指数，调查结果显示，2007~2009 年中国居民健康满意度指数分别为 56.7、56.9 和 59.8，从得分上看满意度是不断提高的。

健康实际上涉及医学、公共卫生、人口统计、社会学、经济学等诸多领域，不同领域对健康的理解略有差别。医学界很早就提出健康是个系统观①，健康本身是一种协调关系，要与自然系统、生态环境条件相协调，健康是人作为个体能长时间地适应环境的身体、情绪、精神和社会方面的能力。医学的角度认为，人在生存过程中要不停地与外界（自然界和社会）进行物质和信息交流，健康实质上就是人在与外界交流的过程中保持动态平衡的状态，如果动态平衡关系失调了，人的身体、精神或心理就会生病。

世界卫生组织（WHO）认为，一个健康的人应当身体健康、心

① 杜治政：《健康定义的面面观》，《医学与哲学》1990 年第 7 期，第 19~22 页。

理健康、社会适应良好、道德健康。[①] 其中身体健康就是指机体机能和生命活动正常运行，心理健康包括以下三个方面的标准：一是具备完整的人格，有稳定的情绪，有良好的自我感觉，可以很好地控制和管理自己的情绪，积极情绪多于或大于消极情绪，可以在心理上自我平衡，因此能够自爱、自尊、自信，且有自知之明；二是对自己所处的环境有充足的安全感，与他人有正常的人际关系，得到别人信任和喜欢；三是对自己的未来具有明确的目标，有进取心，为自己生活或事业中的理想和信念而努力。所谓社会适应良好是指行为个体的心理和行为能够适应环境的变化，且其行为方式被他人理解和接受。而道德健康是一个人不在为自己谋利益时损害其他人的利益，可以按照社会统一的准则辨别是非、真假、美丑、荣辱等，能按社会规范约束自己的行为，支配自己的行动。在这个意义上理解，健康就不单纯是身体上无疾病、无缺陷，还应该在心理和社会交往方面状态良好。

董希望和王弟海认为，理解现代意义上的健康应把握好以下四点：一是健康涉及的内容包括身体健康、心理健康、社会适应良好和道德健康；二是健康的各内容间应平衡，还应与外部环境相平衡；三是健康是个人对自己在现在和未来自我感觉良好的状态；四是这种良好的状态也是一种资源，借助这种资源个体可以实现自己的生活、工作目标，在这个意义上讲，健康就是个人实现自身理想和目标的保障和基础，因此追求健康本身也是个体的目标。[②]

从经济学角度讲，可以从宏观和微观两个层面来衡量健康水平。宏观层面健康是人口整体健康的状态，是测试某一群体或国家人口

① What is the WHO Definition of Health, World Health Organization, http://www.who. int/about/who-we-are/frequently-asked-questions.

② 董希望、王弟海：《经济学中的“健康”：定义与度量——学科比较的视角》，《福建论坛》(人文社会科学版) 2014 年第 12 期，第 19~26 页。

的整体健康状况，一般用公共健康（Public Health）测试指数或总体人口健康指数来测度。参考医学或流行病学一般用死亡率、患病率和伤残率等作为衡量指标，宏观经济学中经常采用初生婴儿死亡率、5 岁以下儿童死亡率、出生时预期寿命等指标来描述总体人口健康水平。在微观层面，由于需要了解掌握微观个体的健康状况，就需要通过对微观个体进行相应的健康调查获取数据。Strauss 和 Thomas 提出微观测试个人健康水平的指标有疾病健康状况（Disease-oriented Definitions of Health Statue）、GHS 指数（General Health Status, 总体健康状态）、身体功能（Physical Functioning）以及营养状态（Nutrition-based indicators）等。[①] 一般要依据医学诊断的结果对一个人的健康状况做出相应的评价。如美国的国家营养健康检测调查就运用 GHS 指数，虽然该调查也是被调查者根据自己的主观感受做的自我评估，但因为从医学角度问十分专业的问题，操作起来成本很高，在实际调查中经常会以调查者本人对自己健康状态的主观感受作为衡量指标，可以通过询问被调查者最初是否可以从事某些特定活动，如移动重物、上楼梯等，选项可以分为容易、可以、困难等，以此来判断受访者的健康程度，如 ADL(Activities of Daily Living，日常活动量）调查。

综上所述，从经济学研究领域看，国内外现有的研究已经从宏观和微观层面明确指出了健康的重要性，从居民个体角度而言，健康程度无疑影响生存和生活质量，其不但是个体实现自身经济目标的资源，也是宏观层面经济社会发展的重要资源。据此，在中国城市化水平不断加深的情况下，有必要对城市居民的健康自我评价水平进行追踪测度，并对其影响因素进行深入剖析。下面将采用中国 35 个城市

① J.Strauss，D.Thomas，"Health, Nutrition and Economic Development," *Journal of Economic Literature* 36（1998）: 766-817.

的居民健康满意度调查结果数据，分析不同城市和地区间居民健康满意度的变化和异质性及其影响因素。

二　对35个城市居民健康满意度指数的分析

根据对微观主体进行健康自我评价的理论设计调查问卷，问题如14~17所示。问题14评价分数为0~100，分数越高代表满意度越高，问题15~17的答案为天数，天数越多则表明健康状态越不好。

14、总体而言，您觉得您的健康情形如何？

15、回顾过去30天，您有多少天身体有疾病或创伤（身体不很健康）？

16、回顾过去30天，您有多少天在心理上有焦虑、抑郁或情绪失控（心理不很健康）？

17、在过去的30天内，您有多少天因为身体或心理的健康问题而限制了日常活动（例如自理生活、工作或娱乐）？

将上述四个问题的答案进行加权平均后，就可以得到35个城市居民的健康自我评价指数，即居民健康满意度指数。

（一）描述性统计

从整体上看，如表1所示，2019年中国35个城市居民的健康满意度平均值为57.26，而2018年为64.48，因此整体居民对健康的自我评价是下降的，下降幅度为12.6%。2019年居民健康满意度指数极小值为50.94，低于2018年的57.36，极大值为61.50，也低于2018年的70.58。从2018年和2019年35个城市居民健康满意度指数的统计分布情况看，2019年居民健康满意度指数的方差为7.07，标准差为 2.66，而 2018 年居民健康满意度指数的方差为 9.05，标准差为 3.01，可见 2019 年中国 35 个城市居民健康满意度的离散程度缩小了，一致性有所增强。

表 1　2018 年和 2019 年中国 35 个城市居民健康满意度指数描述性统计

年份	极小值	极大值	均值	方差	标准差	偏度	峰度
2018	57.36	70.58	64.48	9.05	3.01	–0.46	0.29
2019	50.94	61.50	57.26	7.07	2.66	–0.54	–0.19

图 1 为 2018 年和 2019 年中国 35 个城市居民健康满意度分布的直方图，从分布的偏度上很容易看出，2018 年和 2019 年的数值分布虽然都是左偏分布，但 2019 年数据的左侧拖尾较长，表明 2019 年居民健康满意度低于平均值的人数较 2018 年要多一些；而从峰度分布看，2018 年 35 个城市居民健康满意度评价指数高的人数比较多，而 2019 年则分布较为平缓，进一步证实了相对于 2018 年，2019 年 35 个城市居民的健康满意度没有过高水平的。

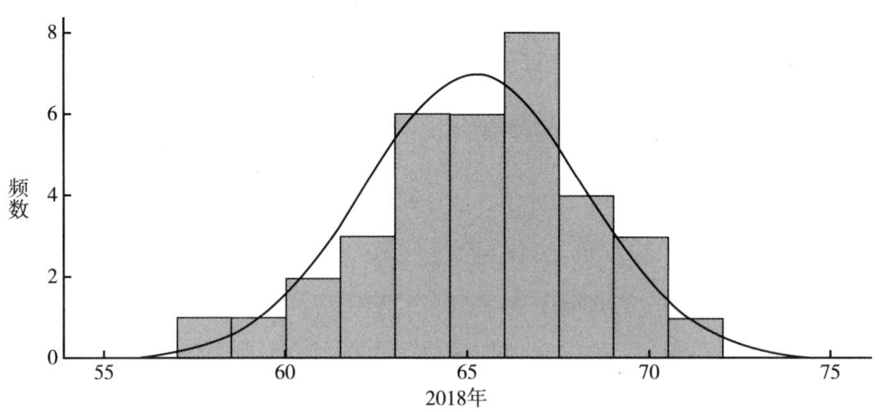

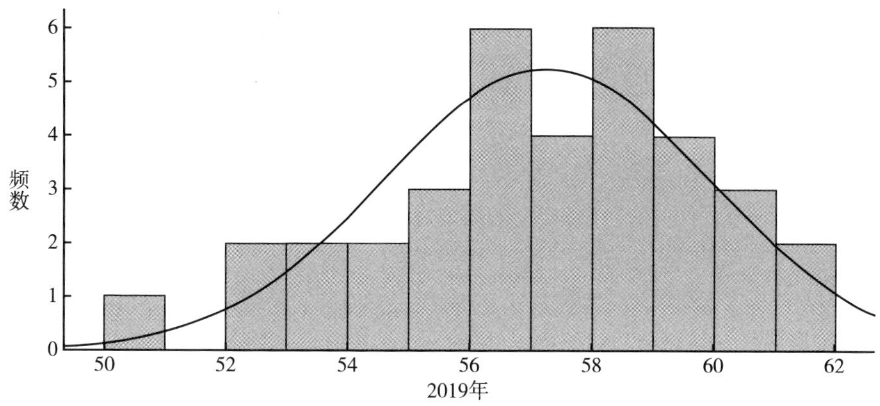

图1 2018年和2019年35个城市居民健康满意度直方图

35个城市居民30天内感觉身体不健康的天数描述统计如表2所示，2019年城市居民身体不健康的天数极小值为2.25天，极大值为4.44天，平均值为2.87天，均高于2018年的对应值。从数据的分布看，2018年和2019年居民身体不健康天数分布的偏度均右偏，这表明实际多数人感觉身体不适的天数大于均值。

表2 2018年和2019年中国35个城市居民身体不健康天数描述性统计（问题14）

年份	极小值	极大值	均值	方差	标准差	偏度	峰度
2018	1.55	4.43	2.53	0.53	0.73	0.77	-0.07
2019	2.25	4.44	2.87	0.24	0.49	0.99	1.44

2019年35个城市居民在过去30天内感觉心理不健康的天数如表3所示，极小值为4.14天，极大值为6.86天，均值为5.14天，2018年居民心理不健康的天数极小值为1.83天，极大值为5.25天，均值为3.01天，从数值分布的对比情况看，2019年城市居民心理不健康

的天数略大于 2018 年，分布右偏，峰度增大，表明多数居民心理不健康的天数大于均值。

表 3　2018 年和 2019 年中国 35 个城市居民心理不健康天数描述性统计（问题 15）

年份	极小值	极大值	均值	方差	标准差	偏度	峰度
2018	1.83	5.25	3.01	0.78	0.88	0.84	0.11
2019	4.14	6.86	5.14	0.32	0.56	0.66	1.16

2019 年 35 个城市居民因为身心不健康而使日常活动受限的天数（在过去 30 天内）如表 4 所示，极小值为 2.24，极大值为 5.78，均值为 3.22，而 2018 年的极小值为 1.25，极大值为 4.74，均值为 2.19，方差和标准差与 2019 年的比较接近，表明与 2018 年相比，2019 年居民因健康原因而影响正常工作和生活的天数增加了，除此之外，个体间的差异度并没有太大变化。

表 4　2018 年和 2019 年中国 35 个城市居民日常活动受限天数描述性统计（问题 16）

年份	极小值	极大值	均值	方差	标准差	偏度	峰度
2018	1.25	4.74	2.19	0.59	0.77	1.66	3.05
2019	2.24	5.78	3.22	0.52	0.72	1.32	3.62

综合起来看，从 2019 年居民健康满意度指数（57.26）处于好（50）和很好（75）之间，低于去年 64.48 的水平。从身体健康和心理健康的调查结果看，2019 年每月居民不健康的天数 35 个城市平均合计为 8.14 天，高于去年的 5.5 天。其中心理不健康的天数由 3.01 增加到 5.14 天，身体不健康的天数由 2.53 天增加到 2.87 天。因为健康原

因影响日常生活工作的天数由 2.19 天增加到 3.22 天。可见，整体上 2019 年居民在身体和心理方面的健康自我评价均低于 2018 年。

（二）不同城市和地区间比较

2018 年和 2019 年中国 35 个城市居民健康满意度指数的变化如图 2 所示，除了海口之外，其余城市的 2019 年居民健康满意度均不及 2018 年的水平，其中下降幅度最大的城市是乌鲁木齐，下降了 21.7%。

分地区比较，如表 5 所示，2019 年四大地区的居民健康满意度指数排第一位的是中部地区（58.0），其后依次是东北地区（57.9）、东部地区（57.6）和西部地区（56.1），地区间差异不大。2018 年排第一位的是东北地区（65.5），其后依次是东部地区（65.4）、中部地区（65.1）和西部地区（64.9），地区间的差异也不明显。

表 5　2018 年和 2019 年中国 35 个城市居民健康满意度指数四大地区平均值比较

2018 年排名	地区	平均值	2019 年排名	地区	平均值
1	东北	65.5	1	中部	58.0
2	东部	65.4	2	东北	57.9
3	中部	65.1	3	东部	57.6
4	西部	64.9	4	西部	56.1

如图 3 所示，2019 年中国 35 个城市分四大地区的居民健康满意度指数均有不同程度下降，下降最多的是西部地区，下降幅度为 13.6%，其他地区的下降幅度差别不大。所以，西部地区不仅排名最后，其居民健康满意度水平下降的幅度也是最大的。

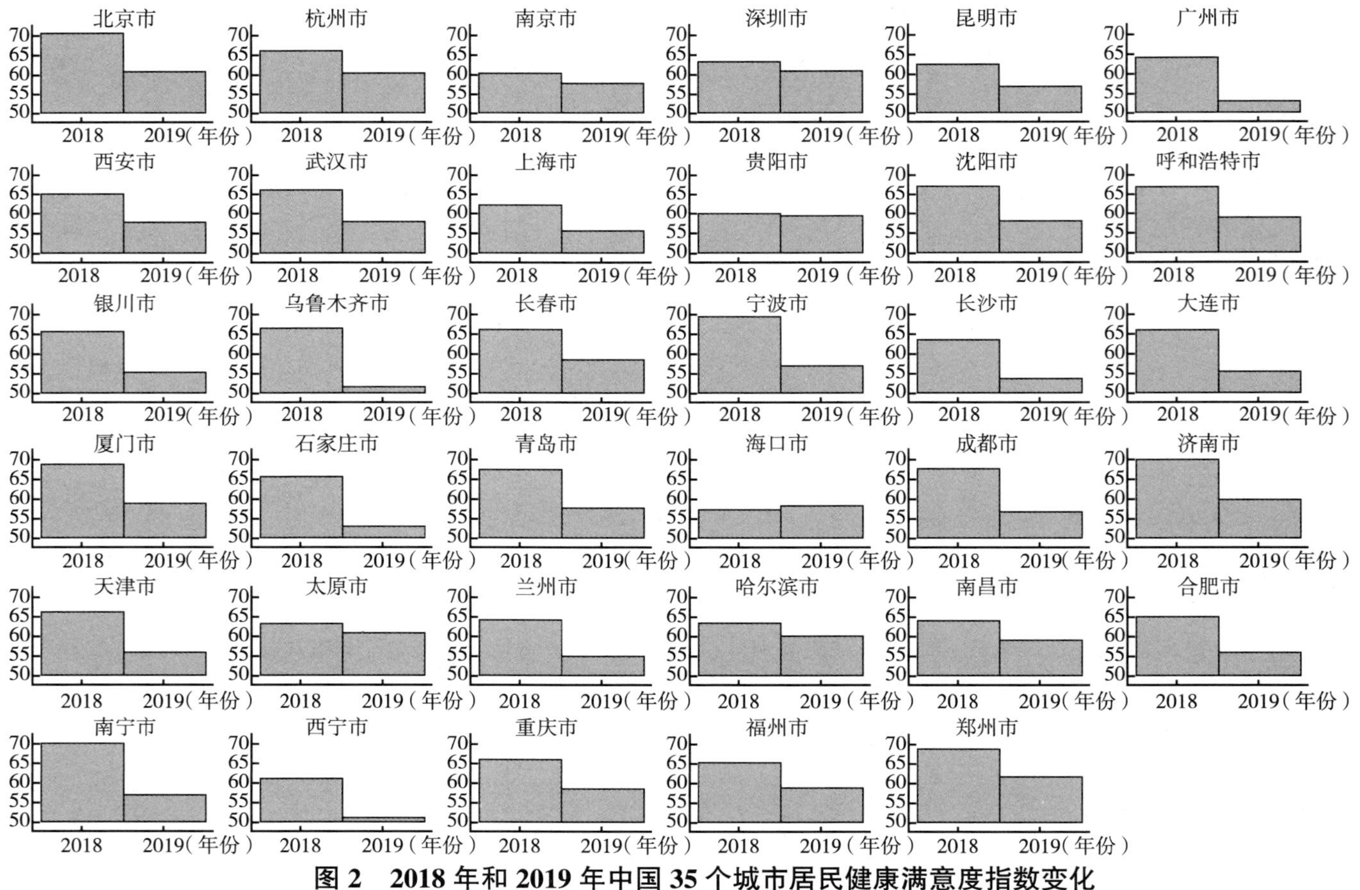

图2 2018年和2019年中国35个城市居民健康满意度指数变化

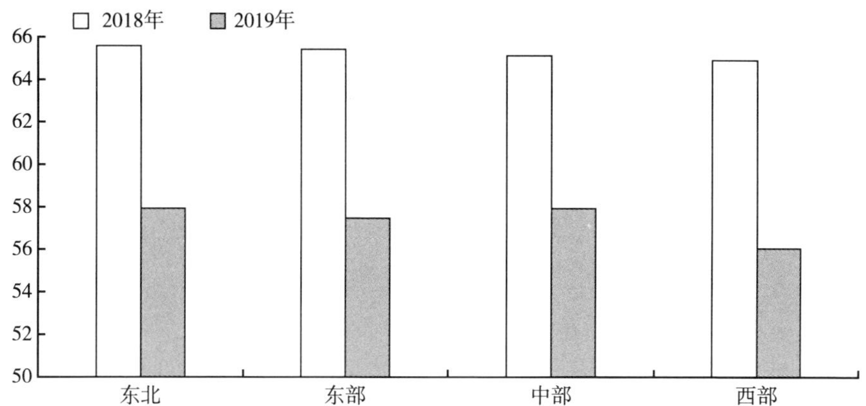

图3　2018年和2019年中国35个城市居民健康满意度指数分四大地区的变化比较

如果分八大综合经济区域进行比较，如表6所示，2019年排第一位的地区是黄河中游地区（59.8），其后依次为南部沿海地区（58.1）、东北地区（57.9）、大西南地区（57.5）、北部沿海地区（57.4）、东部沿海地区（57.3）、长江中游地区（56.4）和大西北地区（53.4），而2018年排第一位的地区是北部沿海地区（67.9），其后依次为黄河中游地区（65.8）、东北地区（65.5）、大西南地区（65.1）、长江中游地区（64.7）、东部沿海地区（64.5）、大西北地区（64.1）和南部沿海地区（63.7）。从地区排名的变化看，南部沿海地区上升最多，由2018年的第8位上升至2019年第2位，北部沿海地区排名下降最多，由2018年的第1位下降至2019年的第5位，其他地区排名相对变化不大或没有变化。

表6　2018年和2019年中国35个城市居民健康满意度指数分八大综合经济区域平均值比较

2018年排名	地区	平均值	2019年排名	地区	平均值
1	北部沿海	67.9	1	黄河中游	59.8
2	黄河中游	65.8	2	南部沿海	58.1
3	东北	65.5	3	东北	57.9

续表

2018 年排名	地区	平均值	2019 年排名	地区	平均值
4	大西南	65.1	4	大西南	57.5
5	长江中游	64.7	5	北部沿海	57.4
6	东部沿海	64.5	6	东部沿海	57.3
7	大西北	64.1	7	长江中游	56.4
8	南部沿海	63.7	8	大西北	53.4

如图 4 所示，与 2018 年相比，2019 年八大综合经济区域的城市居民健康满意度均有所下降，满意度下降最多的是大西北地区，下降幅度为 16.7%，下降幅度最小的是黄河中游地区，下降 8.8%。

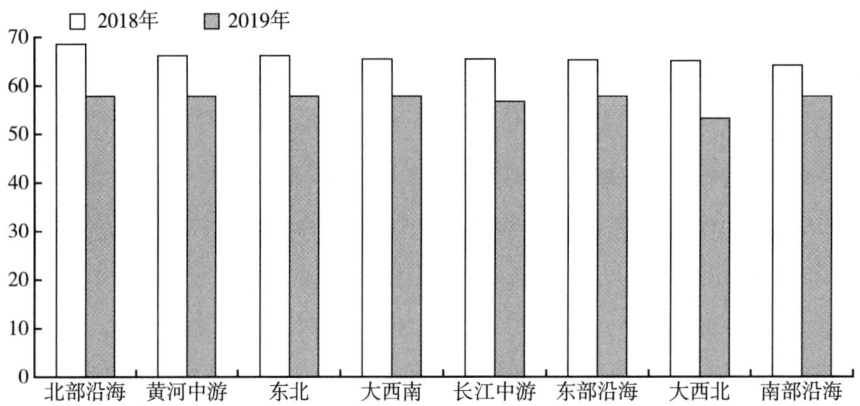

图 4　2018 年和 2019 年中国 35 个城市居民健康满意度指数分八大综合经济区域的变化

三　影响因素分析

为了分析影响城市居民健康满意度的因素，下面将依据现有的研究成果选取相关的变量，通过实证回归找出重要的因素，并为稳定和提高城市居民的健康满意度水平提出相应的建议。

居民对自身健康状态的感知，一方面会影响自身的幸福感水平，已有研究表明居民主观幸福感主要受收入满意度和健康满意度影响，两者对居民主观幸福满意度均有正向影响。[①] 另一方面，居民的健康自我评价也会影响甚至改变社会群体心态，居民健康满意度是社会参与度和社会群体心态的一个中介变量，陈彬等运用中国综合社会调查（CGSS2015）数据证明了居民健康满意度对社会群体心理稳定的重要性。[②]

随着经济发展水平不断提高，居民健康的自我评价对经济发展和社会稳定越来越重要，近年来也开始受到学者们的广泛关注。黄云等利用 CGSS2015 的数据，采用 Ordered Logit 模型分析了影响农村居民身心健康的因素，认为个体和群体收入不平等对农村居民身心健康具有负向影响，其中群体收入的影响呈 U 形。[③] 侯江红、刘文婧也运用 CGSS2015 的数据研究了社会资本对居民健康感知和幸福感的影响，研究结果表明中国居民身心健康水平整体处于良好状态，社会信任和邻里交往对居民健康和幸福感具有正向影响。[④] 张舒怡等通过深入剖析邻里环境对居民健康自我评价的影响发现，对体育休闲设施的感知、归属感和安全感对居民健康的自我评价具有显著且独立的影响。[⑤]

---

① 周春平:《居民主观幸福感影响因素：收入满意度和健康状况——来自江苏的实证分析》,《管理学刊》2012 年第 4 期，第 27~32 页。

② 陈彬、张仁鹏、陈济生:《社会参与、自评健康评价与社会心态关系研究——基于 CGSS2015 数据》,《井冈山大学学报》(社会科学版）2019 年第 5 期，第 79~84 页。

③ 黄云、任国强、周云波:《收入不平等对农村居民身心健康的影响——基于 CGSS2015 数据的实证分析》,《农业技术经济》2019 年第 3 期，第 25~37 页。

④ 侯江红、刘文婧:《社会资本对居民健康与主观幸福感的调节效应——基于中国社会状况综合调查的分析》,《武汉理工大学学报》(社会科学版）2019 年第 2 期，第 105~112 页。

⑤ 张舒怡等:《邻里环境感知对中国城市居民自评健康影响研究——以武汉市为例》,《人文地理》2019 年第 2 期，第 32~40 页。

欧阳文静认为改善和发展民生离不开住房和健康，运用 2010~2014 年"中国家庭追踪调查（CFPS）"数据对房价对城市居民身心健康的影响进行研究，研究发现一般而言房价对城市居民的身心健康无显著影响，但进一步根据异质性深入研究，结果表明房价上升（买房困难）显著降低了年轻人的身心健康水平。[①] 李骁天等通过研究体育锻炼、医疗费用、居民个人特征对居民健康自我评价的影响发现，体育锻炼日益受到居民重视，其对居民健康满意度具有持续显著促进作用，居民实现健康的思想理念正由"医疗"向"非医疗"方面转变。[②] 张文宏、于宜民根据对中国 10 个城市的随机问卷调查结果，对影响居民健康自我评价的社会因素进行了分析，发现居民的社会经济地位、社会资本质量均具有积极作用。[③]

（一）回归模型

2019 年中国 35 个城市居民健康满意度指数下降可能有多方面的原因，结合已有的研究结果，可以将个体因素之外的原因归结为三类：一是收入因素，包括城市居民的收入水平、收入差距；二是住房因素；三是社区环境因素，包括生活便利和生态环境因素。参考 Grossman 的健康生产函数构建模型[④]，对应选取人均可支配收入、基尼系数、房屋销售价格、房价收入比、交通提供能力、人均绿地面积和空气质量作为自变量。以健康满意度指数作为被解释变量，记为

---

① 欧阳文静：《房价与城市居民身心健康——来自 CFPS 数据的证据》，《财经研究》2019 年第 9 期，第 141~153 页。

② 李骁天等：《体育锻炼活动、医疗消费与健康满意度——基于京津冀城市居民体育参与的调查研究》，《武汉体育学院学报》2019 年第 7 期，第 34~42 页。

③ 张文宏、于宜民：《居民自评健康的社会影响因素研究》，《东岳论丛》2019 年第 9 期，第 31~41 页。

④ Michael Grossman, "The Demand for Health: A Theoritical and Empirical Investigation," NBER Press, 1972.

Health，解释变量人均可支配收入记作 *Income*，基尼系数记作 *Gini*，房屋销售价格记作 *Houseprice*，房价收入比记作 *Houseincomeratio*，交通提供能力记作 *Trafficsupply*，人均绿地面积记作 *Greenspace*，空气质量记作 *Airquality*，构建模型如下：

$$Health=\alpha+\beta_1 Income+\beta_2 Gini+\beta_3 Houseprice+\beta_4 Houseincomeratio+\beta_5 Trafficsupply+\beta_6 Greenspace+\beta_7 Airquality+\varepsilon$$

通过回归结果可以分析居民健康自我评价状况的客观影响因素，可以进一步分析影响城市居民身心健康的主要因素存在于经济方面，还是生活条件和环境方面，以便为进一步提高城市居民健康满意度提供有效的建议。

（二）变量分析

回归方程中使用的变量包括 35 个城市的人均可支配收入、基尼系数、房屋销售价格、房价收入比、交通提供能力、人均绿地面积和空气质量，数据来自《中国城市统计年鉴》和 CEIC 数据库，为了具有可比性，上述数据均进行了标准化处理。

回归方程中的自变量在 2019 年的数值以及 35 个城市对应指数的排名如表 7 所示（人均可支配收入不再列出），基尼系数排前 5 位的城市分别为西安（1.32）、长沙（1.28）、北京（1.27）、上海（1.26）和广州（1.25），排后 5 位的城市分别为哈尔滨（0.81）、银川（0.80）、成都（0.80）、海口（0.80）和武汉（0.79），排名处于 6~30 位的城市依次是兰州（1.21）、石家庄（1.19）、杭州（1.19）、厦门（1.14）、重庆（1.13）、宁波（1.09）、昆明（1.07）、大连（1.07）、南昌（1.02）、福州（1.01）、合肥（0.99）、沈阳（0.98）、南宁（0.97）、天津（0.97）、济南（0.93）、郑州（0.91）、长春（0.91）、青岛

（0.90）、呼和浩特（0.87）、太原（0.86）、南京（0.85）、深圳（0.84）、乌鲁木齐（0.84）、西宁（0.84）、贵阳（0.82）。

2019 年 35 个城市的房屋销售价格排前 5 位的城市分别是厦门（1.10）、深圳（1.10）、上海（1.09）、南京（1.09）、天津（1.08），排后 5 位的城市分别是昆明（0.94）、贵阳（0.93）、呼和浩特（0.91）、海口（0.90）、西安（0.90）。排 6~30 位的城市分别是北京（1.07）、合肥（1.06）、杭州（1.04）、宁波（1.04）、乌鲁木齐（1.03）、广州（1.02）、福州（1.01）、南宁（1.01）、银川（1.01）、南昌（1.01）、郑州（1.00）、武汉（0.99）、兰州（0.99）、长沙（0.99）、太原（0.99）、重庆（0.99）、长春（0.98）、西宁（0.98）、沈阳（0.98）、成都（0.98）、青岛（0.97）、哈尔滨（0.96）、大连（0.96）、石家庄（0.96）和济南（0.95）。从排名可以看出，经济发达地区的房屋销售价格较高，经济欠发达地区房屋销售价格较低。

表 7　回归方程中的自变量 2019 年数值及 35 个城市对应指数排名

	城市	*Gini*		*Houseprice*		*Houseincomeratio*		*Traffic-supply*		*Greenspace*		*Airquality*	
		数值	排名	数值	排名	数值	排名	数值	排名	数值	排名	数值	排名
1	北京	1.27	3	1.07	6	0.42	34	0.87	23	1.32	8	0.72	32
2	天津	0.97	19	1.08	5	0.63	29	0.92	21	0.82	20	0.82	29
3	石家庄	1.19	7	0.96	29	1.03	15	1.57	1	0.60	30	0.57	35
4	太原	0.86	25	0.99	20	0.66	28	1.14	12	1.29	9	0.61	34
5	呼和浩特	0.87	24	0.91	33	1.83	2	1.20	10	1.48	5	1.02	17
6	沈阳	0.98	17	0.98	24	1.28	8	0.93	20	1.51	4	1.03	16
7	长春	0.91	22	0.98	22	1.08	13	1.21	9	1.08	14	1.05	15
8	哈尔滨	0.81	31	0.96	27	0.95	21	1.14	11	0.70	23	1.12	10
9	上海	1.26	4	1.09	3	0.50	32	0.74	31	1.15	10	1.00	18
10	南京	0.85	26	1.09	4	0.73	24	0.91	22	1.67	3	0.95	22
11	杭州	1.19	8	1.04	8	0.47	33	0.84	27	1.01	15	0.94	23

续表

	城市	Gini		Houseprice		Houseincomeratio		Traffic-supply		Greenspace		Airquality	
		数值	排名	数值	排名	数值	排名	数值	排名	数值	排名	数值	排名
12	合肥	0.99	16	1.06	7	0.73	25	1.05	15	0.70	24	0.97	20
13	福州	1.01	15	1.01	12	0.74	23	0.99	18	0.60	31	1.22	7
14	南昌	1.02	14	1.01	15	1.31	7	1.36	6	0.62	29	1.15	8
15	济南	0.93	20	0.95	30	0.94	22	0.75	30	0.42	34	0.73	30
16	郑州	0.91	21	1.00	16	0.96	19	0.26	34	0.62	28	0.73	31
17	武汉	0.79	35	0.99	17	1.00	18	1.24	8	0.95	18	0.89	26
18	长沙	1.28	2	0.99	19	1.52	6	0.53	33	0.64	26	0.97	21
19	广州	1.25	5	1.02	11	0.61	30	1.06	14	2.07	2	1.12	11
20	南宁	0.97	18	1.01	13	0.95	20	0.84	26	0.81	21	1.26	6
21	海口	0.80	34	0.90	34	0.52	31	1.54	2	1.14	11	1.31	1
22	重庆	1.13	10	0.99	21	1.10	12	0.20	35	1.13	12	1.09	13
23	成都	0.80	33	0.98	25	1.02	17	0.87	25	0.69	25	0.91	25
24	贵阳	0.82	30	0.93	32	1.02	16	0.73	32	0.96	16	1.27	5
25	昆明	1.07	12	0.94	31	2.16	1	0.99	19	0.82	19	1.31	3
26	西安	1.32	1	0.90	35	1.10	11	1.03	16	0.63	27	0.68	33
27	兰州	1.21	6	0.99	18	1.23	9	0.80	29	0.57	33	0.98	19
28	西宁	0.84	29	0.98	23	1.60	3	0.87	24	0.77	22	0.83	28
29	银川	0.80	32	1.01	14	1.57	5	1.25	7	1.12	13	0.93	24
30	乌鲁木齐	0.84	28	1.03	10	1.59	4	1.09	13	1.42	6	0.89	27
31	大连	1.07	13	0.96	28	1.04	14	1.01	17	0.96	17	1.15	9
32	宁波	1.09	11	1.04	9	0.71	26	0.81	28	0.36	35	1.12	12
33	厦门	1.14	9	1.10	1	0.66	27	1.44	3	1.35	7	1.31	2
34	青岛	0.90	23	0.97	26	1.13	10	1.42	5	0.59	32	1.08	14
35	深圳	0.84	27	1.10	2	0.21	35	1.42	4	2.42	1	1.28	4

2019年35个城市的房价收入比排前5位的城市分别为昆明（2.16）、呼和浩特（1.83）、西宁（1.60）、乌鲁木齐（1.59）、银川

（1.57），排后5位的城市依次是海口（0.52）、上海（0.50）、杭州（0.47）、北京（0.42）、深圳（0.21），排6~30位的城市依次是长沙（1.52）、南昌（1.31）、沈阳（1.28）、兰州（1.23）、青岛（1.13）、西安（1.10）、重庆（1.10）、长春（1.08）、大连（1.04）、石家庄（1.03）、贵阳（1.02）、成都（1.02）、武汉（1.00）、郑州（0.96）、南宁（0.95）、哈尔滨（0.95）、济南（0.94）、福州（0.74）、南京（0.73）、合肥（0.73）、宁波（0.71）、厦门（0.66）、太原（0.66）、天津（0.63）和广州（0.61）。通过房价收入比排名和房屋销售价格排名的对比可见，收入高的经济发达地区房屋销售价格虽然高，但房价收入比相对较低，经济欠发达地区的房价收入比反而较高。

2019年35个城市的交通提供能力排前5位的城市分别是石家庄（1.57）、海口（1.54）、厦门（1.44）、深圳（1.42）、青岛（1.42），排后5位的城市依次是上海（0.74）、贵阳（0.73）、长沙（0.53）、郑州（0.26）、重庆（0.20），排6~30位的城市依次为南昌（1.36）、银川（1.25）、武汉（1.24）、长春（1.21）、呼和浩特（1.20）、哈尔滨（1.14）、太原（1.14）、乌鲁木齐（1.09）、广州（1.06）、合肥（1.05）、西安（1.03）、大连（1.01）、福州（0.99）、昆明（0.99）、沈阳（0.93）、天津（0.92）、南京（0.91）、北京（0.87）、西宁（0.87）、成都（0.87）、南宁（0.84）、杭州（0.84）、宁波（0.81）、兰州（0.80）、济南（0.75）。从排名上看，沿海城市的交通提供能力整体比内陆城市高。

2019年35个城市的人均绿地面积排前5位的城市分别是深圳（2.42）、广州（2.07）、南京（1.67）、沈阳（1.51）、呼和浩特（1.48），排后5位的城市分别是福州（0.60）、青岛（0.59）、兰州（0.57）、济南（0.42）、宁波（0.36），排名处于6~30位的城市依次是乌鲁木齐（1.42）、厦门（1.35）、北京（1.32）、太原（1.29）、上海（1.15）、海口（1.14）、重庆（1.13）、银川（1.12）、长春（1.08）、杭州

（1.01）、贵阳（0.96）、大连（0.96）、武汉（0.95）、昆明（0.82）、天津（0.82）、南宁（0.81）、西宁（0.77）、哈尔滨（0.70）、合肥（0.70）、成都（0.69）、长沙（0.64）、西安（0.63）、郑州（0.62）、南昌（0.62）、石家庄（0.60）。

2019年35个城市的空气质量排前5位的城市分别是海口（1.31）、厦门（1.31）、昆明（1.31）、深圳（1.28）、贵阳（1.27），排后5位的城市分别是郑州（0.73）、北京（0.72）、西安（0.68）、太原（0.61）、石家庄（0.57），排名处于第6~30位的城市依次为南宁（1.26）、福州（1.22）、南昌（1.15）、大连（1.15）、哈尔滨（1.12）、广州（1.12）、宁波（1.12）、重庆（1.09）、青岛（1.08）、长春（1.05）、沈阳（1.03）、呼和浩特（1.02）、上海（1.00）、兰州（0.98）、合肥（0.97）、长沙（0.97）、南京（0.95）、杭州（0.94）、银川（0.93）、成都（0.91）、武汉（0.89）、乌鲁木齐（0.89）、西宁（0.83）、天津（0.82）、济南（0.73）。

模型中的被解释变量和各解释变量的描述性统计结果如表8所示，表中各变量数据均为标准化后的数据。

表8　模型回归变量及其描述性统计

变量类别	变量	英文缩写	均值	标准差	最小值	最大值
被解释变量	健康满意度	*Health*	57.26	2.66	50.94	61.50
解释变量	人均可支配收入	*Income*	1.00	0.22	0.72	1.52
	基尼系数	*Gini*	1.00	0.17	0.79	1.32
	房屋销售价格	*Houseprice*	1.00	0.06	0.90	1.10
	房价收入比	*Houseincomeratio*	1.00	0.43	0.21	2.16
	交通提供能力	*Trafficsupply*	1.00	0.31	0.20	1.57
	人均绿地面积	*Greenspace*	1.00	0.46	0.36	2.42
	空气质量	*Airquality*	1.00	0.21	0.57	1.31

（三）结果讨论

依据前述分析，将表 8 中的变量分为三类，分别对应三个模型。模型一的变量选取人均可支配收入（*Income*）和基尼系数（*Gini*）；模型二的变量在模型一的基础上加入房屋销售价格（*Houseprice*）和房价收入比（*Houseincomeratio*）；模型三在模型二的基础上引入生活环境因素，即交通提供能力（*Trafficsupply*）、人均绿地面积（*Greenspace*）和空气质量（*Airquality*）。

模型的回归结果如表 9 所示，三个模型的回归结果基本结论是一致的，结果表明人均可支配收入对城市居民健康满意度具有正向影响。从模型三的综合结果看，人均可支配收入每提高 1%，可以使健康满意度提高 1.89%。基尼系数与健康满意度具有负相关关系，同样依据模型三的结果，基尼系数每提高 1%，健康满意度下降 4.8%。房屋销售价格和房价收入比对居民健康具有负向影响，房屋销售价格每提高 1%，健康满意度下降 16.70%；而房价收入比每上升 1%，则健康满意度下降 3.38%。在生活环境因素中，人均绿地面积和空气质量对健康满意度均具有正向影响，人均绿地面积每提高 1%，健康满意度将提高 0.06%；而空气质量每改善 1%，健康满意度会提高 0.26%。通过回归结果可见，对健康满意度具有正向影响的最主要因素是人均可支配收入水平，而具有负向影响的最重要的因素就是房屋销售价格，而人均绿地面积和空气质量的提高虽然对健康满意度具有促进作用，但作用比较弱。收入分配不平等和房价收入比提高，对城市居民也会造成一定的心理压力，虽然影响不及房屋销售价格，但也是比较重要的因素。交通提供能力不断提高，正常应提高居民出行的便利化程度，可能由于调查的城市均是省会或发达城市，过于繁忙的交通系统会有诸如交通拥堵等问题，导致交通出行压力较大，因此交通提供能力的提高给人的感受并不很愉快。

表 9　模型回归结果

变量	模型一		模型二		模型三	
	系数	P 值	系数	P 值	系数	P 值
Income	2.67	0.25	2.04	0.42	1.89	0.48
Gini	-4.56	0.14	-4.47	0.12	-4.80	0.12
Houseprice			-15.54	0.12	-16.70	0.12
Houseincomeratio			-3.22	0.10	-3.38	0.10
Trafficsupply					-4.43	0.36
Greenspace					0.06	0.91
Airquality					0.26	0.58
R^2	0.28		0.52		0.55	

四　结论与建议

本报告分析了 2019 年中国 35 个城市居民健康满意度的变化情况，并对不同区域的变化情况进行了比较，在此基础上进一步采用定量方法分析了影响城市居民健康满意度的因素。

（一）结论

现代人们对健康的认识有所扩展，除了身心健康外，还包括有较好的社会经济环境适应能力和较高的道德标准。问卷调查的结果显示，2019 年中国 35 个城市居民的健康满意度指数比 2018 年有所下降，均值为 57.26，略高于好（50）的标准。从地域分布上看，城市居民健康满意度下降最多的是西部地区，其他地区降低的幅度差别不大。西部地区不仅排名最后，而且健康满意度水平下降的幅度也是最大的。从八大综合经济区域视角看，南部沿海地区城市居民健康满意度指数上升最多，由 2018 年的第 8 位上升至 2019 年第 2 位，北部沿海地区排名下降最多，由 2018 年的第 1 位下降至 2019 年的第 5 位，其他地区排名相对变化不大或没有变化。

对城市居民健康满意度影响因素的分析和实证结果表明，当前对中国城市居民健康满意度影响较大的因素是房屋销售价格，其次是基尼系数、交通提供能力和房价收入比，这些因素对城市居民健康满意度都具有负向影响；对健康满意度有正向影响的因素包括人均可支配收入、人均绿地面积和空气质量，其中影响比较大的是人均可支配收入，其次是空气质量，正向影响最小的因素是人均绿地面积。

（二）建议

依据前述分析结果，提高居民健康满意度需要从以下几个方面入手。

第一，不断提高人均可支配收入水平。改革开放以来，人均可支配收入已经得到了大幅提高，城镇居民生活不断向小康迈进，为中国在 21 世纪中叶成为中等发达国家奠定了雄厚的基础。为了进一步提高居民收入水平，应进一步深化改革，扩大开放，消除体制机制障碍，特别是进行供给侧结构性改革，激发要素活力。此外，还要不断加强社会保障体系建设。党的十九大报告提出，加强社会保障体系建设，要建成覆盖全民、城乡统筹、权责清晰、保障适度的社会保障体系，党的初心和使命就是为中国人民谋幸福，为中华民族谋复兴。这个初心和使命激励中国共产党人不断前进，按照“幼有所育（生育保障，包括儿童福利等）、学有所教（教育保障）、劳有所得（就业保障，包括工资收入等）、住有所居（住房保障）、病有所医（医疗保障）、老有所养（养老保障）、弱有所扶（贫困保障）”的总要求，进一步完善社会保障体系，不断提高人民群众的获得感。

第二，改善城市绿化和交通环境条件。随着人均收入水平不断提高，居民对生活环境的要求越来越高，对城市绿化环境的要求不断提高。城市生态环境建设和改善不仅可以保持水土，维持生态平衡，吸收二氧化碳和有害气体等，净化空气，提高空气质量，调节温度气候，还可以为市民提供美丽安静的休闲环境，陶冶情操，使人可以回归自然，放松心情，对于提高城市居民健康满意度具有良好的促进作用。另外，随着经济发展水平的提高，家庭汽车拥有率不断提高，城市中的停车难、行车难、交通拥堵等问题亟须解决。为此，应整体上进行城市的长远交通发展规划，发展立体交通，建立体停车场，同时还应整治交通违法行为，提高市民的交通规则意识。

第三，稳定房价，多途径提供住房。继续坚定贯彻房住不炒的理念，稳定房价，防止房价过快上涨。2016 年中央经济工作会议就提出了房子是用来住的，此后为了抑制房价过快上涨，让住房回归其本来属性，政府甚至采用了行政手段，有效地控制了房价的过快上涨。十九大中央再次强调了这一理念，并开始实行“多主体供应、多渠道保障、租购并举”的方针措施，在多地开始进行构建房地产市场长效发展机制的尝试。从更高的层面看，稳定房价不但可以使居民改善生活条件，还有利于实体经济的发展和经济转型的实现。

综上，健康满意度的提高根本上来源于生活和工作的幸福感，是不断改善民生的目标之一，使人民过上美好幸福的生活，身心健康，一直是我们党和政府的奋斗目标。

B.5
中国35个城市居民医疗服务满意度指数报告

王　钰*

摘　要： 提高医疗服务水平，促进全国人民健康水平提高已经纳入国家战略层面，而优质高效的医疗卫生服务是保障人民得到全方位全周期健康服务的保障和实现途径。通过对35个城市居民医疗服务满意度的问卷调查，得到2019年中国35个城市居民医疗服务满意度指数加权平均值为63.04，介于一般（50）和满意（75）之间，整体上略低于2018年的满意度水平（65.31）。通过四个维度分析影响35个城市居民医疗服务满意度的因素，回归结果表明对提高城市居民医疗服务满意度具有正向作用的因素包括人均可支配收入增长率、医疗服务提供能力、基本医疗保险覆盖率，而基尼系数、30天内身体和心理不健康天数对医疗服务满意度具有负向作用。据此，建议稳步提高医疗服务提供能力，扩大优质医疗服务资源的利用范围，同时提高和稳定基本医疗保险覆盖率，并做好保险基金的使用和管理工作。

关键词： 医疗服务满意度　医疗服务提供能力　基本医疗保险覆盖率　优质医疗资源下沉

---

* 王钰，博士，首都经济贸易大学经济学院教授，主要研究方向为经济增长与经济周期。

一 引言

2016年在全国卫生与健康大会上，习近平总书记提出了大健康的理念[①]，党的十九大报告提出了建设“健康中国”的路线图，进一步明确了大健康的要义是“为人民群众提供全方位全周期的健康服务”，人民健康长寿是民族昌盛和国家富强的重要标志。为了确保大健康战略的实现，2017年5月5日，国务院办公厅颁布了《深化医药卫生体制改革2017年重点工作任务》，具体列出了为建立中国特色基本医疗卫生制度的70项任务内容。十九大报告进一步提出构建并完善医药卫生四大体系，即公共卫生服务体系、医疗服务体系、医疗保障体系和药品供应保障体系，以确保中国特色医疗卫生系统能够提供“优质高效的医疗卫生服务”。由此可见，提高中国的医疗服务水平，促进全国人民健康水平不断提升已经纳入国家战略层面。

对医疗服务的满意度问题进行研究，首先要研究满意度水平。学者们运用不同来源的数据、多元的研究方法对不同层次、不同地区和不同医疗环节患者对医疗服务的满意度及其影响因素进行广泛的调查研究，研究结论表明中国居民对医疗服务的满意度水平测算结果分布于满意度较低到满意度较高之间，说明居民医疗服务满意度差异较大，不同人群、不同地区间存在差异，城乡间也存在差异，影响居民医疗服务满意度的因素也是不尽相同的，但同时学者们也不约而同地指出居民医疗服务满意度还有上升空间。因此，进一步追踪调查居民对医疗服务的满意度水平及其影响因素是必要的。

---

① 《习近平总书记在全国卫生与健康大会上的讲话引起强烈反响》，新华网，2016年8月21日，http://www.xinhuanet.com/politics/2016-08/21/c_1119428119.htm?from=singlemessage&isappinstalled=0。

二　对35个城市居民医疗服务满意度指数的分析

根据研究中心调查问卷中的问题18~20，得到居民对医疗服务评价的微观数据。问题19~20评价分数为0~100，分数越高代表满意度越高。

18、在过去的一年中，您是否因为自己的健康问题或陪同亲友去过医院或诊所就诊（请选择最近一次经历）?

19、考虑您最近一次的就诊经历（自己或陪同亲友），您对该医疗机构的服务质量（包含诊疗水平、服务态度、就诊环境）是否满意?

20、总体而言，您对医疗保险个人负担部分是否满意?

将上述问题的答案根据李克特五级评价法设置赋值标准，对被调查者选择答案的结果进行加权平均就可以得到35个城市居民2019年对医疗服务的满意度结果。

（一）描述性统计

2019年中国35个城市的居民医疗服务满意度指数的描述性统计结果如表1所示。2019年35个城市居民医疗服务满意度指数极小值为59.16，极大值为66.79，均值为63.04，2018年35个城市居民医疗服务满意度指数极小值为53.91，极大值为70.58，均值为65.31，与2018年相比，极小值有所提高，极大值有所下降，均值下降，可见，整体满意度比2018年有所下降。从结果的分布看，2019年满意度指数的方差为3.93，标准差为1.98，而2018年方差为13.95，标准差为3.73，与2018年相比，2019年的不同受访者的满意度水平差距缩小了。如图1所示，从分布的偏度和峰度值看，偏度都小于零，即左偏，说明多数受访者的医疗服务满意度水平是高于平均值的，而2018年满意度数值分布的峰度比2019年陡峭，表明2019年医疗服务满意度高的受访者没有2018年的人数多。

表1 2018年和2019年中国35个城市居民医疗服务满意度指数描述性统计

年份	极小值	极大值	均值	方差	标准差	偏度	峰度
2018	53.91	70.58	65.31	13.95	3.73	-0.65	0.61
2019	59.16	66.79	63.04	3.93	1.98	-0.04	-0.80

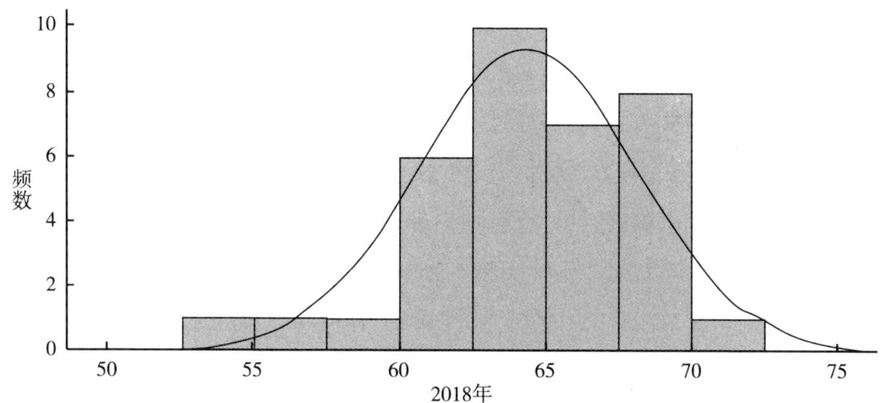

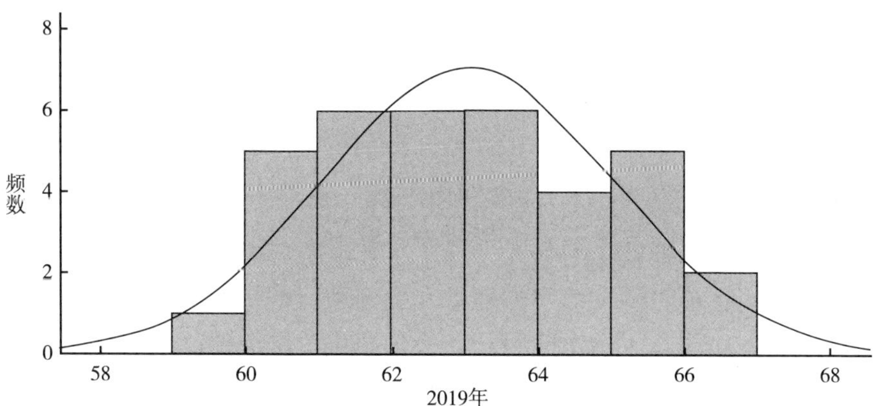

图1 2018年和2019年中国35个城市居民医疗服务满意度直方图

（二）不同城市和地区比较

2018 年和 2019 年中国 35 个城市居民医疗服务满意度的变化如图 2 所示，从整体情况看，与 2018 年相比，2019 年各个城市的满意度变化方向并不一致。满意度下降的城市包括昆明（–13.06%）、哈尔滨（–11.61%）、太原（–11.11%）、深圳（–10.94%）、贵阳（–10.14%）、青岛（–9.98%）、大连（–9.57%）、长春（–9.20%）、合肥（–6.07%）、天津（–5.18%）、福州（–4.94%）、成都（–4.54%）、呼和浩特（–4.45%）、西安（–3.78%）、济南（–3.72%）、长沙（–3.11%）、上海（–2.56%）、郑州（–1.47%）、厦门（–1.42%）、北京（–1.35%）、南宁（–1.20%）、武汉（–0.12%）、西宁（–0.09%），满意度上升的城市包括杭州（22.29%）、广州（8.51%）、银川（8.40%）、石家庄（6.05%）、南京（4.88%）、南昌（4.43%）、宁波（4.14%）、沈阳（3.39%）、海口（1.77%）、乌鲁木齐（1.59%）、重庆（1.19%）、兰州（0.69%）。由于满意度下降的城市多于满意度上升的城市，因此 35 个城市居民医疗服务满意度整体呈下降趋势。

从地区分布上看，35 个城市按四大地区进行比较，结果如表 2 所示，2019 年四大地区居民医疗服务满意度排名第一的是东部地区（63.8），其次是中部地区（63.4），排后两位的地区分别是西部地区（62.5）和东北地区（61.0）。2018 年排第一的是东北地区（65.5），排名最后的是东部地区（63.8），与 2018 年相比，2019 年东部和东北地区的排名发生了对调，而中部地区和西部地区的排名没有变化。发生这种变化的原因在于 2019 年与 2018 年相比，东部地区的居民医疗服务满意度分值没有发生变化，均为 63.8，而东北地区的居民医疗服务满意度发生了较大幅度的下降。

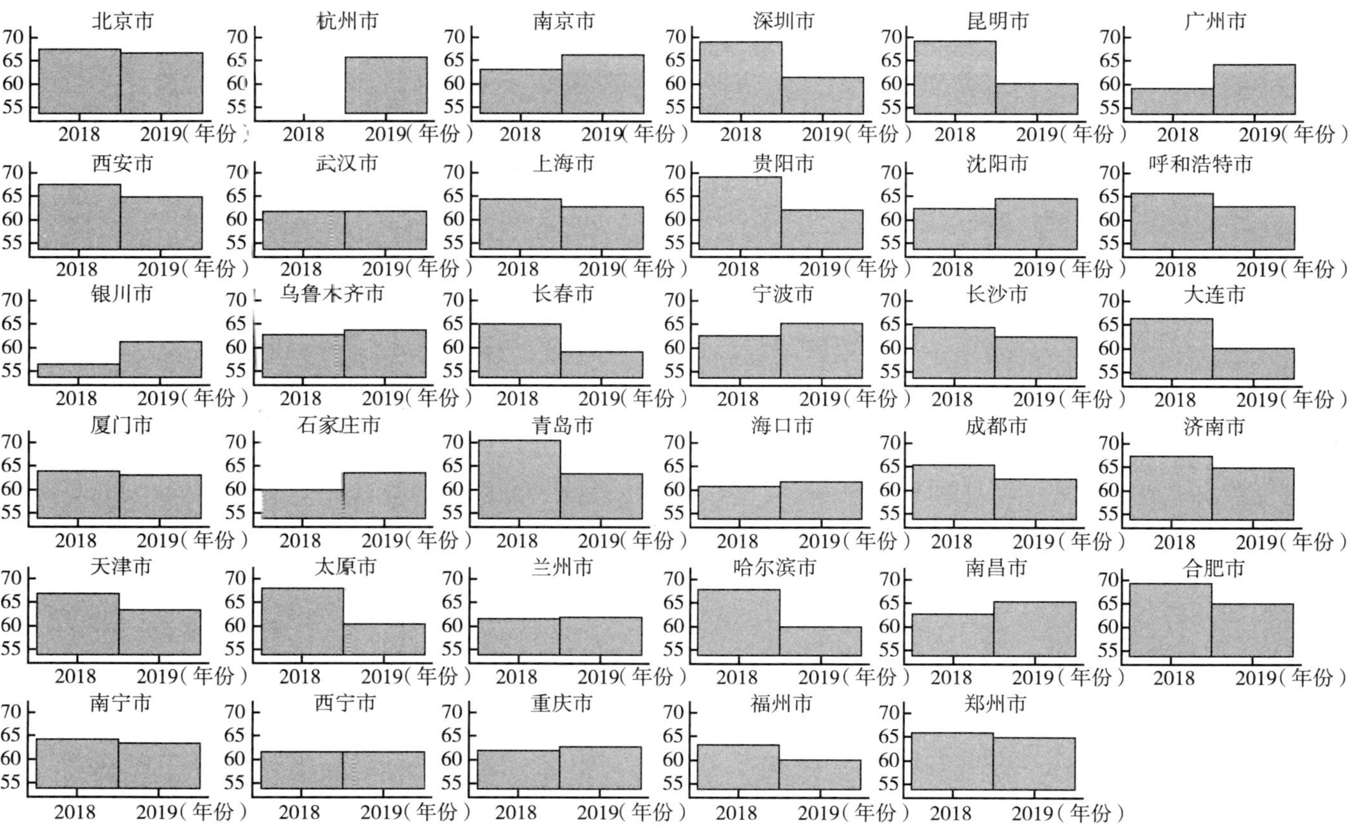

图 2　2018 年和 2019 年中国 35 个城市居民医疗服务满意度变化

表 2　2018 年和 2019 年中国 35 个城市居民医疗服务满意度分四大地区平均值比较

2018 年排名	地区	平均值	2019 年排名	地区	平均值
1	东北	65.5	1	东部	63.8
2	中部	65.4	2	中部	63.4
3	西部	64.2	3	西部	62.5
4	东部	63.8	4	东北	61.0

如图 3 所示，除了东部地区外，其余三大地区居民医疗服务满意度指数均相比 2018 年发生了明显的下降，东北地区下降的最多，下降了 6.9%，中部地区下降了 3.1%，西部地区下降了 2.6%。

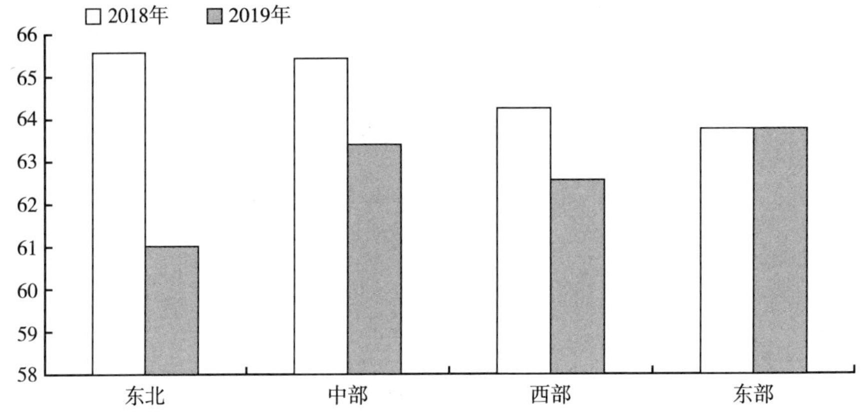

图 3　2018 年和 2019 年中国 35 个城市居民医疗服务满意度指数分四大地区变化比较

从八大综合经济区域的角度比较，如表 3 所示，2019 年城市居民医疗服务满意度指数排第 1 位的地区是东部沿海地区（65.1），其后依次是北部沿海地区（64.5）、长江中游地区（63.7）、黄河中游地区（63.4）、大西北地区（62.2）、大西南地区（62.2）、南部沿海地区（62.2），排最后的是东北地区（61.0）。其中大西北地区、大西南地区和南部沿海地区满意度分数相同。

表3 2018年和2019年中国35个城市居民医疗服务满意度指数八大综合经济区域平均值比较

2018年排名	地区	平均值	2019年排名	地区	平均值
1	黄河中游	66.9	1	东部沿海	65.1
2	北部沿海	66.6	2	北部沿海	64.5
3	大西南	66.0	3	长江中游	63.7
4	东北	65.5	4	黄河中游	63.4
5	长江中游	64.6	5	大西北	62.2
6	南部沿海	63.3	6	大西南	62.2
7	东部沿海	61.1	7	南部沿海	62.2
8	大西北	60.7	8	东北	61.0

与2018年相比，如图4所示，2019年东部沿海地区和大西北地区城市居民的医疗服务满意度指数呈现上升趋势，东部沿海地区上升了6.5%，大西北地区上升了2.5%，其他地区均有不同程度下降，东北地区下降的幅度最大，其后依次是大西南地区（–5.76%）、黄河中游地区（–5.23%）、北部沿海地区（–3.15%）、南部沿海地区（–1.74%）、长江中游地区（–1.39%）。

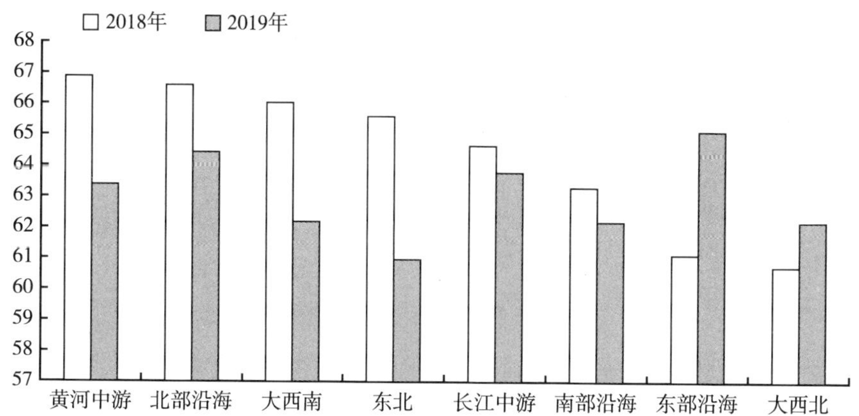

图4 2018年和2019年中国35个城市居民医疗服务满意度指数分八大综合经济区域比较

从比较结果可见，与2018年相比，2019年大多数城市居民医疗服务满意度指数下降，少数城市满意度指数上升；分四大地区进行比较，2019年四个地区城市居民医疗服务满意度指数基本表现为下降；分八大综合经济区域进行比较，也是多数地区表现为满意度指数下降，只有两个地区表现为满意度指数上升。就整体结果看，满意度指数分布为60~70，即处于基本满意的水平。可见，城市居民医疗服务满意度还有很大的提升空间。

三　影响因素分析

为了对城市居民医疗服务满意度不高，且2019年有所下降进行解释，并提出相应的建议，将进一步对影响城市居民医疗服务满意度的因素进行实证分析。

赵大海在研究中国公众对医疗系统的信任度及其影响因素时发现，公众对医疗系统的信任度仅为25.12%，其中对医疗服务的满意度和对政府的信任度是影响公众对医疗系统信任度的因素，中国公众具有较高的政府信任度和较低的医疗服务满意度，较高的政府信任度对医疗系统信任度具有正向影响，而较低的医疗服务满意度是拉低信任度的重要原因。① 翟瑜菲等对海口市运用分层抽样电话调查的方法，抽取872人询问其对医疗服务的满意度，结果显示海口市居民对医疗服务的整体满意度为76.37%，城市居民满意度高于农村居民，不同行政区的居民满意度差异较大。②

居民对医疗服务的满意度实际会受到多方面因素的影响，对此

① 赵大海：《中国公众对医疗卫生系统的信任及其影响因素研究》，《浙江大学学报》（人文社会科学版）2019年第1期，第67~79页。

② 翟瑜菲、寇毛毛、王扬冰、董春波、李娜、刘玉梅：《海口市居民对基本公共卫生服务项目知晓率和满意度调查》，《中国公共卫生管理》2019年第2期，第153~156页。

学者们也展开了广泛的实证。徐广路和沈惠璋运用 2008 年中国社会调查数据研究了基本医疗保险对基本医疗服务和社会冲突感的影响，研究结果表明三种医疗保险对于提高居民医疗服务满意度均有正向作用，其中新农合对满意度的提高作用最大，对降低社会冲突感的作用也最大，而城镇职工基本医疗保险对居民医疗服务满意度的提高作用略低于新农合，对降低社会冲突感的作用也略低于新农合，而城镇居民基本医疗保险对提升医疗服务满意度的作用最弱，对降低社会冲突感没有显著作用。[①] 王晓燕和杭丹对新医改背景下，三医（医保、医疗、医药）联动对医疗服务满意度的影响进行了研究，研究发现在三医联动中医疗是影响医疗服务满意度的主要因素，医保和医药对医疗服务满意度也具有正向影响。[②] 范静波运用结构方程对居民医疗服务的感知结构进行了研究，认为居民对医疗服务的满意度整体上还有很大的上升空间。[③] 雷咸胜运用 CGSS2015 数据对城乡居民医疗服务满意度的影响因素进行了比较研究，研究结果表明影响城市居民医疗服务满意度的主要因素是医疗资源的充足程度，而影响农村居民医疗服务满意度的因素主要是医疗服务获取的便利性，导致差异的原因在于城乡医疗资源配置水平不同，而在政策影响层面，基本医疗保险的覆盖率是最重要的影响因素，特别是对城市居民而言，这涉及政策的公平性。[④] 徐宁等基于 CGSS2013 调查问卷 A 卷中的“医疗公共服务”

---

① 徐广路、沈惠璋:《基本医疗保险对基本医疗服务满意度及社会冲突感的影响》,《保险研究》2015 年第 2 期，第 117~127 页。

② 王晓燕、杭丹:《基于结构方程模型的新医改背景下医疗服务满意度影响因素分析》,《数学的实践与认识》2016 年第 22 期，第 83~89 页。

③ 范静波:《当前居民医疗卫生公共服务满意度感知结构研究》,《华东师范大学学报》（哲学社会科学版）2018 年第 6 期，第 163~177 页。

④ 雷咸胜:《城乡居民医疗服务满意度比较研究——基于 CGSS（2015）数据的实证分析》,《农业技术经济》2019 年第 4 期，第 16~28 页。

中的数据，对影响居民医疗服务满意度的因素进行了相应的分析，认为中国城乡居民对医疗服务的满意度为一般，影响满意度的因素包括居民的经济收入、文化程度、养老保险、4 周内心理健康状况。①

王保前和李自炜基于 CGSS2015 调查数据对农村居民医疗服务满意度进行了研究，认为经济收入水平、对健康的自评情况、社会保险覆盖情况和互联网的使用对医疗服务满意度均具有正向影响，从地区分布情况看，相对于中部地区，西部地区居民对医疗服务的满意度更高。②

还有学者对不同地区医院以及社会医疗服务中心等不同层级的医疗机构的医疗服务满意度进行了调查研究。戴士媛等运用江苏省第六次卫生调查数据，对住院患者医疗服务满意度进行了研究，总体满意率为 76%，影响满意率的因素包括家庭收入、医保报销比率、诊疗过程服务水平等。③王梦圆等对南京患者对三甲医院的非医疗技术满意度进行了测算，调查了 820 例患者，满意度处于比较高的水平。④邵宏燕和汪曦对上海市闵行区江川路街道鹤北邻里社区医疗服务中心的满意度进行了问卷调查，抽样调查了 540 例患者，认为患者总体满意度较高，但仍有提升空间。⑤

---

① 徐宁等:《基于中国综合社会调查对我国居民医疗卫生公共服务满意度的分析》,《中国医疗管理科学》2019 年第 2 期，第 61~66 页。

② 王保前、李自炜:《农村居民医疗卫生服务满意度影响因素分析》,《医学与社会》2019 年第 7 期，第 28~31 页。

③ 戴士媛、顾新月、徐爱军:《住院患者医疗服务满意度及影响因素分析——基于江苏省第六次卫生调查数据》,《卫生经济研究》2019 年第 11 期，第 41~43 页。

④ 王梦圆等:《南京市三甲医院门诊患者非医疗技术服务满意度因子分析》,《医学与社会》2019 年第 3 期，第 95~111 页。

⑤ 邵宏燕、汪曦:《上海市某邻里中心医疗服务居民满意度调查研究》,《重庆医学》2019 年第 12 期，第 2133~2135 页。

（一）回归模型

结合已有的研究分析，2019年35个城市居民医疗服务满意度（记作 *Medicalsatisfaction*）整体呈现下降趋势的原因可以从四个维度上进行分析，一是经济因素，包括城市居民的收入水平、收入差距；二是医疗服务提供能力，包括每万人拥有的执业医师数量、每万人拥有的医疗机构床位数、每万人拥有的医院数量；三是社会保险能力，包括基本医疗保险覆盖率；四是个体健康差异性，包括居民近期身体健康自我评价状况和居民心理健康自我评价状况。综上，回归模型中拟选取的自变量包括人均可支配收入增长率，记作 *Incomegrowth*；基尼系数，记作 *Gini*；医疗服务提供能力，记作 *Medicalsupply*；基本医疗保险覆盖率，记作 *Medicalins*；30天内身体不健康天数，记作 *Physicalhealth*；30天内心理不健康天数，记作 *Mentalhealth*。回归模型构建如下：

$$Medicalsatisfaction=\alpha+\beta_1 Incomegrowth+\beta_2 Gini+\beta_3 Medicalsupply+\beta_4 Medicalins+\beta_5 Physicalhealth+\beta_6 Mentalhealth+\varepsilon$$

通过回归结果可以分析不同维度的影响因素对城市居民医疗服务满意度的影响水平，再根据回归的结果给出相应的对策建议。

（二）变量分析

回归模型中的数据来源于国家统计局官方网站、《中国城市统计年鉴》、《中国卫生和计划生育统计年鉴》和CNKI的中国经济社会大数据研究平台。为了便于分析和比较，本报告对所有数据都进行了标准化处理，使其成为指数化数据。回归方程中的自变量在2019年的数值以及35个城市对应指数的排名如表4所示（基尼系数、基本医疗保险覆盖率不再列出）。

2019 年中国 35 个城市的人均可支配收入增长率排前 5 位的城市分别为天津（1.44）、沈阳（1.28）、乌鲁木齐（1.22）、合肥（1.10）、武汉（1.09），排后 5 位的城市分别为南昌（0.84）、深圳（0.82）、西安（0.69）、大连（0.65）、成都（0.56），排名处在第 6~30 位的城市依次是贵阳（1.09）、厦门（1.07）、南京（1.07）、杭州（1.06）、上海（1.06）、福州（1.05）、海口（1.05）、重庆（1.04）、郑州（1.04）、兰州（1.04）、广州（1.04）、长沙（1.03）、西宁（1.03）、宁波（1.02）、昆明（1.02）、石家庄（1.02）、银川（1.02）、青岛（1.01）、济南（0.99）、呼和浩特（0.96）、太原（0.96）、长春（0.93）、哈尔滨（0.93）、南宁（0.91）、北京（0.84）。

2019 年中国 35 个城市的医疗服务提供能力排前 5 位的城市分别为西宁（2.17）、成都（1.79）、昆明（1.44）、合肥（1.35）、乌鲁木齐（1.33），排后 5 位的城市分别为南京（0.68）、厦门（0.61）、上海（0.58）、宁波（0.58）、深圳（0.40），排名处在第 6~30 位的城市依次是贵阳（1.26）、南昌（1.24）、兰州（1.19）、太原（1.19）、银川（1.17）、长沙（1.09）、沈阳（1.05）、西安（1.04）、重庆（1.02）、长春（1.00）、青岛（0.97）、杭州（0.96）、哈尔滨（0.90）、济南（0.89）、南宁（0.88）、福州（0.87）、北京（0.87）、海口（0.86）、武汉（0.84）、大连（0.84）、天津（0.82）、广州（0.82）、石家庄（0.80）、呼和浩特（0.76）、郑州（0.75）。从排名情况看，如果按人均医疗资源占有情况来分析医疗服务提供能力，城市人口规模大的医疗资源会相对紧张，相对医疗服务提供能力就低，反之则高些。

2019 年中国 35 个城市居民 30 天内身体不健康天数排前 5 位的城市分别为西宁（4.44）、乌鲁木齐（3.71）、呼和浩特（3.51）、大连（3.44）、长春（3.40），排后 5 位的城市分别为厦门（2.32）、成都（2.30）、南京（2.27）、宁波（2.25）、深圳（2.25），排名处在第6~30位的城市依次是银川（3.34）、沈阳（3.31）、海口（3.31）、兰州（3.30）、太原（3.07）、长沙（3.05）、昆明（3.05）、南宁（3.03）、哈尔滨（3.01）、石家庄（2.92）、北京（2.85）、贵阳（2.84）、上海（2.79）、青岛（2.76）、广州（2.75）、天津（2.72）、重庆（2.70）、西安（2.63）、郑州（2.55）、杭州（2.52）、济南（2.49）、武汉（2.47）、福州（2.43）、合肥（2.39）、南昌（2.36）。总体比较而言，经济欠发达地区居民感觉身体不适的天数比经济发达地区多。

2019年中国35个城市居民30天内心理不健康天数排前5位的城市分别为乌鲁木齐（6.86）、石家庄（5.95）、呼和浩特（5.91）、哈尔滨（5.88）、银川（5.73），排后5位的城市分别为广州（4.52）、宁波（4.46）、福州（4.31）、厦门（4.26）、武汉（4.14），排名处在第6~30位的城市依次是西宁（5.67）、长春（5.63）、贵阳（5.56）、昆明（5.45）、北京（5.43）、天津（5.43）、兰州（5.37）、沈阳（5.29）、太原（5.24）、大连（5.22）、成都（5.21）、南宁（5.14）、西安（5.14）、郑州（5.04）、青岛（5.03）、南昌（5.01）、海口（4.95）、重庆（4.93）、合肥（4.85）、杭州（4.83）、长沙（4.76）、深圳（4.72）、南京（4.69）、上海（4.63）、济南（4.61）。可见总体来讲，经济欠发达地区的城市居民心理健康水平比较低，而经济发达地区的居民心理健康水平较高。

回归方程中各变量的描述性统计结果如表5所示，其中人均可支配收入增长率的最小值为0.56，最大值为1.44，标准差为0.16，峰度值为正且较大，表明城市间的差异性较大。医疗服务提供能力的均值为1.00，最小值为0.40，最大值为2.17，标准差为0.34，从数值分布上看，两端的差异性较大。

表 4　2019 年回归方程中的自变量数值及 35 个城市对应指数的排名

	城市	人均可支配收入增长率		医疗服务提供能力		30 内身体不健康天数		30 天内心理不健康天数	
		数值	排名	数值	排名	数值	排名	数值	排名
1	北京	0.84	30	0.87	22	2.85	16	5.43	10
2	天津	1.44	1	0.82	26	2.72	21	5.43	11
3	石家庄	1.02	21	0.80	28	2.92	15	5.95	2
4	太原	0.96	26	1.19	9	3.07	10	5.24	14
5	呼和浩特	0.96	25	0.76	29	3.51	3	5.91	3
6	沈阳	1.28	2	1.05	12	3.31	7	5.29	13
7	长春	0.93	27	1.00	15	3.40	5	5.63	7
8	哈尔滨	0.93	28	0.90	18	3.01	14	5.88	4
9	上海	1.06	10	0.58	33	2.79	18	4.63	29
10	南京	1.07	8	0.68	31	2.27	33	4.69	28
11	杭州	1.06	9	0.96	17	2.52	25	4.83	25
12	合肥	1.10	4	1.35	4	2.39	29	4.85	24
13	福州	1.05	11	0.87	21	2.43	28	4.31	33
14	南昌	0.84	31	1.24	7	2.36	30	5.01	21
15	济南	0.99	24	0.89	19	2.49	26	4.61	30
16	郑州	1.04	14	0.75	30	2.55	24	5.04	19
17	武汉	1.09	5	0.84	24	2.47	27	4.14	35
18	长沙	1.03	17	1.09	11	3.05	11	4.76	26
19	广州	1.04	16	0.82	27	2.75	20	4.52	31
20	南宁	0.91	29	0.88	20	3.03	13	5.14	17
21	海口	1.05	12	0.86	23	3.31	8	4.95	22
22	重庆	1.04	13	1.02	14	2.70	22	4.93	23
23	成都	0.56	35	1.79	2	2.30	32	5.21	16
24	贵阳	1.09	6	1.26	6	2.84	17	5.56	8
25	昆明	1.02	20	1.44	3	3.05	12	5.45	9
26	西安	0.69	33	1.04	13	2.63	23	5.14	18
27	兰州	1.04	15	1.19	8	3.30	9	5.37	12
28	西宁	1.03	18	2.17	1	4.44	1	5.67	6
29	银川	1.02	22	1.17	10	3.34	6	5.73	5
30	乌鲁木齐	1.22	3	1.33	5	3.71	2	6.86	1
31	大连	0.65	34	0.84	25	3.44	4	5.22	15
32	宁波	1.02	19	0.58	34	2.25	34	4.46	32
33	厦门	1.07	7	0.61	32	2.32	31	4.26	34
34	青岛	1.01	23	0.97	16	2.76	19	5.03	20
35	深圳	0.82	32	0.40	35	2.25	35	4.72	27

表5　回归方程各变量及其描述性统计

变量类别	变量	英文缩写	均值	标准差	最小值	最大值
被解释变量	医疗服务满意度	*Medicalsatisfaction*	63.04	1.98	59.16	66.79
解释变量	人均可支配收入增长率	*Incomegrowth*	1.00	0.16	0.56	1.44
	基尼系数	*Gini*	1.00	0.17	0.79	1.32
	医疗服务提供能力	*Medicalsupply*	1.00	0.34	0.40	2.17
	基本医疗保险覆盖率	*Medicalins*	1.05	0.53	0.29	2.26
	30天内身体不健康天数	*Physicalhealth*	2.87	0.49	2.25	4.44
	30天内心理不健康天数	*Mentalhealth*	5.14	0.56	4.14	6.86

注：数据均为标准化后的数据。

（三）结果讨论

依据前述分析，将表5中的变量分为四个维度，分别对应四个模型。模型一为收入维度，选取人均可支配收入增长率（*Incomegrowth*）和基尼系数（*Gini*）作为变量；模型二是医疗供给维度，变量为医疗服务提供能力（*Medicalsupply*）；模型三为社会保险能力维度，变量为基本医疗保险覆盖率（*Medicalins*）；模型四为个体健康差异维度，变量为30天内身体不健康天数（*Physicalhealth*）和30天内心理不健康天数（*Mentalhealth*）。

模型的回归结果如表6所示，四个模型的定性结论基本一致，即人均可支配收入增长率、医疗服务提供能力、基本医疗保险覆盖率会对居民医疗服务满意度提高起到正向促进作用，而基尼系数、30天内身体不健康天数和30天内心理不健康天数对医疗服务满意度提高具有负向影响。从模型四的综合回归结果看，对居民医疗服务满意度作用较大的因素为收入因素，其次是居民个体对健康状况的自我评价因素，再次是医疗供给资源的人均配置状况，最后是基本医疗保险覆盖率。人均可支配收入增长率每提高 1%，医疗服务满意度将提高 2.930%，而基尼系数每提高 1%，医疗服务满意度将下降 4.003%，其负面影响比人均可支配收入增长率提高的正向促进作用还要大。在医疗供给和保障方面，医疗服务提供能力每提高 1%，居民对医疗服务的满意度将提高 0.655%，基本医疗保险覆盖率每提高 1%，满意度将提高 0.146%，医疗服务提供能力提高的作用大于基本医疗保险覆盖率提高的作用。30 天内居民身体不健康天数每增加 1%，则居民对医疗服务的满意度将下降 2.430%，而 30 天内居民心理不健康天数每增加 1%，满意度将下降 0.964%，可见身体健康对医疗服务满意度的作用比心理健康的作用要高。

表 6　模型回归结果

变量	模型一		模型二		模型三		模型四	
	系数	P 值	系数	P 值	系数	P 值	系数	P 值
Incomegrowth	1.990	0.330	1.858	0.3672	1.948	0.368	2.930	0.154
Gini	–4.084	0.044	–3.843	0.07	–3.820	0.730	–4.003	0.047
Medicalsupply			0.507	0.06	0.408	0.720	0.655	0.577
Medicalins					0.143	0.845	0.146	0.829
Physicalhealth							–2.430	0.012
Mentalhealth							–0.964	0.215
R^2	0.371		0.381		0.382		0.571	

四　结论与启示

中国长期以来面临着医疗资源紧张的状况，特别是人口规模较大的城市，“看病难”和“看病贵”的问题比较突出。医疗卫生服务一直备受党和国家领导人的关注，医疗服务的水平和质量是人民健康长寿的根本保障，也是推动社会公共服务均等化的重要内容之一。2019 年 7 月国务院印发了《“健康中国 2030”规划纲要》，提出要强化覆盖全民的公共卫生服务，具体措施包括控制重大传染性疾病，防控慢性病和推进基本公共服务均等化，同时提出为了提供优质高效的医疗服务，应完善医疗卫生服务体系。全国卫生健康系统全力贯彻党中央和国务院的战略部署，提高医疗服务能力和预防能力，有效地提高了婴幼儿、老年人口的卫生健康水平，疾病防控能力显著增强，有力地促进了居民健康水平的提高。《2018 年我国卫生健康事业发展统计公报》的数据显示，2017 年居民的人均预期寿命为 76.7 岁，2018 年提高到 77.0 岁，婴儿死亡率由 6.8‰下降至 6.1‰，同时孕产妇的死亡率也显著下降。这表明中国的医疗卫生服务已经对人口的健康发展起到了重要作用。

（一）结论

本报告通过发放问卷，对 2019 年中国 35 个城市居民的医疗服务满意度进行调查，结果表明医疗服务满意度比 2018 年有所下降。居民对医疗服务的最高评分有所下降，但最低评分显著上升，由 2018 年的 53.91 上升至 2019 年的 59.16。因此，2019 年居民的平均满意度虽然有所下降，但最低满意度水平是有所上升的，这表明中国的城市医疗服务在内容上是有一定程度提升的。

从居民的个体特征差异性看，20~29 岁居民医疗服务满意度指数为 65.16，30~39 岁居民的医疗服务满意度指数为 63.08，40 岁及以上居民的医疗服务满意度指数为 59.95，可见从年龄上看，年龄越大的居民对医疗服务的满意度越低。这可能是由于年龄大的居民受健康状况影响，看病的次数比年轻人多，去医院的次数较多，受就医等候时间长、医疗负担、一次所开药品受限等客观因素影响，满意度降低。从性别角度看，女性的医疗服务满意度指数为 63.53，而男性的医疗服务满意度指数为 64.32，可见女性居民对医疗服务的满意度低于男性。从学历角度来看，大学本科以下居民的医疗服务满意度指数为 61.93，大学本科学历居民的满意度指数为 63.94，研究生及以上学历居民的满意度指数为 65.68，说明学历越高的居民对医疗服务的满意度越高。

从不同城市的比较情况看，2019 年多数城市居民的医疗服务满意度比 2018 年有所下降，只有少数城市居民的医疗服务满意度比 2018 年有所上升。从区域分布的比较结果看，2019 年东部地区城市居民医疗服务满意度指数与 2018 年得分相同，即满意度水平保持不变，东北、中部和西部地区城市居民医疗服务满意度指数与 2018 年相比均有不同程度的下降，其中东北地区下降最显著。如果按八大综合经济区域的划分进行比较，可以看出东部沿海地区和大西北地区城市居民医疗服务满意度指数比 2018 年有所上升，其中东部沿海地区上升最显著，上升比率为 6.55%，其他地区的城市居民医疗服务满意度指数与 2018 年相比均有不同程度的下降，其中下降最多的还是东北地区，与 2018 年相比下降 6.87%，其次是大西南地区，比 2018 年城市居民医疗服务满意度指数下降 5.76%。

2019 年中国 35 个城市居民医疗服务平均满意度与 2018 年相比呈下降状态，有必要进一步分析影响医疗服务满意度的诸多因素中，哪些是促进城市居民医疗服务满意度提高的因素，哪些又是导致医疗服务满意度下降的因素。结合前述文献综述的内容，选取了代表居民收入水平、收入差距的人均可支配收入增长率和基尼系数表示收入维度对医疗服务满意度的影响因素；选取医疗服务提供能力作为反映医疗供给维度的因素，医疗服务提供能力是由包括每万人拥有的执业医师数量、每万人拥有的医疗机构床位数、每万人拥有的医院数量三个具体体现人均医疗资源拥有量的数据构成的；采用基本医疗保险覆盖率作为说明居民接受医疗服务成本负担情况的因素；采用 30 天内身体不健康天数和心理不健康天数作为反映居民个体健康差异维度的因素。回归结果表明，收入因素对35个城市居民的医疗服务满意度影响程度最大，其次影响比较大的是居民对自身健康的自我评价情况，包括30天内自我感觉身体和心理不健康的天数，自我感觉身体和心理不健康的程度越高，对医疗服务改善目前健康水平的期待就会越高，满意度就会越低。影响程度较小的因素是医疗服务提供能力和基本医疗保险覆盖率。

（二）启示

通过上述回归结果可知，对医疗服务满意度提高具有正向作用的因素包括人均可支配收入增长率、医疗服务提供能力、基本医疗保险覆盖率，其中人均可支配收入增长率属于经济因素，需要在宏观经济整体层面实现，因此从医疗卫生行业自身出发，提高医疗服务满意度最主要的就是提高医疗服务供给能力和水平，其次是从政府构建的社会保障体系内提高和稳定基本医疗保险覆盖率，并做好医疗保险基金的使用和管理工作。

第一，稳步提高医疗服务提供能力。2016年10月国务院印发了《“健康中国2030”规划纲要》，其中提出要强化覆盖全民的公共卫生服务，具体措施包括控制重大传染性疾病，防控慢性病和推进基本公共服务均等化，同时提出为了提供优质高效的医疗服务，应完善医疗卫生服务体系。《2018年我国卫生健康事业发展统计公报》数据显示，2018年中国有医院33009个，基层医疗卫生机构943639个，专业公共卫生机构18033个。与上一年相比，医院增加1953个，基层医疗卫生机构增加10615个，专业卫生机构减少1862个。基层医疗卫生机构中，社区卫生服务中心（站）34997个，乡镇卫生院36461个，诊所和医务室228019个，村卫生室622001个。政府办基层医疗卫生机构121918个。图5为2014~2018年全国医疗卫生机构主要构成数量，可见，2014~2018年中国卫生机构数总体呈增加趋势。

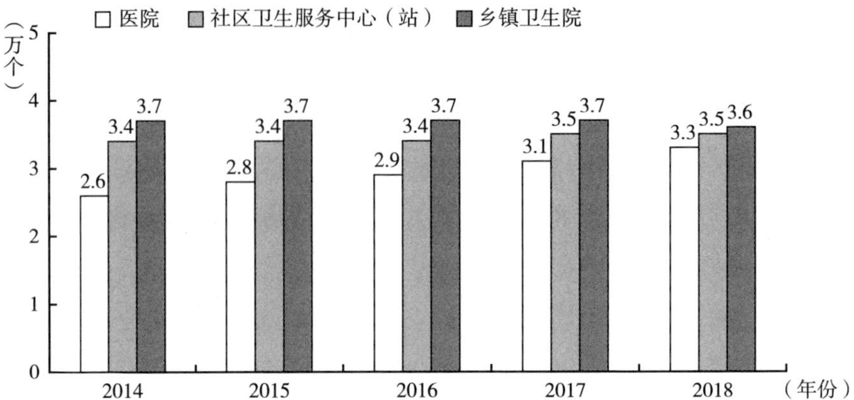

图 5　2014~2018 年全国医疗卫生机构主要构成数量

资料来源:《2018 年我国医疗卫生健康事业发展统计公报》。

随着医疗卫生机构数量的增加，2014~2018 年全国医疗卫生机构的床位数量也不断增加。如图 6 所示，2018 年全国医疗卫生机构床位数为 840.4 万张，比 2017 年增加了 46.4 万张，增长了 5.8%。2017 年每千人拥有的医疗卫生机构的床位数为 5.72 张，2018 年则上升到 6.03 张。

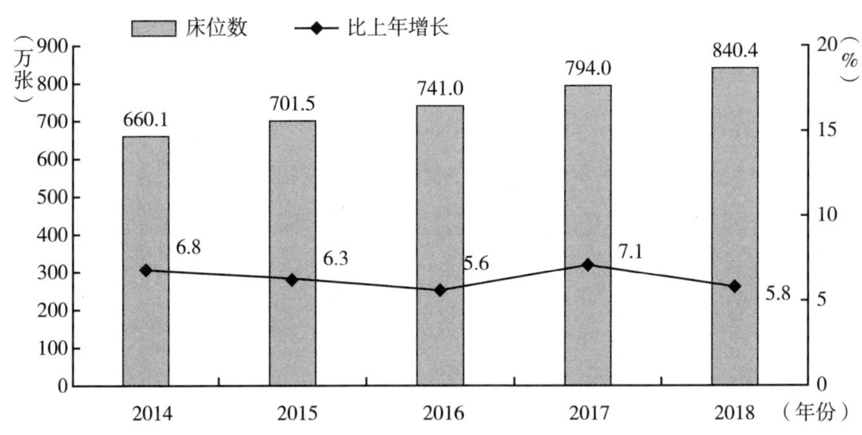

图 6　2014~2018 年全国医疗卫生机构床位数量变化

资料来源:《2018 年我国医疗卫生健康事业发展统计公报》。

如表7所示，2018年全国医疗服务工作量比2017年有所增加，共诊疗83.1亿人次，入院人数达25453万人，人数也比2017年的24436万人有所增加。

为了减少患者等待和排队的时间，至2018年底，45.4%的二级以上公立医院开展了预约诊疗，为了保证和提高医疗服务质量，上述医院还开展了远程医疗服务、优质护理服务等。

由此可见，为了提高医疗卫生的整体水平，改善和提高医疗卫生服务质量，党和政府在硬件建设方面连续多年进行了持续不断的投入，使医疗卫生条件有了根本性的改善，医院卫生人员总数、床位数都增加了，每万人公共卫生人员2018年为6.34人，2017年为6.28人，每千人口医疗卫生机构床位数由2017年的5.72张增加到6.03张。2018年在总诊疗人数大幅增长的情况下，医院医师的日均负责诊疗人数出现微降。

表7　全国医疗服务工作量

机构类别	诊疗人数（亿人次）		入院人数（万人）	
	2017年	2018年	2017年	2018年
医疗卫生机构合计	81.8	83.1	24436	25453
医院	34.4	35.8	18916	20017
公立医院	29.5	30.5	15595	16351
民营医院	4.9	5.3	3321	3666
医院中：				
三级医院	17.3	18.5	8396	9292
二级医院	12.7	12.8	8006	8177
一级医院	2.2	2.2	1169	1209
基层医疗卫生机构	44.3	44.1	4450	4375
其他机构	3.1	3.2	1071	1061
合计中：非公医疗卫生机构	18.4	18.9	3401	3737

资料来源：《2018年我国医疗卫生健康事业发展统计公报》。

在现有硬件建设的基础上，还应进一步做好提高优质医疗资源供给的工作。对于生活在城市中的居民，特别是生活在大城市的居民，看病难通常表现为看名医难、看名科室难、看名院难，这些都是所谓的优质医疗资源。随着经济的发展、人均收入水平的提高，居民对医疗的质量要求也不断提高。因此，只进行硬件的建设和改善是不够的，最重要的是要有一大批值得信任、医德和医术水平都比较高的医生及医生团队。也就是各级政府应不断谋求名医、名院和知名科室的建设，并提高这些优质医疗资源的诊疗率。发达国家为了扩大优质资源的诊疗范围，一般倡导优质医疗资源的下沉，也就是创造各种机制、机会和条件使三甲医院的高水平医生或其团队可以远程辅助下级医疗机构的诊断、治疗或手术，或者是允许三甲医院的医生短期流动到各下级医院出诊。这些都有利于使更多的居民享受到优质医疗资源，提高诊治质量，提高患者的医疗服务满意度。

第二，提高和稳定基本医疗保险覆盖率，并做好医疗保险基金的使用和管理工作。根据国家医保局公布的《2018 年全国基本医疗保障事业发展统计公报》，2018 年全国基本医疗保险的参保人数为 134459 万人，参保率稳定在 95% 以上，基本已经实现全覆盖。2018 年全国基本医疗保险基金总收入为 21384 亿元，总支出为 17822 亿元，累计结存 23440 亿元。基金的收支规模均比 2017 年有所增加，其中总收入比 2017 年增长了 19.3%，总支出比 2017 年增长了 23.6%，分别占 GDP 的 2.4% 和 2.0%。参保人数不断增加，同时医保的受益人数也相应增加。以职工医疗保险为例，参保人数达到 31681 万人，比 2017 年增长了 4.5%，2018 年享受医保待遇的职工人数达到 19.8 亿人次，比 2017 年增长了 9.0%。同时为了降低因病致贫的可能性，自 2018 年起，中央财政连续两年增加 80 亿元医疗求助补助资金，帮助深度贫困地区因病致贫人口摆脱贫困，已取得了显著成效。

另外，为了保障医疗保险基金的安全，2018 年开展了打击医疗保险基金诈骗专项行动，对于违法套取医保基金的行为进行了查处。

随着未来中国社会老龄化的加剧，未来医疗保险基金也可能面临亏空的风险。2018年太保安联联合安永发布了《中国商业健康险白皮书》，指出医保基金将面临赤字危机。为了减轻基本医疗保险基金的压力，应发展商业健康险，这是符合中国的实际发展需要的。

第三，为了进一步提高居民的医疗服务满意度，还应注重居民心理健康的管理和建设工作。现代紧张而具有竞争压力的城市生活，会使居民心理承受较大的压力，使居民身心疲惫，处于亚健康状态。为此，应多提供娱乐休闲的环境，多进行与减压和应对亚健康相关的医疗知识的宣传和普及，从人文关怀的角度提高居民健康感知和认知水平，这也有助于提高居民对医疗服务的满意度。

BLUE BOOK

智库成果出版与传播平台

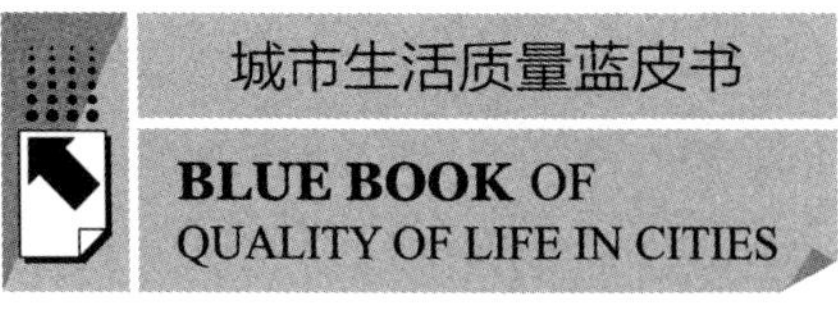

REPORT ON THE QUALITY OF LIFE IN CHINESE CITIES (2020)

NATIONAL INSTITUTE FOR ECONOMIC EXPERIMENTATION

Zhang Liancheng　Zhang Ping
Yang Chunxue　Lang Lihua
Wang Yu　Zhang Ziran

The Author of this Book

Zhang Liancheng, Zhang Ping, Yang Chunxue, Lang Lihua, Wang Yu,
Zhang Ziran, Zhao Jiazhang, Wang Yin, Hao Yubiao, Guo Yi, Yin Shixu

National Institute for Economic Experimentation (NIEE)

"National Institute for Economic Experimentation" is set up by Capital University of Economics and Business (CUEB) and Institute of Economics of China Academy of Social Sciences (CASS)

Early in the year of 2006, CUEB co-founded the "Research Center of China Economic Growth and Business Cycle" with Institute of Economics of CASS. From 2007 to 2019, the Center had successfully held 13 sessions of "Forum on China's Economic Growth and Business Cycle" with Hong Kong Economic Herald. In 2010, the two institutes decided to set up another research center - the "Research Center of the Quality of Life in Chinese Cities (QLICC)", and the Center released the quality-of-life indexes of 30 Chinese provincial capitals in the 5th Forum on China's Economic Growth and Business Cycle in 2011. NIEE was established in 2012 on the basis of the above-mentioned research centers.

At present, NIEE consists of research centers such as the "Research Center of China Economic Growth and Business Cycle", the "Research Center of the Quality of Life in Chinese Cities", the "Research Center of Quantitative Economics" and the "WTO Research Center", and other sectors such as the Economic Operation and International Trade Laboratory, the Economic Warning Laboratories, the Economic Data Processing and Computer Simulation Laboratory, the Digital Investigation Center and the Expert

Committee.

All in all, the purpose of NIEE is to promote economic experimentation research and the study of economics, to push forward the reform of China's economic systems, to improve the quality of economic growth and to drive economic development. NIEE aims to turn itself into an open-minded first-class international research institute in economic study through constant efforts.

Abstract

The Quality of Urban Life Research Center continued with its tracking survey of the quality of life (QOL) in 35 Chinese cities, and obtained related subjective (satisfaction) indices and sub-indices. The subjective data came from the online survey. For the reasonable and extensive spatial distribution of the survey samples, the investigators ensured the widest possible access to the questionnaire during the survey period. There were in total 28,050 visitors to the survey platform, resulting in 8,824 valid responses after screening. Based on statistical analysis of the survey results, the four subjective sub-indices produced are: consumer confidence, education quality, health conditions and medical services, each representing a different aspect of the quality of urban life in China. To facilitate international comparison, the consumer confidence sub-index was calculated in the same way as the Michigan Consumer Sentiment Index (MCSI) which set the US consumer sentiment index of Q1 1966 at 100. A value higher than 100 would thus indicate a stronger consumer confidence than that of US in Q1 1966.

According to the survey findings, in 2019, the weighted mean of the consumer confidence sub-indices of the 35 cities is 138.61, with the sub-index values of all the cities exceeding 100. The US MCSI of the same period (on May 17, 2019) is 102.4 which is lower than the weighted mean of the Chinese sub-indices. The weighted means of education quality, health conditions

and medical services sub-indices are 67.02, 57.26 and 63.04 respectively – all between "acceptable" (50) and "good" (75).

In consideration of international practice and international comparison, the objective (socio-economic data) sub-indices used before are no longer included in the index system this year. However, the objective data reflecting the quality of urban life were still collected to help explain what was really going on in these cities. The objective data were imported from authoritative database containing socio-economic information about the 35 cities, which ensured both the authority and the reliability of the sources. These data were also used as regression variables in the influential factor analysis of urban residents' subjective perceptions of their quality of life in line with relevant theories.

According to the assessment of the Quality of Life in Chinese Cities (QLICC) survey, the domestic consumer confidence has basically remained stable in the process of China's economic transformation to high quality development. Nevertheless, the contradiction between people's ever-growing need for a better life and the unbalanced and inadequate economic development will still exist in the short term, as revealed by residents' perceptions of the education quality, the medical services and their own health conditions. The Chinese government might need to keep on releasing policy and institutional dividends to stimulate the vitality of microeconomic entities, while innovating and refining macro-control measures to promote industrial structure upgrading and economic transformation. It might also need to further ensure "stability in six areas" (employment, financial operations, foreign trade, foreign investment, domestic investment and expectations), and constantly improve the quality of economic growth and public services such as education and healthcare while stabilizing economic development, so as to

provide robust institutional and policy support to a higher quality of life and both physical and mental wellbeing for the residents.

Keywords: Quality of Urban Life (QOUL); Consumer Confidence Sub-indices; Education Quality Sub-indices; Health Conditions Sub-indices; Medical Services Sub-indices

CONTENTS

I General Report

II Topical Reports

General Report

B.1
Report on the Quality of Life in Chinese Cities (2019)

Quality of Urban Life Research Center, NIEE[*]

Abstract: The Quality of Urban Life Research Center continued with its tracking survey of the quality of life (QOL) in 35 Chincse cities, and obtained related subjective (satisfaction) indices and sub-indices. According to the survey findings, in 2019, the weighted mean of the consumer confidence sub-indices of the 35 cities is 138.61 - between the threshold (100) and "confident" (150). Compared with the value of 2018 (115.48), the consumer confidence has obviously been on the rise. The weighted mean of the education quality sub-indices is 67.02 - slightly lower than that of 2018 (69.37). The weighted mean of the health

---

* Members: Zhang Liancheng, Zhang Ping, Yang Chunxue, Lang Lihua, Zhao Jiazhang, Zhang Ziran, Wang Yin, Lu Mingtao, Hao Yubiao, Wang Yu and Guo Yi.

conditions sub-indices is 57.26, also lower than that of last year (64.48). The weighted mean of the medical services sub-indices is 63.04 which is lower than that of 2018 (65.31) as well. All the three mean values fall between "acceptable" (50) and "good" (75). According to the survey findings, the Chinese government might need to keep on releasing policy and institutional dividends to stimulate the vitality of microeconomic entities, while innovating and refining macro-control measures to promote industrial structure upgrading and economic transformation. It might also need to further ensure "stability in six areas" (employment, financial operations, foreign trade, foreign investment, domestic investment and expectations), and constantly improve the quality of economic growth and public services such as education and healthcare while stabilizing economic development, so as to provide robust institutional and policy support to a higher quality of life and both physical and mental wellbeing for the residents.

Keywords: Consumer Confidence; Education Quality; Health Conditions; Medical Services

The *Report on the Quality of Life in Chinese Cities (QLICC)* is a result of continued group studies. Back in 2006, Capital University of Economics and Business (CUEB) and the Institute of Economics Chinese Academy of Social Sciences (CASS) co-founded the Research Center of China's Economic Growth and Business Cycle, and by 2019 have successfully held 13 forums. In 2010, the Quality of Urban Life Research Center ("the Center") was set up,

and the first QLICC report was released in 2011 on the 5th Forum on China's Economic Growth and Business Cycle. As of 2019, the Center has conducted its QLICC survey for nine years. The survey findings have created extensive impacts and thus been of high academic value. From 2012 to 2019, the Center has published seven annual *Report on the Quality of Life in Chinese Cities* (Chinese/English) in the form of blue books. Having not only enriched the data provided for fellow scholars, but also promoted the research in this filed, the report has been a plus to China's academia. Meanwhile, the researchers involved in the project have also completed a number of reports on the subject.

The creation of the QLICC system was the first attempt of its kind in China. More than 20 scholars across the world had looked extensively into the QOL index systems of the European Union, the United States and other countries, while taking into consideration the present socio-economic characteristics of China. The system was eventually set up after over a year of research and years of revision, in order to evaluate the quality of life in Chinese cities and provide guidance on the pathway and direction of QOL improvement. Despite its current defects, the QLICC system has filled in a gap in the field, and provided a reference system and a direction to work on for the assessment of the present quality of life in Chinese cities, for government decision-making and urban development, and for the improvement in urban residents' welfare and the quality of economic growth. This is consistent with the ruling conception of the CPC and the State Council. Meanwhile, the QLICC system has also laid the foundation for Chinese economists to conduct in-depth study on the QOL of Chinese residents and create a more scientific index system.

Most foreign QOL studies have been based merely on satisfaction surveys.

In the *QLICC Report* however, the system included both subjective and objective indices from the beginning. Related comparisons were also made between the two to determine whether residents' subjective perceptions were consistent with the objective quality of life, so as to provide more useful information for decision-makers and city managers and to help them better focus on the work of improving residents' quality of life. Besides, in order to build a scientific objective index system, the project team was very careful when making choices among the numerous indicators released by the authorities. At the same time, to provide extra proof of residents' QOL and expectations, special surveys have also been carried out on the greatest influential factors of QOL, house price expectation and job prospects, in addition to the QLICC survey.

The Center continued with its tracking survey of QLICC in the 35 Chinese cities from April to May, 2019. It is the 9th annual survey since 2011. Related subjective (satisfaction) indices (QLICCs) were obtained through statistical analysis and calculation for the evaluation of China's quality of urban life in 2019. The results were presented on the 13th Forum on China's Economic Growth and Business Cycle (2019) and reflected in the report.

1.1 Constitution of QLICC Survey (2019)

The 2019 survey retains the set of adopted techniques, index system setup and sample choosing method used in 2018. The method used for questionnaire distribution is as follows: to ensure the reasonable and extensive spatial distribution of survey samples, residents of the 35 cities were first screened out based on IP address segments, and then the questionnaire was distributed and recovered through WJX.cn (an online

survey platform). There were in total 28,050 visitors to the platform, resulting in 8,824 valid responses.

1.1.1 Subjective index systems of previous surveys

The QLICC system created by NIEE in 2011 consisted of two sections: the subjective (satisfaction) index system and the objective (socio-economic data) index system. The same system was used from 2012 to 2016 (See Table 1).

Table 1 Subjective index system of QLICC (2012-2016)

Satisfaction (subjective) sub-index	Indicator	Answers & Values				
		100	75	50	25	0
Living standard	Income status (50%)	Excellent	Good	Acceptable	Unacceptable	Poor
	Income expectation (50%)	Very optimistic	Optimistic	Acceptable	Pessimistic	Very pessimistic
Living cost	Living cost	Very low	Low	Acceptable	High	Very high
Human capital	Human capital	Excellent	Good	Acceptable	Unacceptable	Poor
Social security	Healthcare and elderly support (50%)	Excellent	Good	Acceptable	Unacceptable	Poor
	Public order (50%)	Excellent	Good	Acceptable	Unacceptable	Poor
Living experience	Pace of life (50%)	Very slow	Slow	Acceptable	Quick	Very quick
	Living convenience (50%)	Excellent	Good	Acceptable	Unacceptable	Poor

The 2017 survey basically retained the index system setup and the methods of questionnaire distribution and sample choosing used in the past, while making small adjustments. Considering that the communication habits of Chinese residents had changed greatly – from landlines to mobile phones – the sample population was switched to mobile phone users and was surveyed through the CATI (computer-assisted telephone interview) method. Of the

11 digits of a mobile phone number, the first three are network operator codes, while the middle four are region codes, and the last four personal codes. Therefore, the regional distribution of the users can be told by their phone numbers. The survey team first selected the region codes representing the 35 cities, and then chose the last 4 digits of telephone numbers randomly to generate a sample library, so as to ensure that all the 35 cities were covered with a balanced sample size for each city in the spatial distribution.

In 2017, the QLICC system still consisted of the subjective index system and the objective (socio-economic data) index system. The subjective / objective index could be further divided into five sub-indices - living standard, living cost, human capital, social security and living experience (health conditions) - each representing a particular aspect of urban residents' QOL in China.

There were mainly two changes in the 2017 subjective index system. One was in the connotation of the social security subjective sub-index. From 2012 to 2016, this sub-index had come from the weighted mean of the subjective healthcare and elderly support indicator and the subjective public order indicator. In 2017, however, the part of questionnaire concerning this sub-index was mainly designed to focus on whether residents were satisfied with the non-reimbursable part of their medical insurance, so as to make the questions more targeted and to generate results of greater practical significance. The other lay in the introduction of the survey on residents' health conditions, while replacing the subjective living experience sub-index with the subjective health conditions sub-index. From 2012 to 2016, the subjective sub-index of living experience had been obtained by calculating the weighted mean of the subjective pace of life indicator and the subjective living convenience indicator. In 2017 however, the health conditions sub-

index was generated using the international Short Form-8 (SF-8) scale instead. The new method could more accurately reflect residents' perceptions of their quality of life, and was more convenient for international comparison. The health conditions subjective sub-index concerned both physical and mental health (of equal weighting). The final values (range: 0-100) were obtained by processing the survey data with the T-score method (See Table 2).

Table 2 Subjective index system of QLICC (2017)

Satisfaction (subjective) sub-index	Indicator	Answers & Values				
		100	75	50	25	0
Living standard	Income status (50%)	Excellent	Good	Acceptable	Unacceptable	Poor
	Income expectation (50%)	Very optimistic	Optimistic	Acceptable	Pessimistic	Very pessimistic
Living cost	Living cost	Very low	Low	Acceptable	High	Very high
Human capital	Human capital	Excellent	Good	Acceptable	Unacceptable	Poor
Social security	Healthcare	Excellent	Good	Acceptable	Unacceptable	Poor
Health conditions	SF-8 physical health (50%)	Range: 0-100. Related values are obtained by processing the survey data with the T-score method.				
	SF-8 mental health (50%)					

1.1.2 Adjustments of subjective index system in 2018

In 2018, the QLICC system still consisted of the subjective (satisfaction) index system and the objective (socio-economic data) index system. The survey basically retained the set of adopted techniques, index system setup and sample choosing method used in the past, while making major adjustments to the subjective index system.

In view of further changes in the communication habits of Chinese

residents, both telephone interviews and online survey were conducted in 2018. In the former, mobile phone users were surveyed through the CATI method: According to the distribution of the samples, the digit segments representing the 35 cities were first selected. Then the last 4 digits of residents' telephone numbers were randomly chosen to generate a sample library. In the latter, residents of the 35 cities were first screened out based on IP address segments. Then the samples were randomly selected from valid questionnaire responses. The combination of the two methods fully ensured the reasonable and extensive spatial distribution of the survey samples.

In accordance with related international criteria, and to facilitate further international comparison, the team made major adjustments to the subjective index system to better present the QOL of the time and the sense of gain among urban residents in China. The 2018 subjective index system was made up of four subjective sub-indices: consumer confidence, education quality, health conditions and medical services, each representing a different aspect of the quality of urban life in China. Among them, the consumer confidence sub-index was calculated in the same way as the Michigan Consumer Sentiment Index (MCSI), and was comparable internationally. Since the developers of the questionnaire set the US results for Q1 1966 at 100, a value higher than 100 would therefore indicate a stronger consumer confidence than that of US in Q1 1966. The education quality sub-index was a simplification of the five indices proposed by Department II of Basic Education, Ministry of Education in J.J.E. [2013] No.2 of the "Opinions of the Ministry of Education on Promoting the Reform of Education Quality Evaluation in Primary and Secondary Schools" for the purpose of "setting up and improving the comprehensive evaluation system of education quality in primary and secondary schools". As for the health conditions sub-index, the

team adopted a health metric developed by the Centers for Disease Control and Prevention of the United States (CDC) – the number of physically or mentally unhealthy days in the past 30 days. If the total number of physically and mentally distressed days was greater than 30, then it was counted as 30 days. The bigger the number, the worse the physical or mental health in the past 30 days.

1.1.3 Adjustments of index system in 2019

In 2019, the team made great changes to the QLICC system by removing the objective (socio-economic data) index system. The new system consists only of the subjective index system, to be aligned with international criteria and to facilitate further international comparison. The subjective index system remains the same as in 2018. That is, it is still composed of four satisfaction sub-indices: consumer confidence, education quality, health conditions and medical services. Of the four sub-indices, the team referred to the setup and assessment approach of the MCSI (US) for the consumer confidence sub-index, and the value range was set at 0-200. The education quality sub-index was developed based on the five indices proposed by Department II of Basic Education, Ministry of Education in J.J.E. [2013] No.2 of the "Opinions of the Ministry of Education on Promoting the Reform of Education Quality Evaluation in Primary and Secondary Schools"① for the purpose of "setting up and improving the comprehensive evaluation system of education quality in primary and secondary schools". The health conditions sub-index

① "Opinions of the Ministry of Education on Promoting the Reform of Education Quality Evaluation in Primary and Secondary Schools" (J.J.E. [2013] No.2), MOE website, Jue 3 2013 http://old.moe.gov.cn/publicfiles/business/htmlfiles/moe/s7054/201306/153185.html.

was derived from a health metric developed by the CDC, concerning both physical and mental health. The medical services sub-index was used mainly to measure how satisfied residents were with healthcare services and the non-reimbursable part of the medical insurance. The value ranges of the last three sub-indices were all set at 0-100.

In consideration of the changes in Chinese residents' means of communication, the survey method was also different from that of 2018. That is, it changed from a combination of telephone interviews and online survey to using merely the website platform, identifying survey samples in the 35 cities based on IP address segments.

1.2 Subjective Sub-indices of the 35 Cities (2019)

In 2019, the subjective (satisfaction) index of QLICC is explained from four aspects: consumer confidence, education quality, health conditions and medical services.①

1.2.1 Consumer confidence sub-index

Table 3 summarizes the results of the 2019 consumer confidence survey. Overall, the weighted mean of the consumer confidence sub-indices of the 35 cities is 138.61 – between the threshold (100) and "confident" (150), indicating that consumers are optimistic about the current economic situation and the economic outlook in the next five years, and are satisfied with their personal income and income expectation. Compared with that of the same

---

① The main findings below have been published earlier. For details, see: Zhang Liancheng et al., NIEE, "Quality of Life for Urban Residents: Stability with Worry - Report on Resident Quality of Life in 35 Chinese Cities (2019)," *Economic Perspectives* 9 (2019): 3~17.

period in 2018 (115.48), the consumer confidence sub-index is on the rise as a whole. It is also higher than the US MCSI released on May 17, 2019 (102.4).

From the performance of individual cities, the consumer confidence sub-indices of all the 35 cities are above the threshold (100). In terms of ranking, the top 10 cities are: Nanning (145.35), Chongqing (143.36), Nanchang (143.03), Jinan (142.10), Qingdao (142.01), Guiyang (141.87), Changchun (141.44), Zhengzhou (141.27), Urumqi (140.83) and Nanjing (140.40). Among them, there are three eastern, three central and four western cities. The bottom 10 cities are: Hohhot (137.50), Fuzhou (137.08), Shanghai (136.78), Tianjin (136.64), Shenyang (135.39), Yinchuan (135.34), Beijing (135.09), Guangzhou (134.03), Shijiazhuang (130.35) and Chengdu (129.63). Compared with that of 2018, the consumer confidence has greatly increased in seven cities (Chongqing, Changchun, Urumqi, Nanjing, Haikou, Xi'an and Hangzhou), and declined significantly in six cities (Shanghai, Shenyang, Guangzhou, Shenzhen, Lanzhou and Changsha).

Table 3 Consumer confidence sub-indices of the 35 cities (2019)

Ranking		City	Value in 2019	Ranking		City	Value in 2019
2019	2018			2019	2018		
1	7	Nanning	145.35	12	13	Taiyuan	139.96
2	28	Chongqing	143.36	13	8	Hefei	139.77
3	5	Nanchang	143.03	14	35	Xi'an	139.74
4	2	Jinan	142.10	15	4	Changsha	139.68
5	9	Qingdao	142.01	16	24	Dalian	139.15
6	6	Guiyang	141.87	17	17	Xiamen	139.02
7	29	Changchun	141.44	18	30	Hangzhou	138.85
8	18	Zhengzhou	141.27	19	19	Kunming	138.49
9	22	Urumqi	140.83	20	15	Harbin	138.04
10	34	Nanjing	140.40	21	20	Xining	137.93
11	33	Haikou	140.26	22	14	Wuhan	137.85

Continued

Ranking		City	Value in 2019	Ranking		City	Value in 2019
2019	2018			2019	2018		
23	21	Ningbo	137.85	30	3	Shenyang	135.39
24	11	Lanzhou	137.69	31	32	Yinchuan	135.34
25	12	Shenzhen	137.63	32	25	Beijing	135.09
26	16	Hohhot	137.50	33	10	Guangzhou	134.03
27	23	Fuzhou	137.08	34	27	Shijiazhuang	130.35
28	1	Shanghai	136.78	35	31	Chengdu	129.63
29	26	Tianjin	136.64			Mean	138.61

In the QLICC system, the consumer confidence sub-index is composed of indicators including personal income changes, income expectation, anticipation of China's economic situation in 1-5 years and timing of consumer durable purchase. In 2019, the consumer confidence is generally stable among Chinese urban residents. According to the changes of these five indicators, it mainly results from residents' faith in both the stability of their own future income level and the momentum of China's economic development in the coming 1-5 years. At a time of weaker investment / export growth and greater pressure of economic slowdown, such a strong consumer confidence indicates that consumer demand is likely to become a stabilizer for China's economic growth in the following 1-2 years.

From the backgrounds of the respondents, as shown in Table 4, consumer confidence varies by gender, age and education, and there are individual differences. Firstly, by gender, the sub-index of the male consumers is slightly higher than that of the females. Secondly, by age, the 20-29 age group has the highest consumer confidence, while the ≥ 40 age group has the lowest. It can be observed that residents of different ages are faced with varying degrees of pressure in life, and are thus of different consumer confidence. Finally, by

education, the consumer confidence sub-index is positively correlated with the educational level. The consumers with the strongest confidence have at least a master's degree, and the consumers with lower confidence are those without a bachelor's degree. This is because the gaps in educational qualifications might result in different employment opportunities and income potentials, and thus lead to the differences in consumer confidence.

Table 4 Consumer confidence by gender, age and education

Group		Consumer confidence
Gender	Male	139.44
	Female	138.99
Age	20-29	140.19
	30-39	139.50
	≥40	134.23
Education	< Bachelor	138.86
	Bachelor	139.06
	≥ Master	140.80

1.2.2 Education quality sub-index

The education quality sub-index is a measure of residents' opinions about whether schools are focusing on education for all-around development. In terms of values, 100 stands for "excellent", 75 for "good", 50 for "acceptable", 25 for "unacceptable" and 0 for "poor". Table 5 summarizes the results of the 2019 education quality sub-indices. As shown in the table, the weighted mean of the education quality sub-indices is 67.02 - between "acceptable" (50) and "good" (75), and slight lower than that of 2018 (69.37). The sub-index is composed of three indicators, as one of the key survey questions is: "In your opinion, do ordinary primary / secondary schools nowadays emphasize

1. moral education; 2. the comprehensive improvement of both physical and mental qualities; 3. the development of hobbies and talents". Based on the mean values of the three indicators, schools are perceived to have done best in moral education (70.64), followed by the improvement of physical and mental qualities (65.73), and the development of hobbies and talents comes last (64.76). All the mean values fall between "acceptable" (50) and "good" (75).

Table 5 Education quality sub-indices of the 35 cities (2019)

Ranking		City	Value in 2019	Ranking		City	Value in 2019
2019	2018			2019	2018		
1	7	Xiamen	73.02	19	19	Nanchang	66.73
2	31	Qingdao	70.99	20	32	Hefei	66.67
3	33	Haikou	70.75	21	15	Xining	66.62
4	13	Changsha	70.08	22	18	Nanjing	66.55
5	8	Guiyang	69.94	23	21	Dalian	66.40
6	14	Yinchuan	69.17	24	16	Chongqing	66.27
7	11	Shenzhen	69.00	25	29	Beijing	66.19
8	35	Hangzhou	68.83	26	30	Xi'an	65.76
9	28	Zhengzhou	68.80	27	22	Wuhan	65.74
10	25	Ningbo	68.76	28	20	Fuzhou	65.55
11	2	Urumqi	67.98	29	34	Guangzhou	65.30
12	3	Lanzhou	67.97	30	4	Tianjin	65.17
13	5	Nanning	67.96	31	26	Harbin	63.49
14	9	Taiyuan	67.61	32	23	Shijiazhuang	63.45
15	1	Jinan	67.54	33	27	Shanghai	62.84
16	6	Hohhot	67.43	34	12	Chengdu	61.86
17	24	Changchun	66.82	35	17	Shenyang	61.70
18	10	Kunming	66.75			Mean	67.02

By ranking, the top 10 cities are: Xiamen (73.02), Qingdao (70.99), Haikou (70.75), Changsha (70.08), Guiyang (69.94), Yinchuan (69.17),

Shenzhen (69.00), Hangzhou (68.83), Zhengzhou (68.80) and Ningbo (68.76). The bottom 10 cities are: Xi'an (65.76), Wuhan (65.74), Fuzhou (65.55), Guangzhou (65.30), Tianjin (65.17), Harbin (63.49), Shijiazhuang (63.45), Shanghai (62.84), Chengdu (61.86) and Shenyang (61.70). In terms of economy, Beijing, Shanghai and Guangzhou are the most developed among the 35 cities, and can thus provide the best education and the richest educational resources. Therefore, the residents of these cities are supposed to be more satisfied with the education quality. However, according to the survey findings, it is quite the contrary. The three cities rank 25th, 33rd and 29th respectively. Compared with that of 2018, the rankings of Qingdao, Haikou, Hangzhou, Zhengzhou, Ningbo and Hefei have significantly improved, while the rankings of Tianjin, Chengdu, Shenyang, Jinan and Hohhot have declined.

In addition to the regular questions on education quality, the survey also asked supplementary questions about other concerns of the residents, including: student workloads, major obstacles to entering prestigious or key primary / secondary schools, and residents' perceptions of extracurricular education expenses. The results are shown in Table 6, 7 and 8.

Table 6 summarizes residents' satisfaction with their children's student workloads in 2019. The higher the value, the lighter the workload perceived. In terms of value ranges, 100 stands for "very light", 75 for "light", 50 for "acceptable", 25 for "heavy" and 0 for "very heavy". Overall, the mean value of the 35 cities is 26.17 - between "acceptable" and "heavy", but closer to the latter. By rankings, Jinan ranks first (32.02), and Taiyuan ranks last (21.27). That is, residents in Jinan perceived that their children had the lightest student workloads, and those in Taiyuan the heaviest. In terms of values, however, all the respondents felt that the workloads were too heavy.

Table 6 Student workload indicators of the 35 cities (2019)

Ranking		City	Value in 2019	Ranking		City	Value in 2019
2019	2018			2019	2018		
1	22	Jinan	32.02	19	27	Xining	26.31
2	14	Guiyang	30.13	20	9	Wuhan	25.81
3	5	Shenzhen	29.88	21	8	Chengdu	25.61
4	3	Tianjin	29.64	22	15	Yinchuan	25.40
5	1	Qingdao	29.13	23	35	Xi'an	25.35
6	16	Haikou	28.81	24	25	Ningbo	24.81
7	4	Urumqi	28.36	25	6	Fuzhou	24.74
8	33	Nanchang	28.31	26	26	Dalian	24.43
9	13	Beijing	28.12	27	10	Harbin	24.28
10	7	Xiamen	27.81	28	20	Guangzhou	23.93
11	30	Lanzhou	27.40	29	2	Nanjing	23.61
12	17	Changsha	26.88	30	29	Hangzhou	23.55
13	11	Nanning	26.80	31	18	Changchun	23.31
14	21	Kunming	26.78	32	19	Shijiazhuang	22.78
15	28	Chongqing	26.72	33	23	Shenyang	22.53
16	12	Zhengzhou	26.59	34	34	Shanghai	21.70
17	24	Hohhot	26.55	35	32	Taiyuan	21.27
18	31	Hefei	26.53			Mean	26.17

By ranking changes, the indicators of Jinan, Guiyang, Haikou, Nanchang, Lanzhou, Chongqing, Hefei and Xi'an have improved greatly compared to that of 2018; and the indicators of Nanjing, Fuzhou, Harbin, Changchun, Shijiazhuang, Chengdu and Wuhan have declined significantly.

Table 7 summarizes the major obstacles perceived by the residents to entering prestigious or key primary / secondary schools, in the case of their children or students in general. Overall, "school district" is regarded by 32.60% of the respondents as the primary obstacle, followed by "academic performance" (23.30%), "school-selection fee" (20.18%) and "domicile of household register" (19.05%). Compared with that of 2018, the results of

2019 show that the proportions of "school-selection fee" and "academic performance" have risen significantly. Of the four factors, increased importance in "academic performance" indicates improved fairness in education, while the other three remain major obstacles to the balanced development of education.

Table 7 Perceptions of major obstacles to entering prestigious or key primary / secondary schools (2019)

No.	City	%				
		School district	Academic performance	School-selection fee	Domicile of household register	Other factors
1	Beijing	39.95	18.56	21.13	19.85	0.52
2	Chengdu	31.33	21.03	27.90	17.60	2.15
3	Dalian	41.56	22.08	15.15	17.32	3.90
4	Fuzhou	34.20	23.38	14.72	22.94	4.76
5	Guangzhou	21.02	29.30	21.66	23.89	4.14
6	Guiyang	18.39	36.77	12.56	17.94	14.35
7	Harbin	31.62	21.79	26.50	14.10	5.98
8	Haikou	27.19	24.12	15.35	24.56	8.77
9	Hangzhou	32.19	26.18	21.89	15.88	3.86
10	Hefei	39.74	23.08	15.38	17.95	3.85
11	Hohhot	34.20	18.61	20.78	18.61	7.79
12	Jinan	40.17	20.52	18.78	17.90	2.62
13	Kunming	26.43	23.79	24.67	16.74	8.37
14	Lanzhou	30.26	28.07	16.67	14.47	10.53
15	Nanchang	31.76	23.61	15.88	24.03	4.72
16	Nanjing	43.65	17.92	22.48	13.36	2.61
17	Nanning	33.04	19.57	13.48	26.52	7.39
18	Ningbo	32.16	24.67	14.98	22.91	5.29
19	Qingdao	41.63	21.46	15.88	14.59	6.44
20	Xiamen	27.39	23.91	13.48	28.70	6.52
21	Shanghai	35.75	20.47	18.91	20.98	3.89
22	Shenzhen	24.09	21.45	22.11	28.71	3.63
23	Shenyang	47.83	23.04	14.78	13.04	1.30

Continued

No.	City	%				
		School district	Academic performance	School-selection fee	Domicile of household register	Other factors
24	Shijiazhuang	30.87	23.91	20.87	22.61	1.74
25	Taiyuan	29.69	20.52	23.14	19.65	6.99
26	Tianjin	41.37	19.54	19.87	15.31	3.91
27	Urumqi	35.24	27.75	19.82	11.89	5.29
28	Wuhan	37.10	19.68	24.52	15.81	2.90
29	Xi'an	28.88	19.83	34.91	13.79	2.59
30	Xining	23.26	26.51	16.74	21.40	12.09
31	Yinchuan	22.91	36.12	24.67	11.01	5.29
32	Changchun	30.30	19.48	25.11	19.05	6.06
33	Changsha	29.18	28.33	15.88	22.75	3.86
34	Zhengzhou	33.33	18.86	22.81	21.49	3.51
35	Chongqing	25.96	28.53	26.92	17.63	0.96
2019		32.60	23.30	20.18	19.05	4.86
2018		33.50	17.10	17.40	19.20	12.80

Table 8 summarizes residents' perceptions of their children's extra-curricular education expenses in 2019. The value range is 0-100. The lower the value, the higher the expenses, and vice versa. 0 stands for "very high", 25 for "high", 50 for "acceptable", 75 for "low", and 100 for "very low". The mean value of the 35 cities is 24.92 - between "very high" (0) and "high" (25), but closer to the latter. It suggests that extra-curricular education expenses constitute a major part of household expenditure to urban residents.

Table 8 Satisfaction with extracurricular education expenses (2019)

Ranking		City	Value in 2019	Ranking		City	Value in 2019
2019	2018			2019	2018		
1	9	Guiyang	31.33	4	12	Jinan	28.45
2	4	Xiamen	29.60	5	22	Hefei	28.08
3	7	Xining	28.87	6	34	Nanchang	28.05

Continued

Ranking		City	Value in 2019	Ranking		City	Value in 2019
2019	2018			2019	2018		
7	5	Fuzhou	28.03	22	16	Ningbo	23.94
8	6	Haikou	27.89	23	29	Hangzhou	23.72
9	24	Chongqing	27.65	24	11	Lanzhou	23.64
10	10	Kunming	26.73	25	13	Zhengzhou	23.28
11	21	Changsha	26.66	26	28	Taiyuan	22.93
12	27	Shenzhen	26.50	27	32	Chengdu	22.77
13	2	Guangzhou	26.42	28	31	Xi'an	22.75
14	15	Nanning	26.39	29	19	Shijiazhuang	22.31
15	1	Qingdao	26.16	30	17	Nanjing	21.38
16	8	Yinchuan	26.09	31	33	Shenyang	20.94
17	14	Urumqi	25.09	32	25	Dalian	20.51
18	3	Tianjin	24.96	33	35	Harbin	19.65
19	20	Hohhot	24.90	34	18	Changchun	18.98
20	23	Beijing	24.63	35	30	Shanghai	18.58
21	26	Wuhan	24.31			Mean	24.92

Compared with that of 2018, residents are on the whole less satisfied with the education quality, the student workloads and the extracurricular education expenses. It suggests that China might need to further accelerate the reform of the education system, as well as the supply and better allocation of quality educational resources.

1.2.3 Health conditions sub-index

The survey on health conditions is mainly designed to observe urban residents' perceptions of their own health. The value range is 0-100. 0 stands for "poor", 25 for "acceptable", 50 for "good", 75 for "excellent", and 100 for "perfect". The weighted mean of the sub-indices is 57.26 - between "good" (50) and "excellent" (75), but lower than that of 2018 (64.48). Table 9 summarizes the results of the 2019 survey on health conditions.

Table 9 Health conditions sub-indices of the 35 cities (2019)

Ranking		City	Value in 2019	Ranking		City	Value in 2019
2019	2018			2019	2018		
1	14	Zhengzhou	61.50	19	26	Shenyang	57.56
2	6	Taiyuan	61.04	20	28	Wuhan	56.92
3	5	Shenzhen	60.82	21	25	Ningbo	56.79
4	8	Beijing	60.80	22	2	Kunming	56.78
5	35	Hangzhou	60.41	23	15	Chengdu	56.69
6	7	Harbin	59.99	24	19	Nanning	56.62
7	10	Jinan	59.95	25	3	Hefei	56.21
8	20	Xiamen	59.27	26	11	Tianjin	55.81
9	4	Guiyang	59.01	27	34	Yinchuan	55.64
10	13	Hohhot	58.98	28	12	Dalian	55.62
11	24	Nanchang	58.65	29	30	Lanzhou	54.98
12	22	Fuzhou	58.51	30	17	Shanghai	54.33
13	31	Haikou	58.44	31	18	Changsha	53.71
14	16	Changchun	58.44	32	33	Guangzhou	53.32
15	27	Chongqing	58.27	33	32	Shijiazhuang	52.72
16	1	Qingdao	57.89	34	23	Urumqi	52.01
17	21	Nanjing	57.76	35	29	Xining	50.94
18	9	Xi'an	57.70			Mean	57.26

As shown in Table 9, the top 10 cities are: Zhengzhou (61.50), Taiyuan (61.04), Shenzhen (60.82), Beijing (60.80), Hangzhou (60.41), Harbin (59.99), Jinan (59.95), Xiamen (59.27), Guiyang (59.01) and Hohhot (58.98). The bottom 10 cities are: Tianjin (55.81), Yinchuan (55.64), Dalian (55.62), Lanzhou (54.98), Shanghai (54.33), Changsha (53.71), Guangzhou (53.32), Shijiazhuang (52.72), Urumqi (52.01) and Xining (50.94).

By ranking changes, the rankings of Zhengzhou, Hangzhou, Xiamen, Nanchang, Fuzhou, Haikou and Chongqing have greatly improved, while the rankings of Qingdao, Kunming, Hefei, Tianjin, Dalian, Shanghai, Changsha and Urumqi have declined significantly.

The health conditions sub-index is composed of two indicators which correspond to two questions in the questionnaire: the number of physically / mentally unhealthy days in the past 30 days, and the number of days of limited daily activities due to physical / mental distress in the past 30 days. The specific results are summarized in Table 10, 11, 12 and 13.

In the survey on health conditions, the team adopted a health metric developed and used by the CDC – the number of physically / mentally unhealthy days in the past 30 days. Table 10 summarizes the survey findings.

Table 10 Number of physically / mentally unhealthy days in the past 30 days (2019)

Unit: day

Ranking		City	No. of days in 2019	Ranking		City	No. of days in 2019
2019	2018			2019	2018		
1	1	Nanjing	5.78	19	30	Haikou	8.39
2	26	Wuhan	5.88	20	24	Chengdu	8.64
3	3	Shenzhen	6.08	21	8	Taiyuan	8.66
4	2	Fuzhou	6.11	22	21	Dalian	8.75
5	4	Xiamen	6.18	23	28	Tianjin	8.76
6	6	Shanghai	6.55	24	16	Hangzhou	8.85
7	14	Jinan	6.70	25	17	Kunming	8.85
8	15	Guangzhou	6.77	26	33	Yinchuan	9.02
9	9	Ningbo	6.88	27	22	Lanzhou	9.17
10	10	Nanchang	6.89	28	29	Shenyang	9.57
11	20	Beijing	7.10	29	34	Xi’an	9.62
12	12	Nanning	7.45	30	7	Guiyang	9.73
13	11	Zhengzhou	7.56	31	19	Shijiazhuang	9.80
14	5	Qingdao	7.73	32	25	Hohhot	9.82
15	23	Chongqing	7.95	33	35	Changchun	9.82
16	13	Hefei	7.97	34	18	Xining	10.53
17	32	Changsha	7.98	35	31	Urumqi	11.14
18	27	Harbin	8.33		Mean		8.14

As shown in Table 10, the 2019 mean value of the 35 cities is 8.14 days. That is, residents on average perceived themselves to be either physically or mentally unhealthy in 8.14 out of the past 30 days. Nanjing and Wuhan are of the least unhealthy days (< 6 days), and Xining and Urumqi the most (> 10 days).

Compared to that of 2018 (5.5 days), the 2019 mean of unhealthy days has increased by 48%.

Table 11 and 12 present the separate survey findings of physical and mental health in 2019. By comparison, the residents are better off physically than mentally, that is, the major cause of health problems is psychological. In physical health, the means of 2019 (2.87 days) and 2018 (2.53 days) are of little difference, while in mental health, the mean of 2019 (5.14 days) is much higher than that of 2018 (3.01 days). In April 2018, the Chinese Health Management Association of CMA worked together with the National Research Institute for Family Planning, the Holistic Integrative Medicine Branch of CMDA and the Beijing Health Management Association to co-release the *White Paper: Mental Health of Urban Residents in China*. According to the *White Paper*, 73.6% of the population were in a state of mental sub-health; 16.1% were of some psychological problems; and only 10.3% were in good conditions mentally.① It is consistent with the survey findings. All this shows that the mental health of the residents in China requires more concern.

① "*White Paper on Mental Health of Urban Residents in China* published," CCTV.com, Apr 30 2018, http://jiankang.cctv.com/2018/04/30/ARTIWf496N6d9O0lrIdJM4rG180430.shtml.

Table 11　No. of physically unhealthy days in the past 30 days (2019)

Unit: day

Ranking		City	No. of days in	Ranking		City	No. of days in
2019	2018		2019	2019	2018		2019
1	10	Ningbo	2.25	19	3	Guiyang	2.84
2	2	Shenzhen	2.25	20	27	Beijing	2.85
3	1	Nanjing	2.27	21	17	Shijiazhuang	2.92
4	18	Chengdu	2.30	22	32	Harbin	3.01
5	6	Xiamen	2.32	23	13	Nanning	3.03
6	9	Nanchang	2.36	24	20	Kunming	3.05
7	11	Hefei	2.39	25	21	Changsha	3.05
8	5	Fuzhou	2.43	26	8	Taiyuan	3.07
9	25	Wuhan	2.47	27	23	Lanzhou	3.30
10	19	Jinan	2.49	28	28	Shenyang	3.31
11	12	Hangzhou	2.52	29	29	Haikou	3.31
12	4	Zhengzhou	2.55	30	30	Yinchuan	3.34
13	34	Xi'an	2.63	31	35	Changchun	3.40
14	14	Chongqing	2.70	32	22	Dalian	3.44
15	33	Tianjin	2.72	33	26	Hohhot	3.51
16	15	Guangzhou	2.75	34	31	Urumqi	3.71
17	7	Qingdao	2.76	35	24	Xining	4.44
18	16	Shanghai	2.79			Mean	2.87

Table 12　No. of mentally unhealthy days in the past 30 days (2019)

Unit: day

Ranking		City	No. of days in	Ranking		City	No. of days in
2019	2018		2019	2019	2018		2019
1	29	Wuhan	4.14	9	11	Shenzhen	4.72
2	8	Xiamen	4.26	10	34	Changsha	4.76
3	3	Fuzhou	4.31	11	19	Hangzhou	4.83
4	7	Ningbo	4.46	12	13	Hefei	4.85
5	14	Guangzhou	4.52	13	31	Chongqing	4.93
6	4	Jinan	4.61	14	26	Haikou	4.95
7	1	Shanghai	4.63	15	12	Nanchang	5.01
8	2	Nanjing	4.69	16	5	Qingdao	5.03

Continued

Ranking		City	No. of days in 2019	Ranking		City	No. of days in 2019
2019	2018			2019	2018		
17	18	Zhengzhou	5.04	27	16	Kunming	5.45
18	32	Xi'an	5.14	28	10	Guiyang	5.56
19	6	Nanning	5.14	29	35	Changchun	5.63
20	30	Chengdu	5.21	30	17	Xining	5.67
21	23	Dalian	5.22	31	33	Yinchuan	5.73
22	9	Taiyuan	5.24	32	20	Harbin	5.88
23	28	Shenyang	5.29	33	25	Hohhot	5.91
24	24	Lanzhou	5.37	34	22	Shijiazhuang	5.95
25	21	Tianjin	5.43	35	27	Urumqi	6.86
26	15	Beijing	5.43			Mean	5.14

To study the relationship between physical / mental health and daily life, in 2019, the team also surveyed residents on the number of days of limited daily activities due to physical or mental distress in the past 30 days. The findings are summarized in Table 13. The mean of the 35 cities is 3.22 days, higher than that of 2018 (2.19 days). By city, Shenzhen is of the least days (2.24 days), and Guiyang the most (5.78 days).

Table 13 No. of days of limited daily activities due to physical / mental distress

Unit: day

Ranking		City	No. of days in 2019	Ranking		City	No. of days in 2019
2019	2018			2019	2018		
1	4	Shenzhen	2.24	7	10	Guangzhou	2.43
2	8	Nanjing	2.26	8	13	Hangzhou	2.61
3	5	Xiamen	2.27	9	23	Jinan	2.66
4	1	Fuzhou	2.41	10	3	Wuhan	2.72
5	12	Beijing	2.42	11	31	Chongqing	2.81
6	2	Shanghai	2.43	12	22	Tianjin	2.88

Continued

Ranking		City	No. of days in 2019	Ranking		City	No. of days in 2019
2019	2018			2019	2018		
13	9	Qingdao	2.99	25	33	Shenyang	3.52
14	14	Taiyuan	2.99	26	29	Haikou	3.57
15	6	Ningbo	3.03	27	15	Kunming	3.58
16	20	Nanning	3.16	28	35	Yinchuan	3.59
17	30	Zhengzhou	3.21	29	21	Xining	3.63
18	34	Changchun	3.22	30	11	Shijiazhuang	3.71
19	24	Nanchang	3.24	31	26	Xi'an	3.78
20	7	Changsha	3.27	32	28	Lanzhou	3.86
21	19	Harbin	3.30	33	17	Chengdu	3.94
22	18	Hohhot	3.43	34	32	Urumqi	4.64
23	27	Dalian	3.44	35	25	Guiyang	5.78
24	16	Hefei	3.51			Mean	3.22

Table 14 summarizes the impact of gender, age and education on residents' perceptions of their health conditions. By gender, the males are slightly more satisfied with their health conditions than the females. By education, the educational level is proportional to the satisfaction with health conditions. By age, the most satisfied is the 20-29 age group, but at the same time they are also of the greatest number of days of limited daily activity due to physical or mental distress.

Table 14 Satisfaction with health conditions by gender, age and education

Group		Overall health*	"Physically + mentally" unhealthy (day)	Daily activities limited due to physical or mental distress (day)
Gender	Male	59.54	7.39	3.03
	Female	56.68	8.36	3.10
Age	20-29	59.51	8.08	3.25
	30-39	57.22	7.44	2.76
	≥ 40	52.14	8.51	2.96

Continued

Group		Overall health*	"Physically + mentally" unhealthy (day)	Daily activities limited due to physical or mental distress (day)
Education	< Bachelor	57.53	8.48	3.51
	Bachelor	57.67	7.88	3.01
	≥ Master	60.04	7.85	2.97

Note: The overall health indicators were obtained based on the values assigned to respondents' answers to the question "How is your health?"

1.2.4 Medical services sub-index

The survey on medical services mainly investigated residents' opinions on the quality of healthcare services and the non-reimbursable part of the medical insurance. The value range is 0-100. The lower the value, the more unsatisfied the residents, and vice versa. 0 stands for "poor", 25 for "unacceptable", 50 for "acceptable", 75 for "good", and 100 for "excellent".

Table 15 summarizes residents' perceptions of medical services in 2019 and shows the weighted mean of the data provided in Table 16 and 17.

Table 15 Medical services sub-indices of the 35 cities (2019)

Ranking		City	Value in 2019	Ranking		City	Value in 2019
2019	2018			2019	2018		
1	1	Beijing	66.79	11	23	Guangzhou	64.37
2	33	Nanjing	66.31	12	11	Urumqi	63.93
3	15	Hangzhou	65.92	13	18	Shijiazhuang	63.73
4	25	Nanchang	65.54	14	8	Qingdao	63.54
5	3	Ningbo	65.27	15	16	Tianjin	63.47
6	20	Hefei	65.12	16	2	Nanning	63.40
7	21	Xi'an	65.03	17	5	Xiamen	63.05
8	4	Jinan	64.94	18	10	Hohhot	62.99
9	6	Zhengzhou	64.94	19	31	Shanghai	62.87
10	9	Shenyang	64.70	20	17	Chongqing	62.71

Continued

Ranking 2019	Ranking 2018	City	Value in 2019	Ranking 2019	Ranking 2018	City	Value in 2019
21	24	Changsha	62.46	29	19	Yinchuan	61.40
22	7	Chengdu	62.45	30	28	Taiyuan	60.53
23	34	Guiyang	62.19	31	30	Kunming	60.28
24	26	Lanzhou	61.99	32	13	Dalian	60.16
25	35	Haikou	61.91	33	22	Fuzhou	60.08
26	14	Wuhan	61.87	34	29	Harbin	60.00
27	32	Xining	61.62	35	12	Changchun	59.16
28	27	Shenzhen	61.55			Mean	63.04

According to the 2019 survey findings, the weighted mean of the medical services sub-indices is 63.04 – between "acceptable" (50) and "good" (75), but lower than that of 2018 (65.31). By ranking, the top 10 cities are: Beijing (66.79), Nanjing (66.31), Hangzhou (65.92), Nanchang (65.54), Ningbo (65.27), Hefei (65.12), Xi'an (65.03), Jinan (64.94), Zhengzhou (64.94) and Shenyang (64.70). The bottom 10 cities are: Wuhan (61.87), Xining (61.62), Shenzhen (61.55), Yinchuan (61.40), Taiyuan (60.53), Kunming (60.28), Dalian (60.16), Fuzhou (60.08), Harbin (60.00) and Changchun (59.16).

By ranking changes, the rankings of Nanjing and Nanchang have improved greatly compared to that of 2018, rising 31 and 21 places; while the rankings of Changchun and Dalian have dropped 23 and 19 places, respectively. Among the four megacities of Beijing, Shanghai, Guangzhou and Shenzhen, the rankings of Beijing (No.1) and Shenzhen (No.28) have generally remained stable, and the rankings of Shanghai and Guangzhou have gone up over ten places.

The medical services sub-index consists of two indicators: satisfaction with the quality of healthcare services (Table 16) and the non-

reimbursable part of the medical insurance (Table 17). According to the two indicators, the residents are more satisfied with the quality of healthcare services (64.91) than the non-reimbursable part of the medical insurance (61.16).

Table 16 Are you satisfied with the quality of healthcare services (including diagnosis & treatment, service attitude and hospital environment)?

Ranking		City	Value in 2019	Ranking		City	Value in 2019
2019	2018			2019	2018		
1	3	Beijing	69.35	19	21	Hohhot	64.42
2	34	Nanjing	68.82	20	25	Changsha	64.34
3	19	Hangzhou	68.69	21	10	Wuhan	64.31
4	27	Guangzhou	67.45	22	18	Shenzhen	64.22
5	9	Zhengzhou	67.27	23	30	Lanzhou	64.01
6	23	Nanchang	67.26	24	17	Chongqing	63.99
7	6	Jinan	66.81	25	20	Urumqi	63.89
8	11	Xi'an	66.78	26	35	Haikou	63.79
9	7	Shijiazhuang	66.64	27	28	Dalian	63.77
10	4	Tianjin	66.58	28	26	Taiyuan	62.97
11	16	Chengdu	66.48	29	29	Yinchuan	62.37
12	8	Shenyang	66.42	30	32	Xining	62.30
13	14	Qingdao	66.40	31	22	Harbin	61.98
14	13	Hefei	66.35	32	31	Kunming	61.26
15	5	Ningbo	66.34	33	24	Fuzhou	61.11
16	2	Nanning	65.86	34	33	Guiyang	60.39
17	1	Xiamen	64.66	35	15	Changchun	60.17
18	12	Shanghai	64.42			Mean	64.91

Table 17 In general, are you satisfied with the non-reimbursable part of the medical insurance?

Ranking		City	Value in 2019	Ranking		City	Value in 2019
2019	2018			2019	2018		
1	2	Beijing	64.24	19	30	Xining	60.94
2	1	Ningbo	64.19	20	20	Shijiazhuang	60.82
3	31	Guiyang	63.99	21	9	Qingdao	60.67
4	12	Urumqi	63.98	22	25	Changsha	60.57
5	17	Hefei	63.89	23	10	Yinchuan	60.44
6	29	Nanchang	63.81	24	24	Tianjin	60.37
7	33	Nanjing	63.80	25	34	Haikou	60.02
8	26	Xi'an	63.29	26	16	Lanzhou	59.98
9	18	Hangzhou	63.16	27	13	Wuhan	59.42
10	8	Jinan	63.08	28	23	Kunming	59.31
11	21	Shenyang	62.97	29	19	Fuzhou	59.04
12	3	Zhengzhou	62.62	30	32	Shenzhen	58.89
13	6	Hohhot	61.56	31	5	Chengdu	58.43
14	7	Xiamen	61.43	32	15	Changchun	58.14
15	11	Chongqing	61.43	33	28	Taiyuan	58.10
16	35	Shanghai	61.32	34	27	Harbin	58.01
17	22	Guangzhou	61.29	35	14	Dalian	56.55
18	4	Nanning	60.94			Mean	61.16

Table 18 summarizes the impact of gender, age and education on respondents' perceptions of medical services. By gender, the females are slightly less satisfied than the males. By age, the 20-29 age group is the most satisfied. By education, the educational level is proportional to the satisfaction with medical services, but the differences among the groups are insignificant.

Table 18 Satisfaction with medical services by gender, age and education

Group		Medical services
Gender	Male	64.32
	Female	63.53
Age	20-29	65.16
	30-39	63.08
	≥ 40	59.95
Education	< Bachelor	61.93
	Bachelor	63.94
	≥ Master	65.68

To better analyze residents' perceptions of healthcare, the team also investigated the proportion of residents who visited hospital(s) or clinic(s) because of their own health problems or accompanying their relative(s) / friend(s) in the past year. Table 19 is a summary of the results.

Table 19 In the past year, have you visited hospital(s) or clinic(s) because of your own health problems or accompanying your relative(s) / friend(s) (% of the respondents)

Unit: %

No.	City	Never	Community hospital / clinic	General hospital	Special hospital	Other healthcare providers
1	Haikou	37.72	20.61	32.02	6.14	3.51
2	Urumqi	34.80	22.03	36.12	5.29	1.76
3	Hohhot	34.20	18.61	33.77	11.26	2.16
4	Lanzhou	32.46	19.74	33.33	12.72	1.75
5	Yinchuan	32.16	12.33	36.56	15.86	3.08
6	Taiyuan	31.88	27.07	28.38	11.79	0.87
7	Qingdao	30.04	15.45	46.35	7.30	0.86
8	Xiamen	29.57	27.39	31.74	10.43	0.87
9	Guiyang	29.15	29.15	28.70	8.97	4.04

Continued

No.	City	Never	Community hospital / clinic	General hospital	Special hospital	Other healthcare providers
10	Changchun	26.84	20.35	39.39	12.12	1.30
11	Nanchang	26.61	22.75	38.63	9.87	2.15
12	Harbin	25.64	23.08	40.60	7.69	2.99
13	Xining	25.58	20.47	35.35	13.95	4.65
14	Dalian	24.68	19.05	44.59	9.96	1.73
15	Changsha	24.03	30.90	34.33	8.58	2.15
16	Nanjing	22.80	24.43	46.25	4.23	2.28
17	Shenzhen	22.77	37.29	34.65	4.62	0.66
18	Fuzhou	22.08	31.17	37.66	6.06	3.03
19	Shenyang	21.74	22.17	44.35	10.87	0.87
20	Kunming	21.59	22.91	42.73	8.81	3.96
21	Xi'an	21.12	32.33	37.93	7.76	0.86
22	Shijiazhuang	20.00	33.91	38.70	6.52	0.87
23	Chongqing	19.87	28.85	40.06	9.94	1.28
24	Ningbo	19.82	25.99	41.85	10.57	1.76
25	Guangzhou	18.79	33.12	40.45	7.01	0.64
26	Tianjin	18.57	20.85	52.44	6.84	1.30
27	Zhengzhou	18.42	32.46	40.35	8.77	0.00
28	Shanghai	18.13	16.06	55.96	9.59	0.26
29	Hefei	17.52	28.21	43.59	7.69	2.99
30	Wuhan	17.10	31.61	43.87	6.45	0.97
31	Hangzhou	15.88	27.47	47.21	8.15	1.29
32	Beijing	15.46	25.77	52.32	5.93	0.52
33	Chengdu	15.45	25.75	47.64	9.87	1.29
34	Jinan	14.41	33.62	41.92	10.04	0.00
35	Nanning	13.48	27.39	47.39	9.57	2.17
Mean of 2019		23.44	25.44	40.49	8.89	1.74
Mean of 2018		36.00	25.10	27.40	9.00	2.60

According to the survey findings, the mean of the "never" column is 23.44% - 12.56 percentage points lower than that of 2018. That is, 12.56 percentage points more of the respondents have been to a hospital / clinic in 2019. Of all the hospital visitors, 40.49% went to general hospitals 13.09 percentage points higher than that of 2018. The percentage of community hospital or clinic visitors have not changed much. The findings indicate that the hierarchical medical system needs to be further promoted.

By rankings, the top 10 cities in the "never" column are: Haikou (37.72%), Urumqi (34.80%), Hohhot (34.20%), Lanzhou (32.46%), Yinchuan (32.16%), Taiyuan (31.88%), Qingdao (30.04%), Xiamen (29.57%), Guiyang (29.15%) and Changchun (26.84%). The bottom 10 cities are: Tianjin (18.57%), Zhengzhou (18.42%), Shanghai (18.13%), Hefei (17.52%), Wuhan (17.10%), Hangzhou (15.88%), Beijing (15.46%), Chengdu (15.45%), Jinan (14.41%) and Nanning (13.48%).

1.3 Primary Indicator Radar Charts of the 35 Cities

Figure 1 shows the subjective primary indicator radar charts of the 35 cities in 2019 (arranged according to the rankings of the consumer confidence sub-index – one of the primary indicators). As shown in the radar charts, a common characteristic of the primary indicators is that Chinese residents generally have a strong consumer confidence, but are not that satisfied with their health conditions.

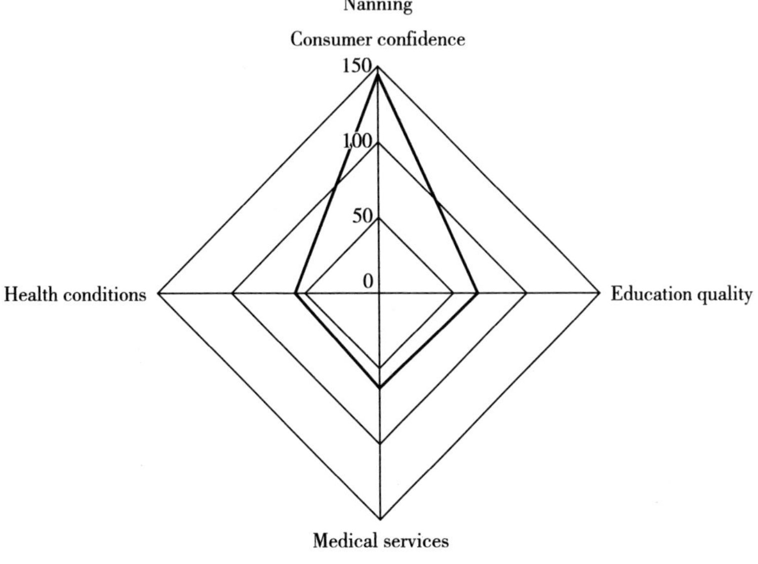
Nanning
Consumer confidence
150
100
50
0
Health conditions
Education quality
Medical services

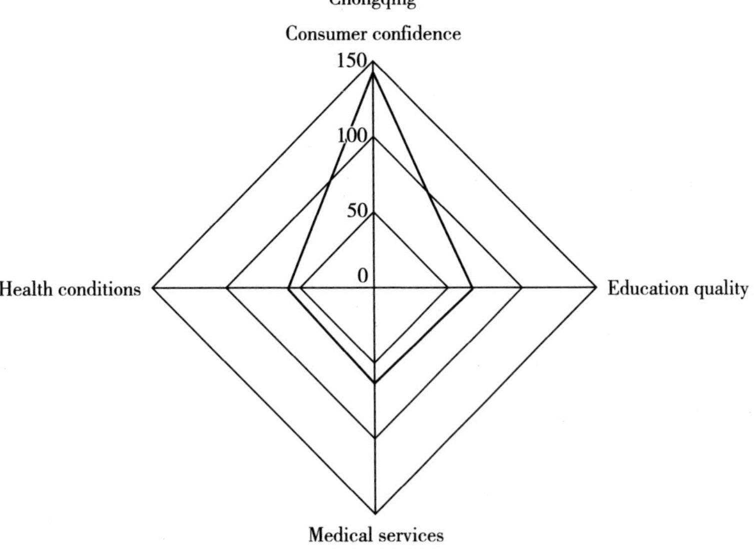
Chongqing
Consumer confidence
150
100
50
0
Health conditions
Education quality
Medical services

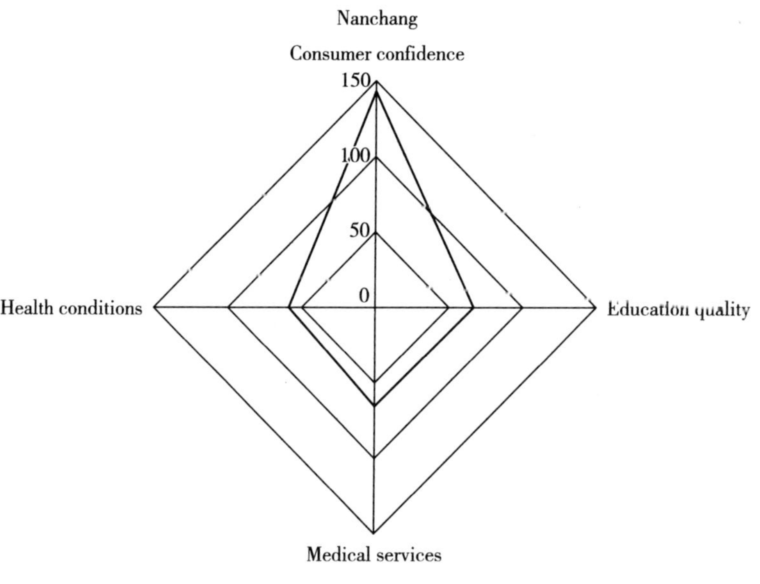
Nanchang
Consumer confidence
150
100
50
0
Health conditions
Education quality
Medical services

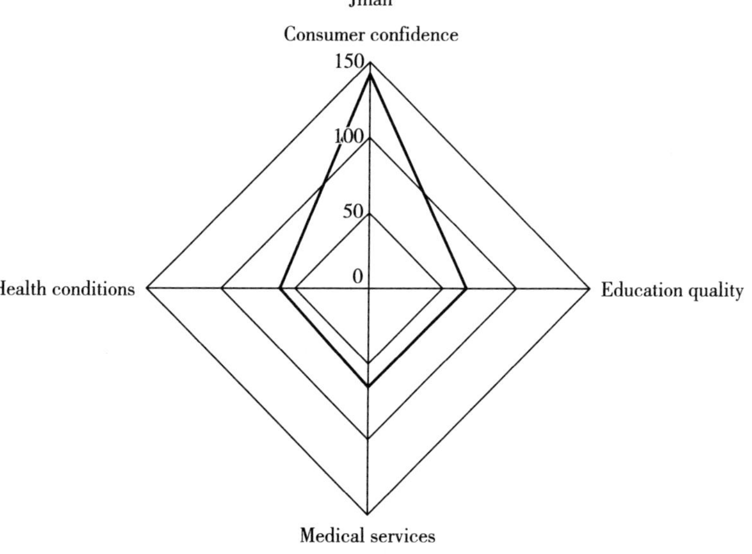
Jinan
Consumer confidence
150
100
50
0
Health conditions
Education quality
Medical services

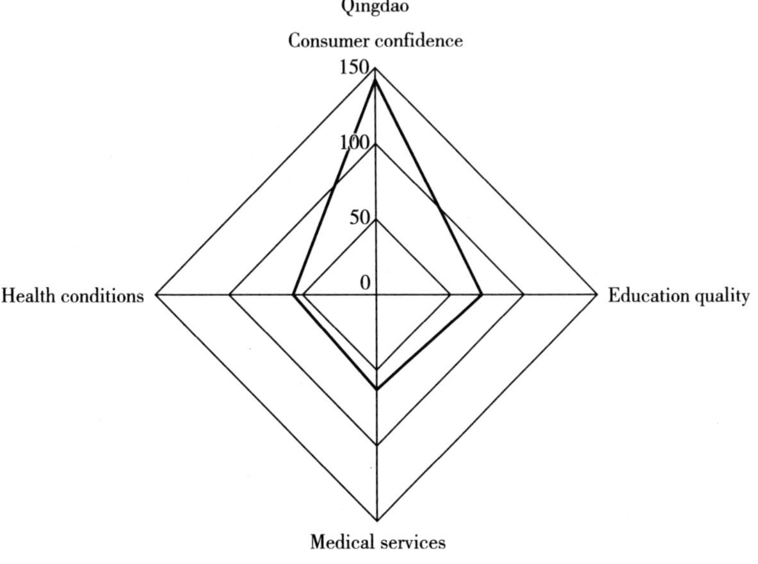
Qingdao
Consumer confidence
150
100
50
0
Health conditions
Education quality
Medical services

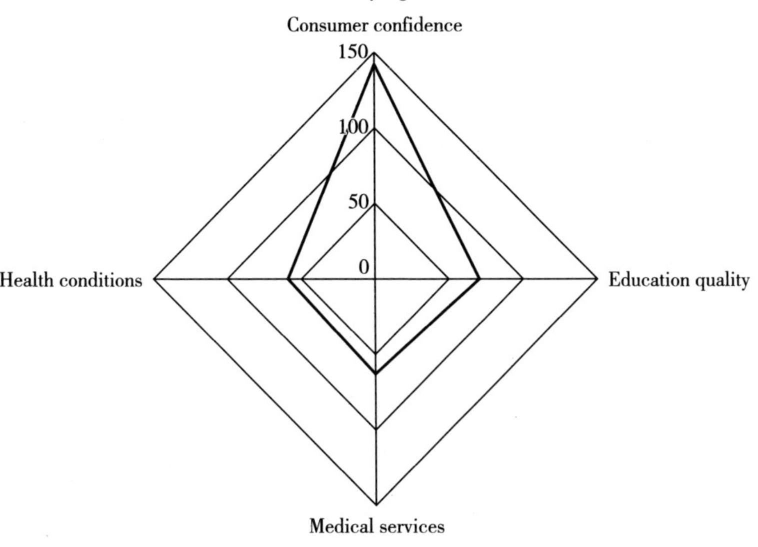
Guiyang
Consumer confidence
150
100
50
0
Health conditions
Education quality
Medical services

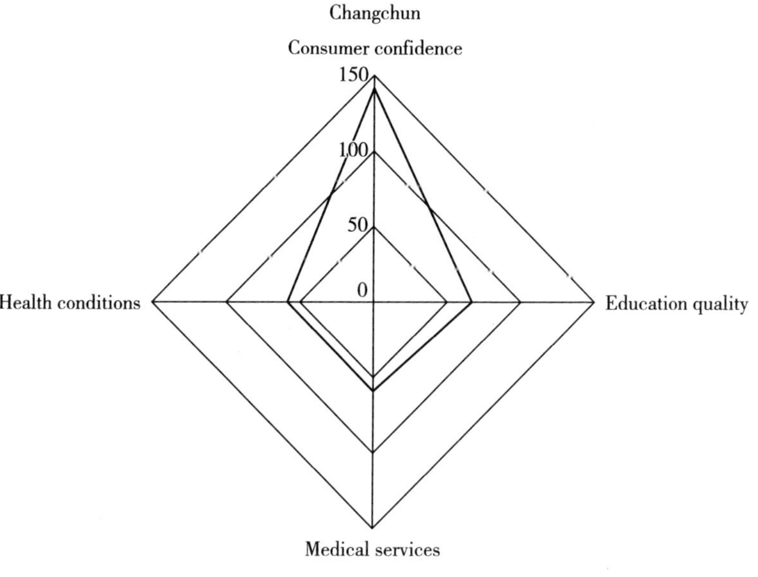
Changchun
Consumer confidence
150
100
50
0
Health conditions
Education quality
Medical services

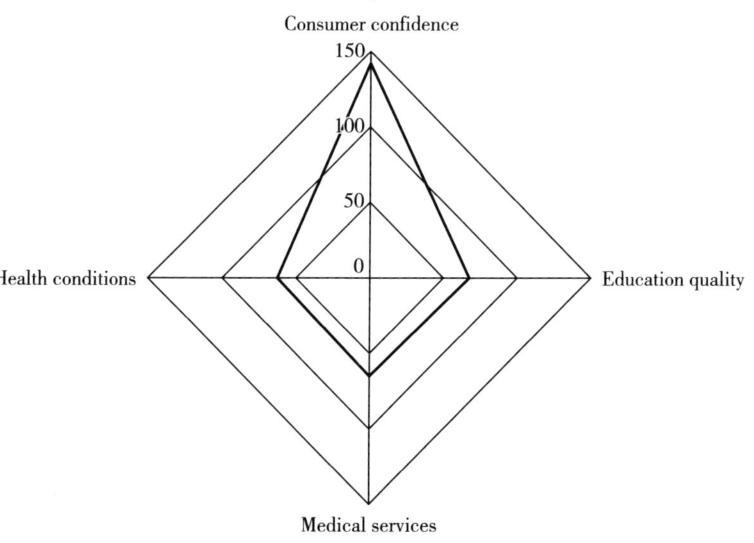
Zhengzhou
Consumer confidence
150
100
50
0
Health conditions
Education quality
Medical services

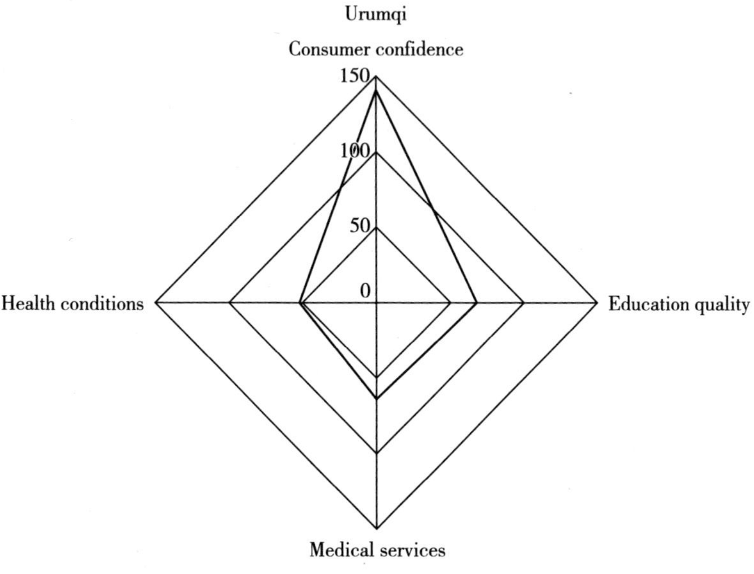
Urumqi
Consumer confidence
150
100
50
0
Health conditions
Education quality
Medical services

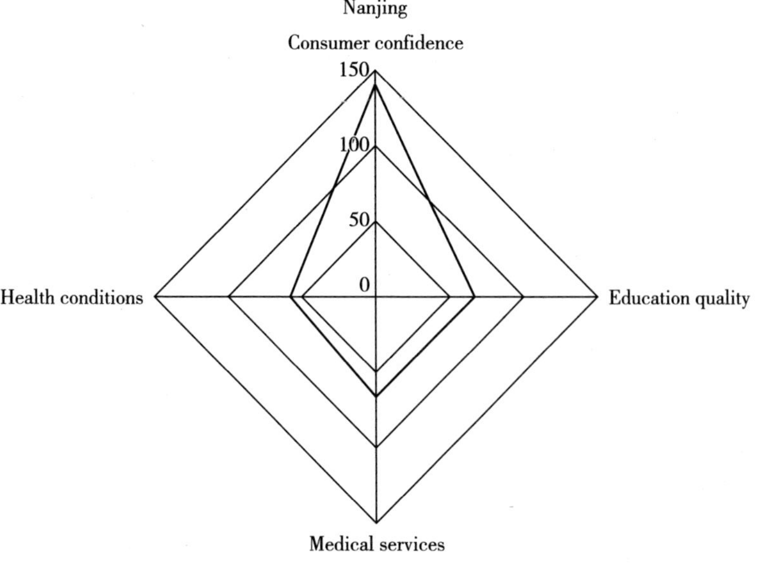
Nanjing
Consumer confidence
150
100
50
0
Health conditions
Education quality
Medical services

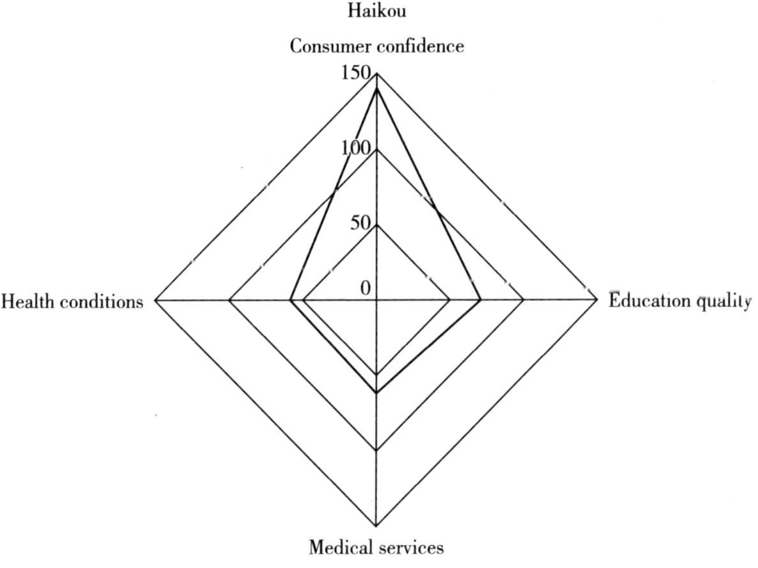
Haikou
Consumer confidence
150
100
50
0
Health conditions
Education quality
Medical services

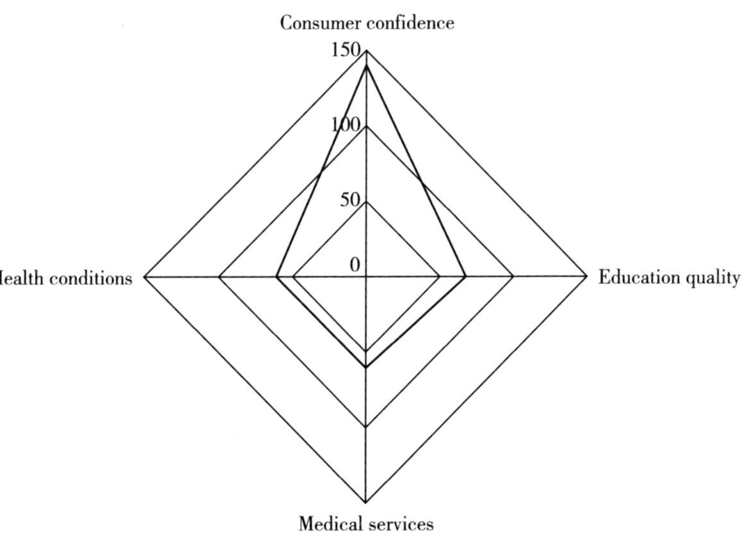
Taiyuan
Consumer confidence
150
100
50
0
Health conditions
Education quality
Medical services

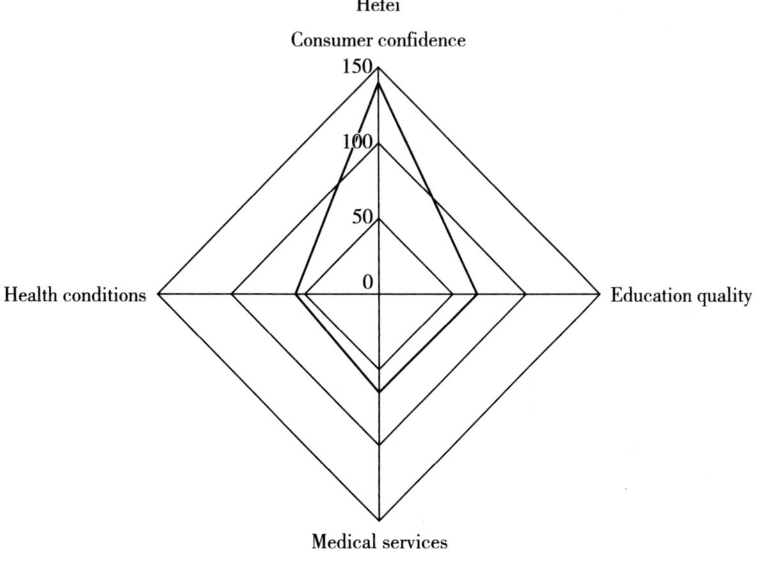
Hefei
Consumer confidence
150
100
50
0
Health conditions
Education quality
Medical services

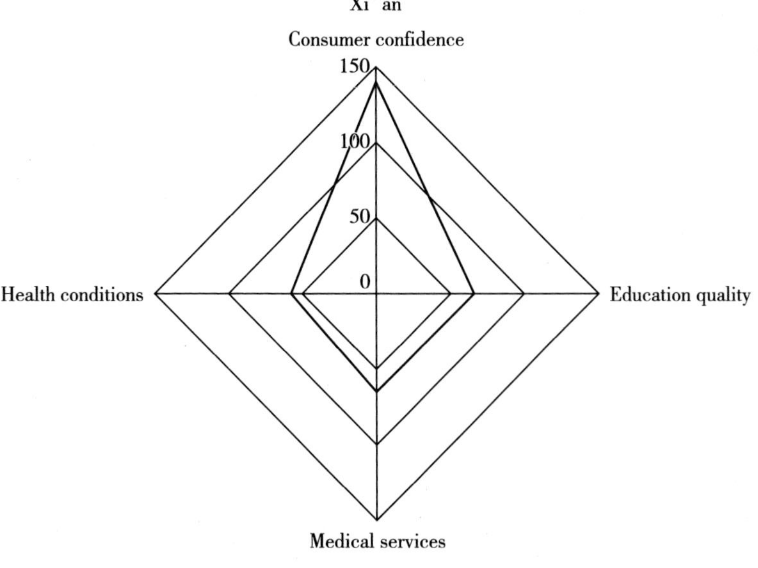
Xi' an
Consumer confidence
150
100
50
0
Health conditions
Education quality
Medical services

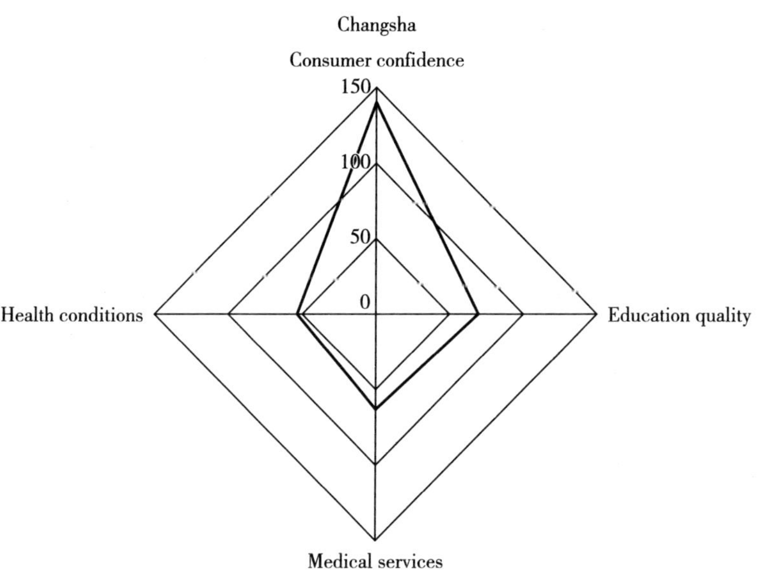

Changsha
Consumer confidence
150
100
50
0
Health conditions
Education quality
Medical services

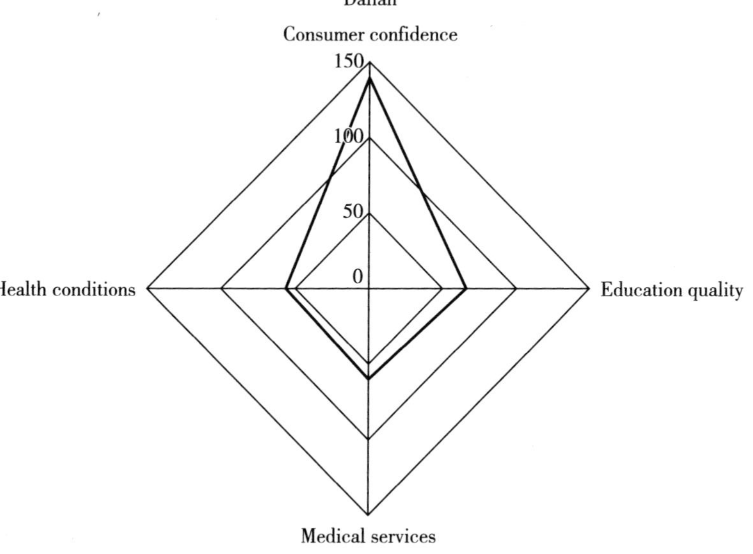

Dalian
Consumer confidence
150
100
50
0
Health conditions
Education quality
Medical services

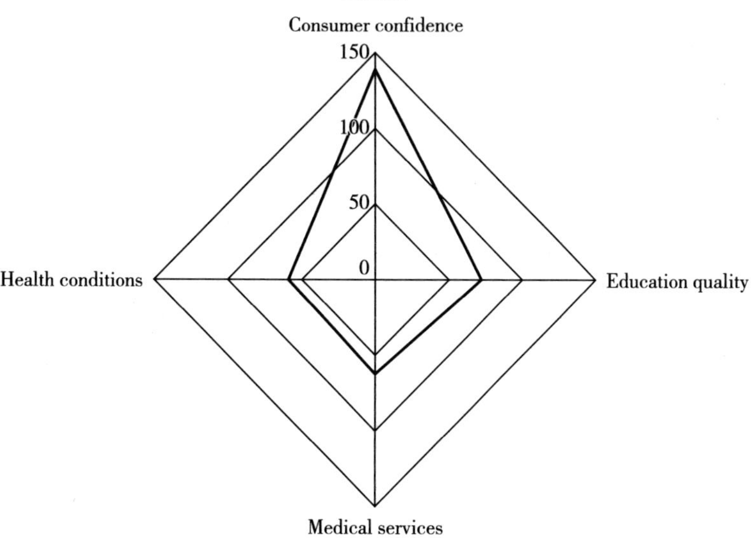
Xiamen
Consumer confidence
150
100
50
0
Health conditions
Education quality
Medical services

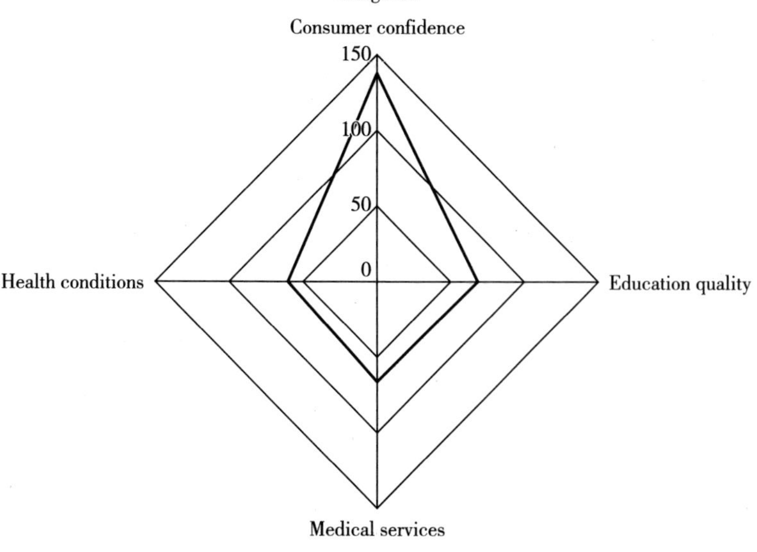
Hangzhou
Consumer confidence
150
100
50
0
Health conditions
Education quality
Medical services

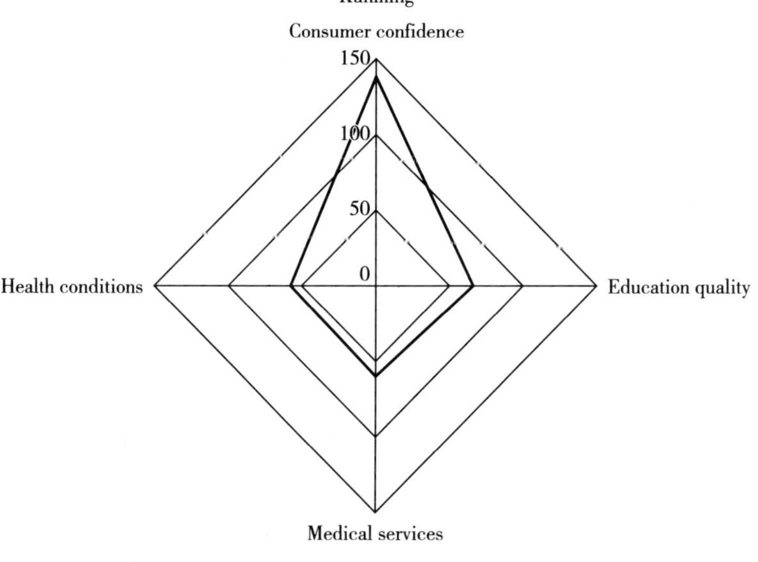
Kunming
Consumer confidence
150
100
50
0
Health conditions
Education quality
Medical services

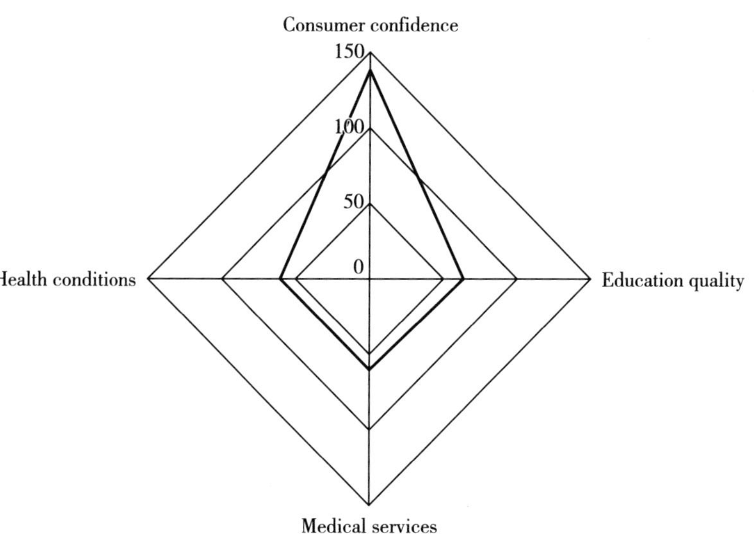
Harbin
Consumer confidence
150
100
50
0
Health conditions
Education quality
Medical services

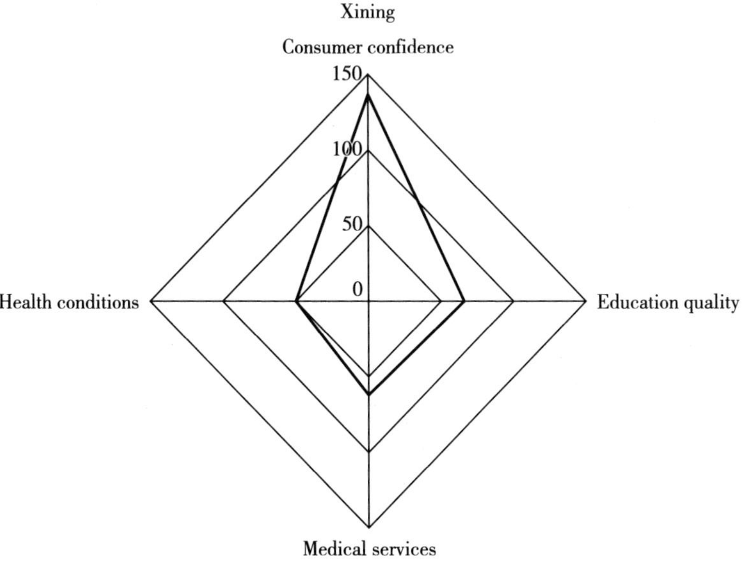
Xining
Consumer confidence
150
100
50
0
Health conditions
Education quality
Medical services

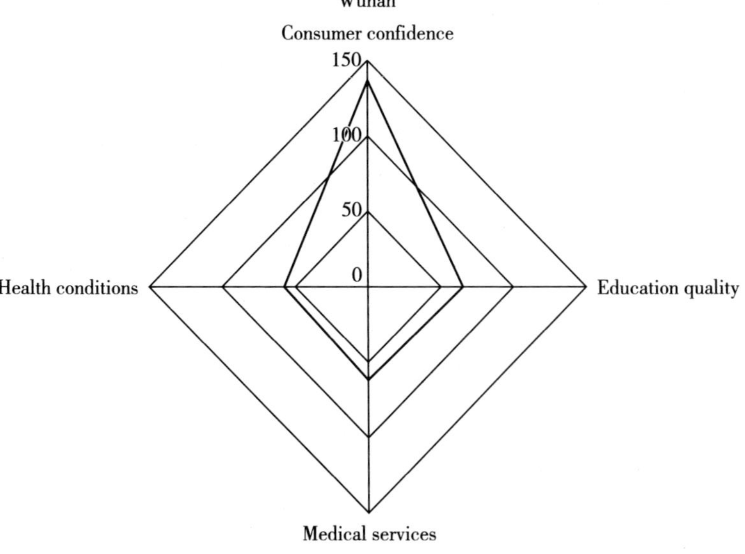
Wuhan
Consumer confidence
150
100
50
0
Health conditions
Education quality
Medical services

Ningbo

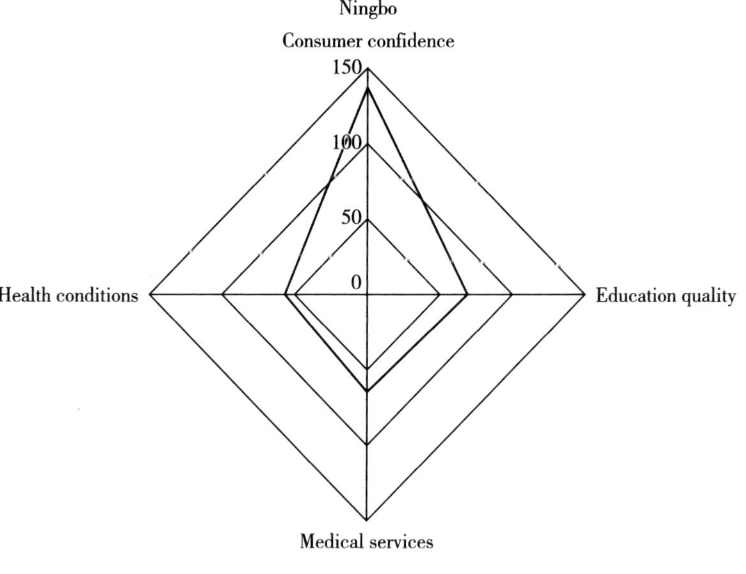

Lanzhou

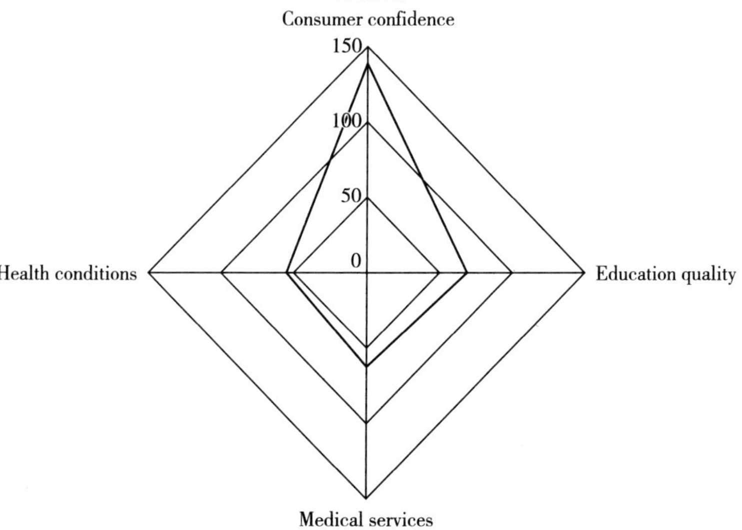

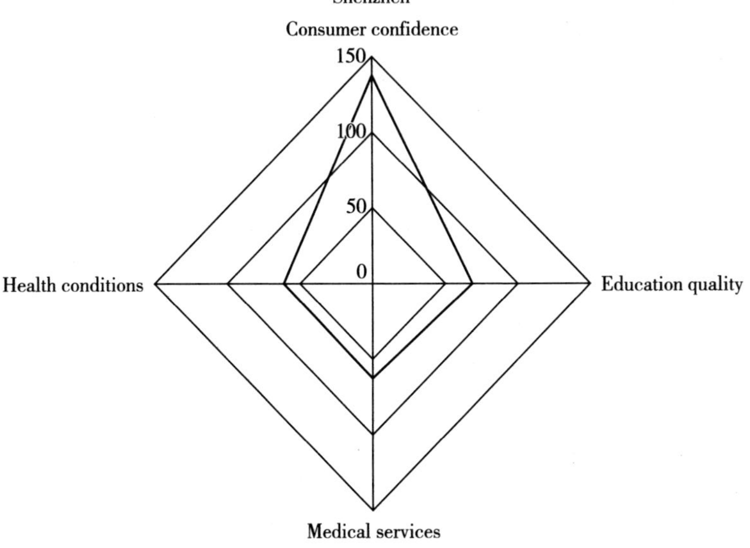
Shenzhen
Consumer confidence
150
100
50
0
Health conditions
Education quality
Medical services

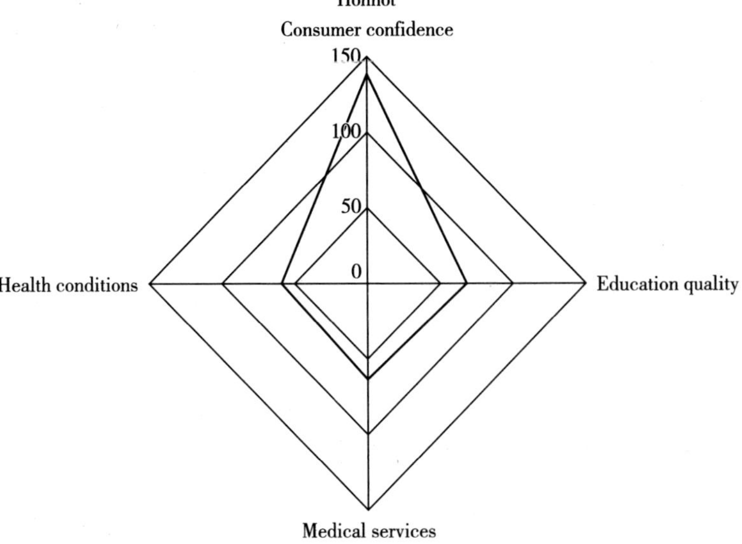
Hohhot
Consumer confidence
150
100
50
0
Health conditions
Education quality
Medical services

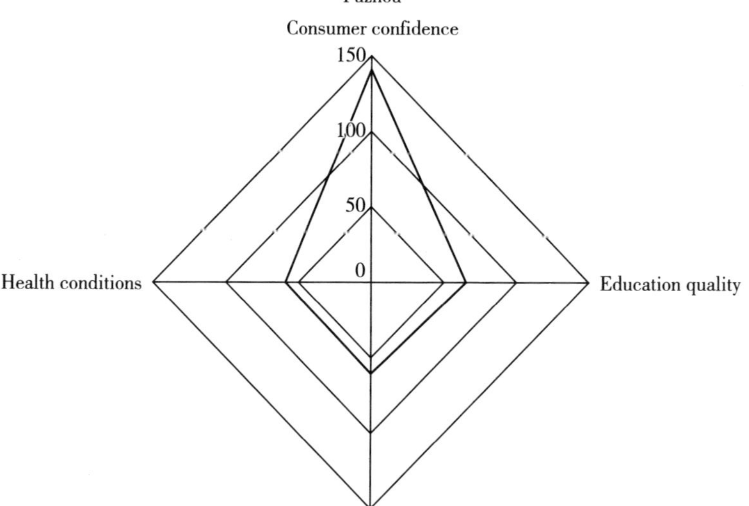
Fuzhou
Consumer confidence
150
100
50
0
Health conditions
Education quality
Medical services

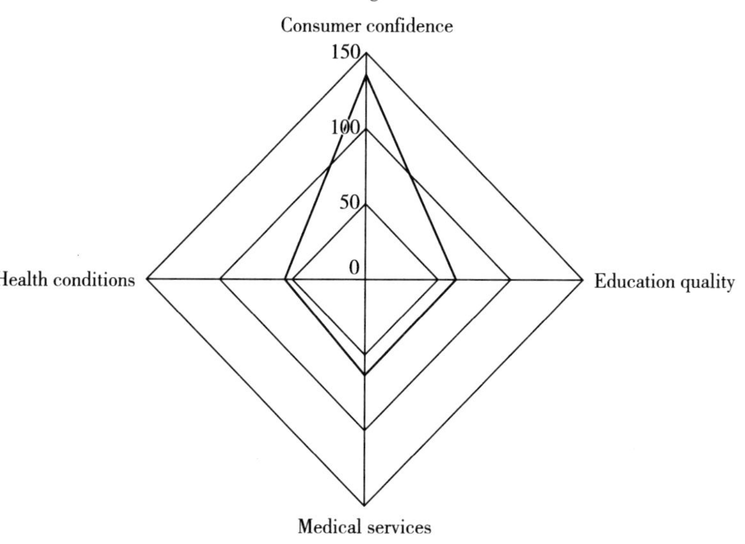
Shanghai
Consumer confidence
150
100
50
0
Health conditions
Education quality
Medical services

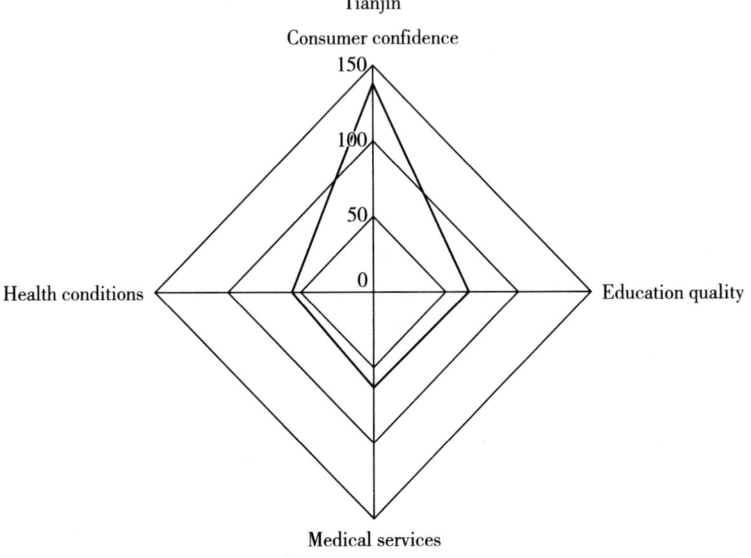
Tianjin
Consumer confidence
150
100
50
0
Health conditions
Education quality
Medical services

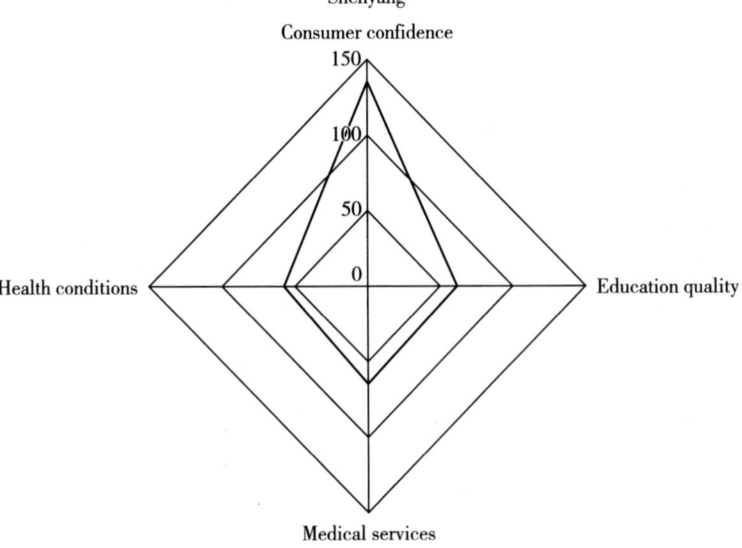
Shenyang
Consumer confidence
150
100
50
0
Health conditions
Education quality
Medical services

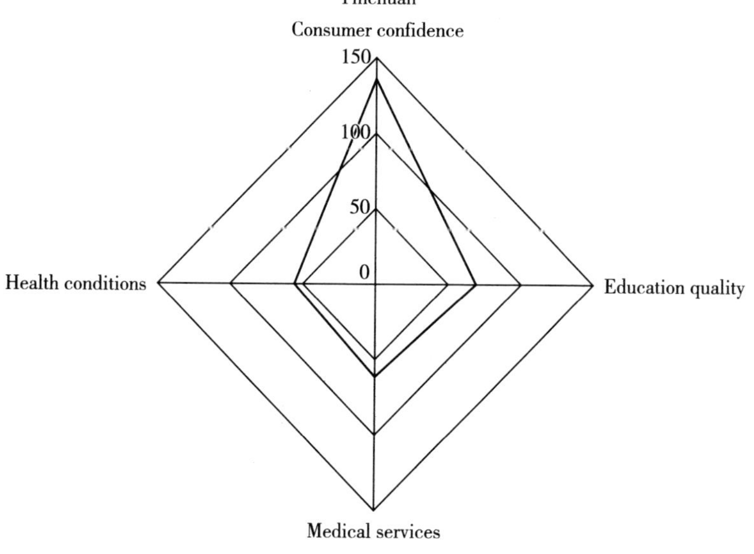
Yinchuan
Consumer confidence
150
100
50
0
Health conditions
Education quality
Medical services

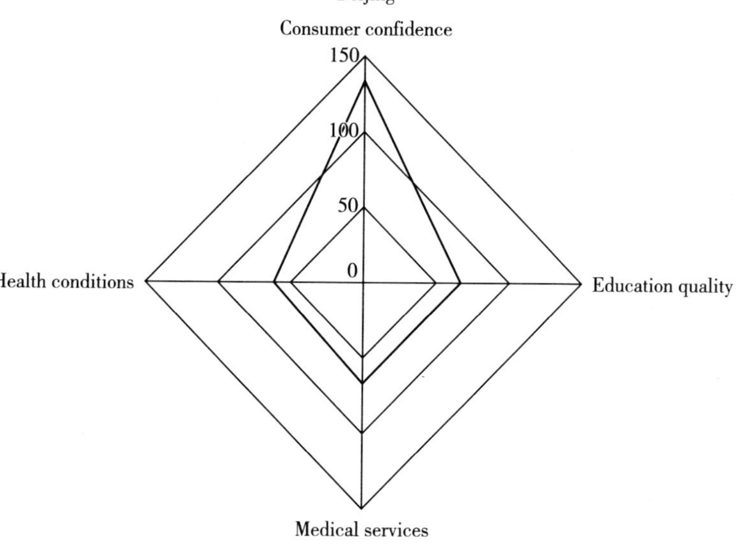
Beijing
Consumer confidence
150
100
50
0
Health conditions
Education quality
Medical services

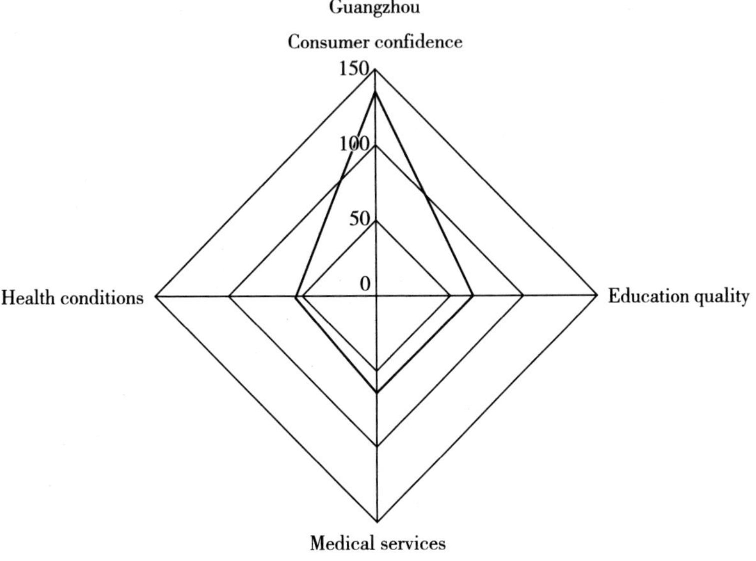
Guangzhou
Consumer confidence
150
100
50
0
Health conditions
Education quality
Medical services

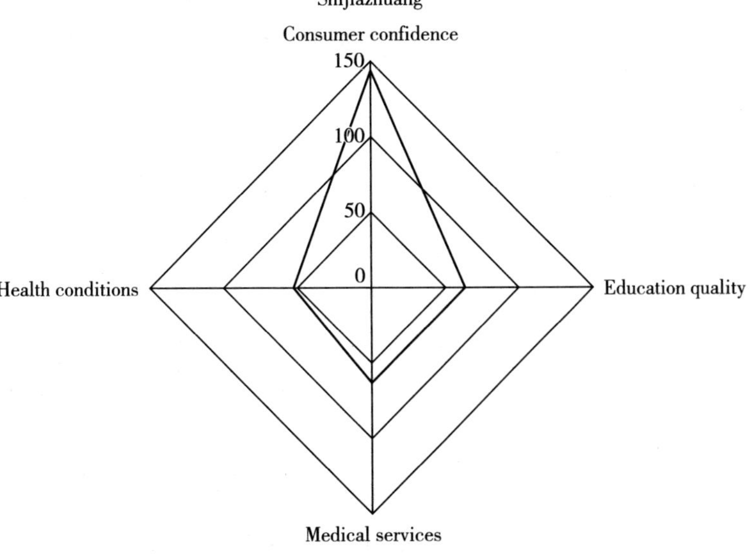
Shijiazhuang
Consumer confidence
150
100
50
0
Health conditions
Education quality
Medical services

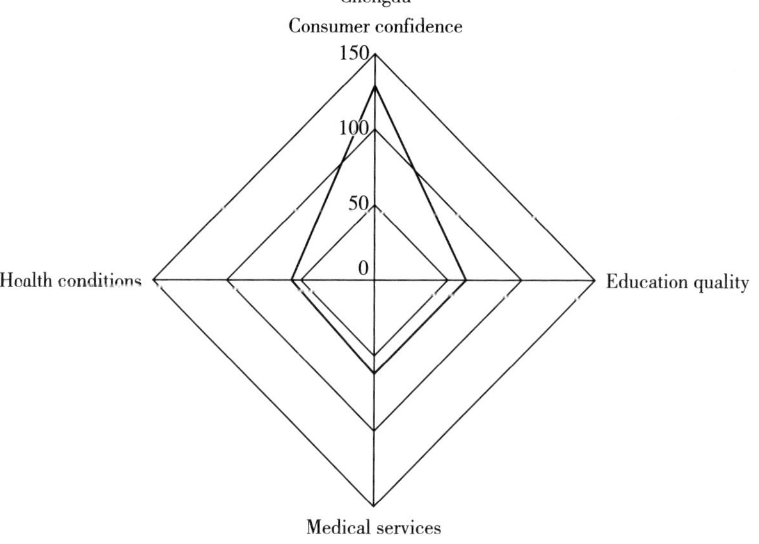

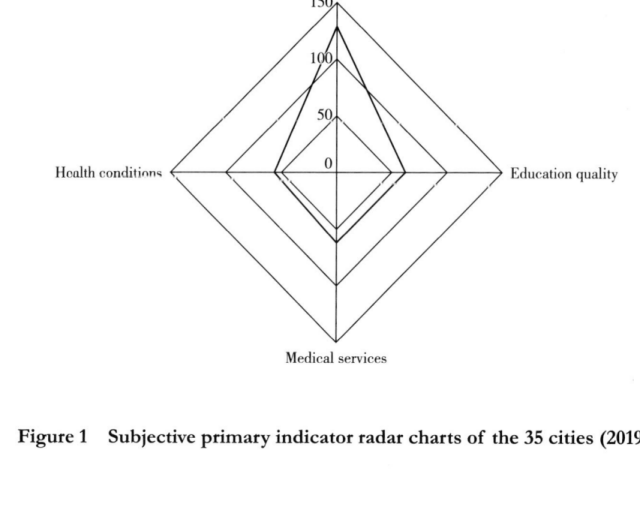

Figure 1 Subjective primary indicator radar charts of the 35 cities (2019)

1.4 Conclusions and Suggestions

After the subprime crisis, the external environment of China's economic development has undergone profound changes. Economic globalization has suffered twists and turns. Multilateralism has been under attack. The trade disputes between China and the United States have brought considerable pressure on China's economic growth. However, according to the QLICC survey findings, the consumer confidence has generally remained stable among Chinese urban residents. At a time of weaker investment / export growth and greater pressure of economic slowdown, such a strong consumer confidence indicates that consumer demand is likely to become a stabilizer for China's economic growth in the following 1-2 years. To achieve this, it is

essential to maintain steady growth and ensure stability in employment and in residents' income and wealth.

As for the sub-indices of education quality, medical services and health conditions, the performances of some indictors are not satisfactory. The consumer confidence sub-index has remained stable and been on the rise, but only to a limited extent. All this shows that there is still a long way to go to address the contradiction between people's ever-growing need for a better life and the unbalanced and inadequate economic development.

As suggested by the survey findings, the government might need to keep on releasing policy and institutional dividends, to stimulate the vitality of microeconomic entities, while innovating and refining macro-control measures to promote industrial structure upgrading and economic transformation. It might also need to further ensure "stability in six areas" (employment, financial operations, foreign trade, foreign investment, domestic investment and expectations), and constantly improve the quality of economic growth and public services such as education and healthcare while stabilizing economic development, so as to lay a solid economic foundation and provide robust institutional and policy support to a higher quality of life and both physical and mental wellbeing for the residents.

References

Zhang Ziran et al., "Two Contrasts in China's Economic Development - Report on Resident Quality of Life in 30 Chinese Cities," *Economics Perspectives* 7 (2011).

Zhang Liancheng et al., "High Living Costs Encumbering Improvement in

Satisfaction with the Urban Quality of Life - Report on Resident Quality of Life in 35 Chinese Cities (2012)," *Economics Perspectives* 7 (2012).

Zhang Liancheng et al., "Quality of Life: Stable Indexes versus Severe Challenges - Report on Resident Quality of Life in 35 Chinese Cities (2013)," *Economics Perspectives* 8 (2013).

Zhang Liancheng et al., "Rising Indexes for Quality of Life, Growing Concerns over Air Quality and Food Safety - Report on Resident Quality of Life in 35 Chinese Cities (2014)," *Economics Perspectives* 8 (2014).

Zhang Liancheng et al., "Economic Challenges vs a Steady Rise in Quality of Life Satisfaction - Report on Resident Quality of Life in 35 Chinese Cities (2015)," *Economics Perspectives* 9 (2015).

Zhao Jiazhang et al., "Expected Stability vs Existing Challenges - Report on Resident Quality of Life in 35 Chinese Cities (2016)," *Economics Perspectives* 8 (2016).

NIEE, *Report on the Quality of Life in Chinese Cities (2012)*, Social Sciences Academic Press (China), 2013.

NIEE, *Report on the Quality of Life in Chinese Cities (2013)*, Social Sciences Academic Press (China), 2014.

NIEE, *Report on the Quality of Life in Chinese Cities (2014)*, Social Sciences Academic Press (China), 2014.

Zhang Liancheng et al. eds., *Report on the Quality of Life in Chinese Cities (2015)*, Social Sciences Academic Press (China), 2015.

NIEE, *Report on the Quality of Life in Chinese Cities (2016)*, Social Sciences Academic Press (China), 2017.

Zhang Liancheng et al., *Report on the Quality of Life in Chinese Cities (2017)*, Social Sciences Academic Press (China), 2017.

Zhang Liancheng et al., *Report on the Quality of Life in Chinese Cities (2018)*, Social Sciences Academic Press (China), 2019.

Topical Reports

B.2

Report on the Consumer Confidence Sub-indices of the 35 Cities

Wang Yu[*]

Abstract: The questionnaire survey investigated the consumer confidence of the 35 Chinese cities. According to the survey findings, in 2019, the weighted mean of the consumer confidence sub-indices is 138.61. The values of all the 35 cities exceed 100 and are higher than that of 2018, indicating that a good foundation has been laid for China's transition into consumer-oriented economy. Regional comparison shows that the sub-indices of the central and the western regions are slightly higher than those of the northeastern and the eastern regions, and that the sub-indices of different regions are generally consistent in the direction

* Prof. Wang Yu, from the School of Economics of CUEB, specializes in the study of economic growth and economic cycle.

and range of changes. Through correlation analysis, it is found that changes of the consumer confidence sub-index are highly and positively correlated with that of the inflation rate and the consumption rate. That is to say, increase in consumer confidence will lead to higher inflation and consumption. According to the regression analysis of the major influential factors of consumer confidence changes, improvements in per capita disposable income or the coverage of basic medical insurance / unemployment insurance have a strong positive impact on the sub-index, but not per capita wealth or social insurance coverage. Therefore, the key to stabilizing consumer confidence lies in the stabilization of residents' income and employment, as well as the coverage of improved social security, along with the continuous development and improvement of the financial market.

Keywords: Consumer Confidence Sub-index; Inflation Rate; Consumption Rate; Per Capita Wealth

2.1 Introduction

After the stage of high economic growth, China has become a country of upper-middle income. With the increase of per capita income, consumer consumption has to a certain extent grown out of the constraint of hard budget. Under such circumstances, consumer confidence comes to have an increasing impact on consumer demand. Moreover, since China is a country of vast territory and large regional disparities in economic development,

during the transition of China's economy from investment- to consumption-orientation, it is necessary to investigate and measure the changes of the consumer confidence, in order to stabilize economic growth and promote economic transformation.

Index of Consumer Sentiment (ICS) or Consumer Confidence Index (CCI) is a concept originated in the United States. ICS was first proposed by George Katona from the Survey Research Center of the University of Michigan (SRC, UMich) in the 1940s. He believed that consumer demand was a function of both income and purchase intention (consumer sentiment), and the latter (including consumer motivation and attitude) was determined by consumer psychology. He also thought that generally consumers' purchase intention could be described with a consumer sentiment / satisfaction index. The index should serve as a comprehensive indicator of the strength of consumer confidence, which quantifies consumers' subjective perceptions of their income status and income expectation, as well as the consumer psychology. It should also be a leading indicator of the current status and future trends of economic operation, mainly used to predict the economic cycle and related fluctuations.

Since the 1940s, UMich has been calculating and releasing ICS on a quarterly basis, which forecasts economic turning points at least nine months in advance, and predicts changes in the unemployment levels. However, studies have spotted its deviations from the economic situation of the United States, which are to be corrected with methods such as scaling and translation.[①] Since the 1960s, the Federal Reserve System of the United States (FRS) has also recognized the importance of the index, and started the development and calculation of CCI. Since then, a total of more than 40 countries including

① Xu Yonghong, Zhu Jianping, "Study on Origin and Elimination of Consumer's Confidence Index," *Journal of Applied Statistics and Management* 5 (2018).

Australia, Japan and Canada have been working on the index as well. In China, the authorities, as well as major financial institutions including CUEB, Shanghai University of Finance and Economics (SUFE) and Southwestern University of Finance and Economics (SWUFE), have started to develop, monitor and release the national / regional consumer confidence index regularly since 1998.

2.2 Analysis of consumer confidence sub-indices

The consumer confidence sub-indices were obtained by calculating the answers to Q 1-5 on the questionnaire in the same way as the MCSI. The higher the value, the stronger the consumer confidence. The value range is 0-200. The developers of the questionnaire set the US consumer confidence index of Q1 1966 at 100. The questions and the 5-point scale used are as follows:

1. What do you think of your income (or the income of your household members) compared to that of last year?

○ Much better ○ Better ○ Same ○ Worse ○ Much worse

2. What do you think your income (or the income of your household members) will be in the coming year?

○ Much better ○ Better ○ Same ○ Worse ○ Much worse

3. In view of the overall economic situation of China, are you confident of the healthy development of the economy in the next year?

○ Very confident ○ Confident ○ Not sure ○ Unconfident ○ Very unconfident

4. In view of the overall economic situation of China, are you confident of the healthy development of the economy in the next 5 years?

○ Very confident ○ Confident ○ Not sure ○ Unconfident ○ Very unconfident

5. Do you think it is a good time to buy durable goods such as cars or

consider home decoration / refurbishment?

○ Yes ○ Not sure ○ No

2.2.1 Descriptive statistics

The mean consumer confidence sub-index of the 35 cities was 115.48 in 2018 and 138.61 in 2019. Table 1 summarizes the descriptive statistics on the consumer confidence sub-indices in the past two years. In 2019, the sub-indices generally range from 129.63 to 145.35. The mean is 138.61 - between the threshold (100) and "confident" (150), that is, in the "confident" interval. The 2018 sub-indices ranged from 104.44 to 122.84, and the mean was 115.48. Compared with that of 2018, the mean sub-index has grown by 20%. As shown in Table 1, the variance of the sub-index is 10.94 this year, and the standard deviation is 3.31; while in 2018, the variance was 16.33, and the standard deviation was 4.04. It can be observed that the dispersion of the consumer confidence sub-indices has narrowed among the 35 cities, and the similarity has improved. It indicates that there has been a general increase in the consumer confidence across the country.

Table 1 Descriptive statistics on consumer confidence sub-indices (2018-2019)

Year	Min	Max	Mean	Variance	Standard deviation	Skewness	Kurtosis
2018	104.44	122.84	115.48	16.33	4.04	-0.39	0.38
2019	129.63	145.35	138.61	10.94	3.31	-0.72	1.27

Figure 1 summarizes the distribution of the consumer confidence sub-indices in 2018-2019. It is clear that in 2019 the sub-indices of the 35 cities are of higher distributional similarity, most of which fall in the range of 135-145,

and a few in 129-130. The distribution is left-skewed. In 2018, the distribution of the sub-indices was also left-skewed, but closer to normal.

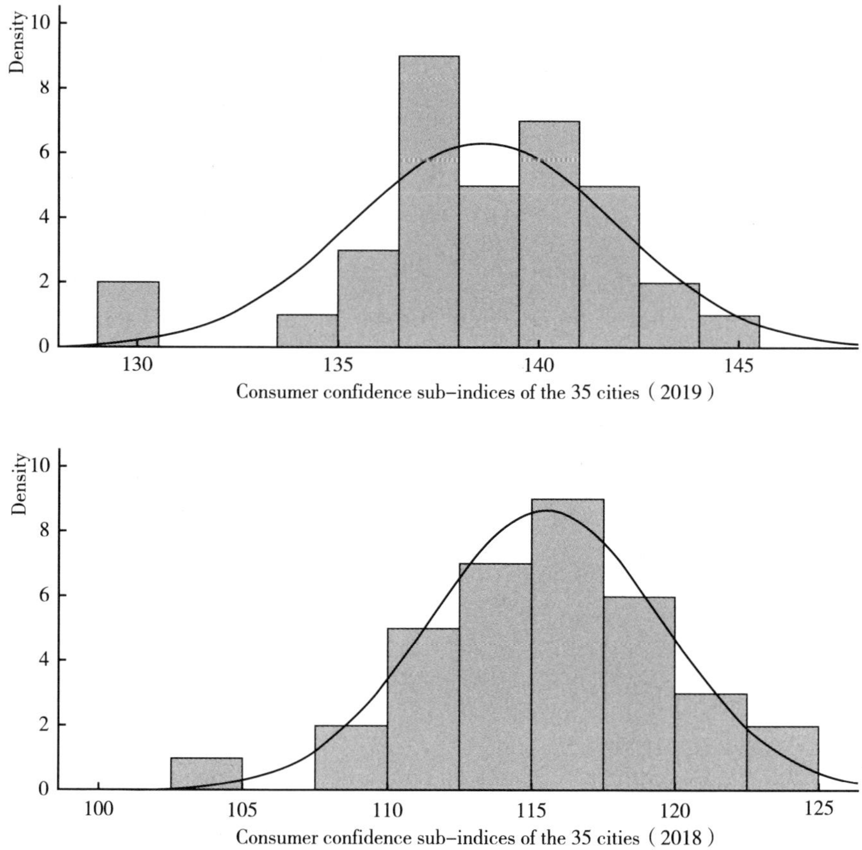

Density
10
8
6
4
2
0
130 135 140 145
Consumer confidence sub–indices of the 35 cities (2019)

Density
10
8
6
4
2
0
100 105 110 115 120 125
Consumer confidence sub–indices of the 35 cities (2018)

Figure 1 Histogram of consumer confidence sub-indices of the 35 cities (2018-2019)

Of roughly the same period, the US MCSI is 97.9 in early June 2019, nearly 1% lower than that of late April and early May 2018 (98.8). That is to say, consumer confidence has increased significantly in China and slightly declined in the United States from 2018 to 2019.

2.2.2 Comparison among different cities and regions

Figure 2 summarizes the changes of the consumer confidence sub-indices of the 35 cities in 2018-2019. Overall, the sub-indices have consistently improved, although the specific range of change may differ. At a time of weaker investment / export growth and greater pressure of economic slowdown, consumer demand is likely to become a stabilizer for China's economic growth in the following 1-2 years.

Geographically, China can be divided into four regions (northeastern, eastern, central and western) or eight integrated economic zones. Table 2 and 3 summarized the distribution of the surveyed 35 cities accordingly.

Table 2 Distribution of the 35 cities by region

No.	Region	Cities
1	Northeastern (4)	Shenyang, Changchun, Harbin, Dalian
2	Eastern (14)	Beijing, Tianjin, Shijiazhuang, Shanghai, Nanjing, Hangzhou, Ningbo, Fuzhou, Xiamen, Jinan, Qingdao, Guangzhou, Shenzhen, Haikou
3	Central (6)	Taiyuan, Hefei, Nanchang, Zhengzhou, Wuhan, Changsha
4	Western (11)	Hohhot, Nanning, Chongqing, Chengdu, Guiyang, Kunming, Xi'an, Lanzhou, Xining, Yinchuan, Urumqi

Table 3 Distribution of the 35 cities by integrated economic zone

No.	Economic zone	Province / autonomous region / municipality
1	Northeast China (4)	Shenyang, Changchun, Harbin, Dalian
2	Northern Coastal (5)	Beijing, Tianjin, Shijiazhuang, Jinan, Qingdao
3	Eastern Coastal (4)	Shanghai, Nanjing, Hangzhou, Ningbo
4	Middlc Yellow River (4)	Xi'an, Taiyuan, Zhengzhou, Hohhot
5	Middle Yangtze River (4)	Wuhan, Changsha, Nanchang, Hefei
6	Southern Coastal (5)	Fuzhou, Xiamen, Guangzhou, Shenzhen, Haikou
7	Great Southwest (5)	Kunming, Guiyang, Chongqing, Chengdu, Nanning
8	Great Northwest (4)	Lanzhou, Xining, Yinchuan, Urumqi

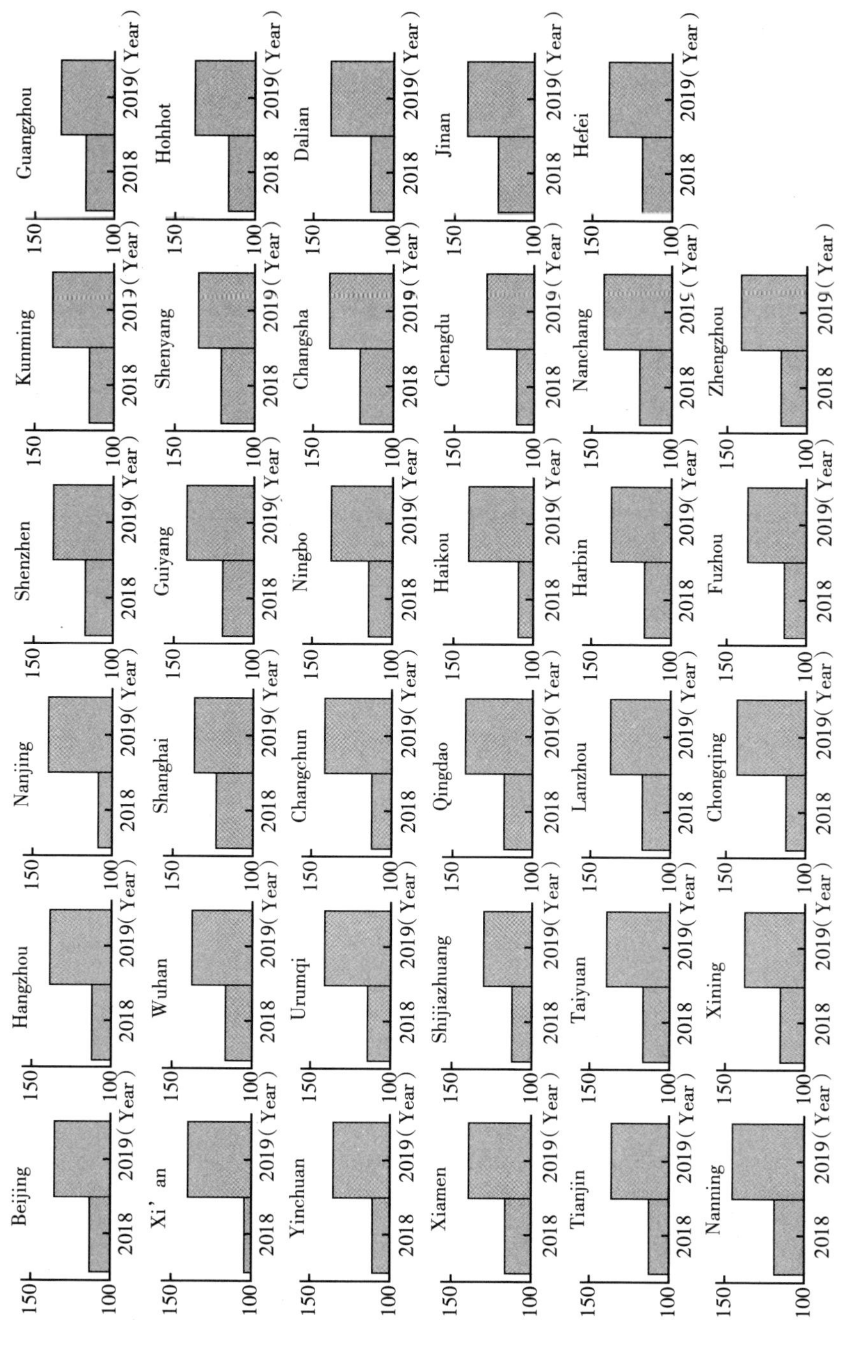

Figure 2 Changes in consumer confidence sub-index by city (2018-2019)

Comparison is made between the mean consumer confidence sub-indices of the four regions in 2018 and 2019. The results are summarized in Table 4 and Figure 3.

Table 4 Mean consumer confidence sub-indices of the four regions (2018-2019)

Ranking in 2018	Region	Mean	Ranking in 2019	Region	Mean
1	Central	118.2	1	Central	140.3
2	Northeastern	116.0	2	Western	138.9
3	Eastern	115.2	3	Northeastern	138.5
4	Western	114.2	4	Eastern	137.7

As shown in Table 4, the central region was of the highest consumer confidence sub-index in 2018 (mean=118.2), followed by the northeastern (mean=116.0), the eastern (mean=115.2) and the western regions (mean=114.2). In 2019, the sub-indices of the four regions have generally improved at similar rates and are of similar rankings. The central region still ranks first, followed by the western region. The difference is that the eastern region ranks last this time, while the western region takes over second place.

As can be seen from Figure 3, the overall performances of the four regions are rather similar, rising from nearly 120 in 2018 to about 140 in 2019. It is clear that, over the past two years, the consumer confidence sub-indices have been of little regional differences and rather consistent changes.

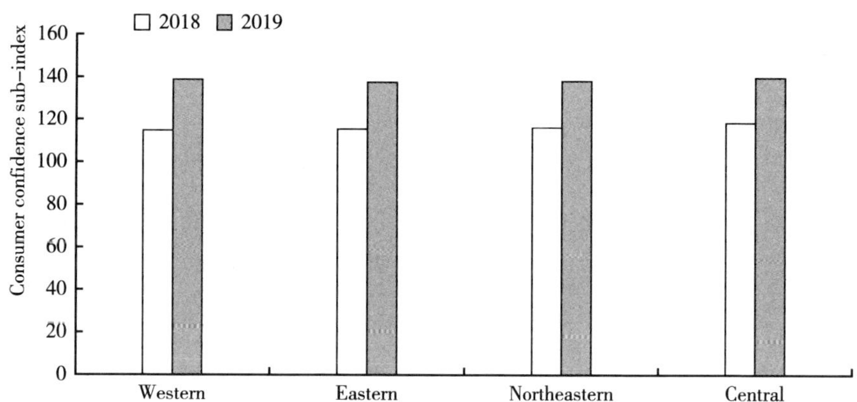

Figure 3　Comparison of consumer confidence sub-indices of the four regions (2018-2019)

As shown in Table 5, among the eight integrated economic zones, the Middle Yangtze River zone (119.1) ranked top in 2018, followed by the Northeast China (116.0), the Northern Coastal (115.8), the Great Southwest (115.6), the Southern Coastal (115.0), the Eastern Coastal (114.6), the Great Northwest (114.5) and the Middle Yellow River zones (113.4). In 2019, the rankings have changed significantly. The Middle Yangtze River zone (140.1) still ranks top, followed by the Great Southwest (139.7), the Middle Yellow River (139.6), the Northeast China (138.5), the Eastern Coastal (138.5), the Great Northwest (138.0), the Southern Coastal (137.6) and the Northern Coastal zones (137.2).

Table 5　Comparison of mean consumer confidence sub-indices of the eight integrated economic zones (2018-2019)

Ranking in 2018	Economic zone	Mean	Ranking in 2019	Economic zone	Mean
1	Middle Yangtze River	119.1	1	Middle Yangtze River	140.1
2	Northeast China	116.0	2	Great Southwest	139.7
3	Northern Coastal	115.8	3	Middle Yellow River	139.6

Continued

Ranking in 2018	Economic zone	Mean	Ranking in 2019	Economic zone	Mean
4	Great Southwest	115.6	4	Northeast China	138.5
5	Southern Coastal	115.0	5	Eastern Coastal	138.5
6	Eastern Coastal	114.6	6	Great Northwest	138.0
7	Great Northwest	114.5	7	Southern Coastal	137.6
8	Middle Yellow River	113.4	8	Northern Coastal	137.2

Overall, the consumer confidence sub-indices of all the eight integrated economic zones have improved in 2019 at similar rates, as shown in Figure 4.

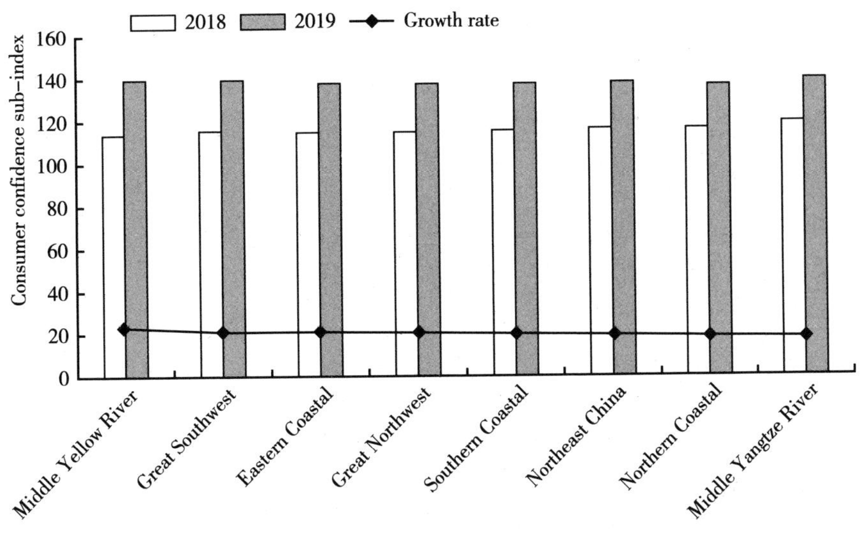

Figure 4 Comparison of consumer confidence sub-indices of the eight integrated economic zones (2018-2019)

It can be seen from the above comparison that consumer confidence has strengthened across the entire country, without significant regional difference. It shows that despite the great pressure brought by the economic slowdown, all the efforts have worked in stabilizing the consumer demand. On the part

of the State Council, it has clearly pointed out the need to pursue the high-quality development of China's economy, to stabilize the property market, and to avoid and manage financial risks proactively and effectively. Meanwhile, on the part of the local governments, measures have been taken to pursue the transition to a new economy, to advance reforms actively, to pay attention to people's living standards, to reinforce environmental protection and to boost people's sense of gain.

2.3 Consumer confidence sub-index and objective economic factors

The consumer confidence sub-index is designed to conduct (subjective) judgments and predictions of (objective) economic conditions, including the forecast of price changes and the analysis of consumer demand, and to understand the correlation between the consumer confidence sub-index and the inflation / consumption rate in the 35 cities.

2.3.1 Consumer confidence sub-index and inflation rate

Table 6 summarizes the 2019 rankings of the inflation rate and the consumption rate indicators of the 35 cities. Among the top 5, Lanzhou (1.021) has the highest inflation rate, followed by Chengdu (1.008), Fuzhou (1.007), Guiyang (1.005) and Kunming (1.005). The bottom 5 cities are: Xining (0.995), Shenzhen (0.994), Shenyang (0.992), Dalian (0.992) and Shanghai (0.987). Figure 5 shows the correlation between the inflation rate and the consumer confidence sub-index in the 35 cities. Lanzhou, Chengdu and Shijiazhuang have experienced the greatest ranking changes. In Lanzhou, the consumer confidence sub-index is positively correlated with inflation, but the inflation

rate is much higher than that of other cities. In Chengdu and Shijiazhuang, the consumer confidence sub-indices are low, but the inflation rates are high. In the rest 32 cities, there is generally a positive correlation between the sub-index and the inflation rate. That is, the higher the sub-index, the higher the inflation rate, and vice versa.

Table 6 Rankings of inflation and consumption rates of the 35 cities (2019)

Ranking	City	Inflation rate	Ranking	City	Consumption rate
1	Lanzhou	1.021	1	Xi'an	1.207
2	Chengdu	1.008	2	Shenzhen	1.151
3	Fuzhou	1.007	3	Guiyang	1.139
4	Guiyang	1.005	4	Tianjin	1.132
5	Kunming	1.005	5	Changchun	1.124
6	Taiyuan	1.004	6	Lanzhou	1.091
7	Xiamen	1.004	7	Urumqi	1.073
8	Wuhan	1.003	8	Shenyang	1.069
9	Xi'an	1.003	9	Dalian	1.062
10	Tianjin	1.002	10	Changsha	1.058
11	Changchun	1.002	11	Harbin	1.057
12	Hefei	1.002	12	Yinchuan	1.047
13	Changsha	1.002	13	Guangzhou	1.028
14	Chongqing	1.002	14	Chongqing	1.012
15	Hohhot	1.001	15	Xining	1.008
16	Qingdao	1.001	16	Haikou	0.995
17	Yinchuan	1.000	17	Hangzhou	0.994
18	Urumqi	1.000	18	Shanghai	0.988
19	Ningbo	1.000	19	Zhengzhou	0.983
20	Shijiazhuang	0.999	20	Fuzhou	0.981
21	Hangzhou	0.999	21	Nanchang	0.964
22	Nanchang	0.999	22	Wuhan	0.963
23	Nanjing	0.998	23	Jinan	0.961
24	Zhengzhou	0.998	24	Nanning	0.958
25	Guangzhou	0.998	25	Chengdu	0.947

Continued

Ranking	City	Inflation rate	Ranking	City	Consumption rate
26	Haikou	0.998	26	Qingdao	0.946
27	Beijing	0.997	27	Beijing	0.943
28	Harbin	0.997	28	Hohhot	0.941
29	Nanning	0.997	29	Xiamen	0.938
30	Jinan	0.996	30	Kunming	0.907
31	Xining	0.995	31	Ningbo	0.892
32	Shenzhen	0.994	32	Shijiazhuang	0.888
33	Shenyang	0.992	33	Taiyuan	0.864
34	Dalian	0.992	34	Hefei	0.862
35	Shanghai	0.987	35	Nanjing	0.826

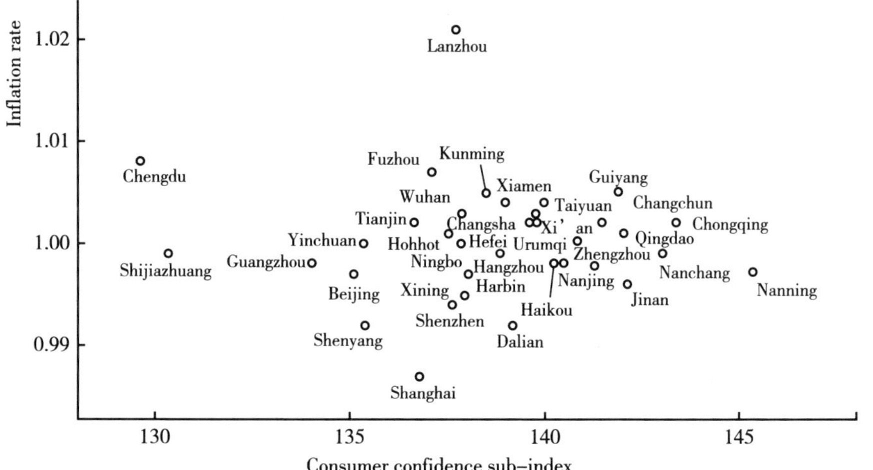

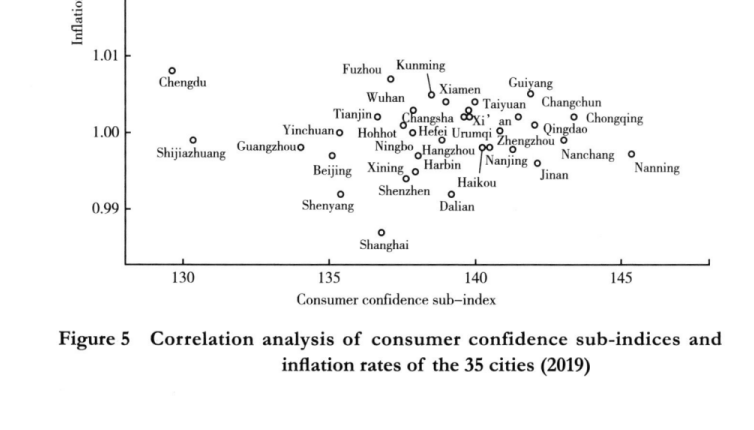

Figure 5 Correlation analysis of consumer confidence sub-indices and inflation rates of the 35 cities (2019)

2.3.2 Consumer confidence sub-index and consumption rate

The consumer confidence sub-index is positively correlated with the consumption rate in all the 35 cities in 2019. That is, the higher the consumer

confidence sub-index, the higher the consumption rate. It indicates that when per capita income continues to increase, subjective factors will have greater impacts on the consumption. As shown in Figure 6, Xi'an, Chengdu and Shijiazhuang have seen the greatest changes among the 35 cities. Chengdu and Shijiazhuang are of low consumer confidence sub-indices and low consumption rates, while Xi'an is of a high consumer confidence sub-index and a high consumption rate. Compared with the analysis in Figure 5, it can be found that the consumer confidence sub-indices of Chengdu and Shijiazhuang are lower than that of other cities, which lead to lower consumption rates. The high inflation rates in the two cities probably result from the rise in agricultural commodity prices in 2019.

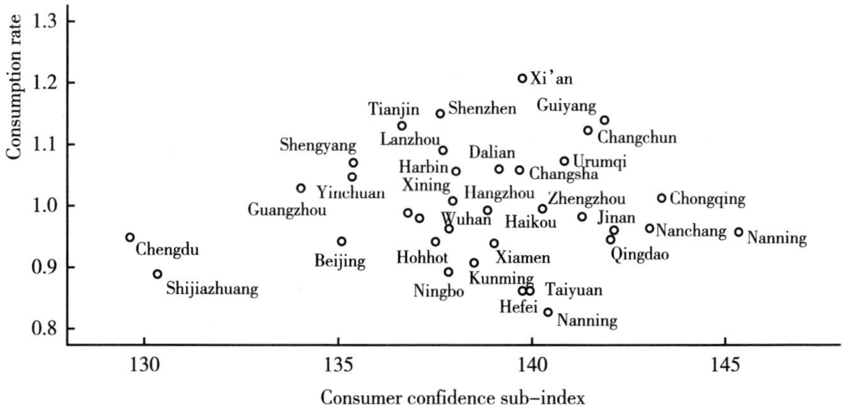

Figure 6 Correlation analysis of consumer confidence sub-indices and consumption rates of the 35 cities (2019)

2.4 Analysis of influential factors

Although consumer confidence index mainly measures the subjective

perceptions of consumers, these perceptions are derived from the objective economic environment. Thus, it is also necessary to analyze the influential factors that affect consumer confidence from the perspective of consumption and identify the major influential factors, in order to facilitate effective intervention and management of consumer confidence for the stabilization of the macroeconomy.

Consumption is under the influence of consumer preference, as well as the level of income, wealth and social security. The higher the actual income and the income expectation, or the more the wealth and the higher the consumption capacity, or the better the social security and the less the anxieties of life, the stronger the consumer confidence. Based on the above principles, a regression analysis can be made on the influential factors of consumer confidence in the 35 cities.

Consumer confidence index reflects the subjective / psychological feelings of consumers, and is a manifestation of collective social psychology.[①] Therefore, it is usually necessary to collect samples by means of questionnaires and make calculations correspondingly. Consumer confidence index mirrors changes in the economic situation perceived by consumers.[②] Most traditional theories explaining consumer behaviors are based on Franco Modigliani's Life-cycle Theory and Milton Friedman's Permanent Income Hypothesis (PIH). However, Mclntyre held that consumption should not be explained only from the perspective of long-term income, because consumer confidence was of short-term changes, and that changes in consumption levels were sensitive to

---

① G.Katona, "Psychology and Consumer Economics,"*Journal of Consumer Research* 1(1974):1-8.

② M.W.Roos, "Willingness to Consume and Ability to Consume," *Journal of Economic Behavior and Organization* 66(2008):387-402.

consumer confidence. He also believed that changes in consumer confidence could be monitored on a monthly or quarterly basis, to predict the volatility of total consumer demand in advance.[①] In fact, consumer confidence index has long been discovered as a precursor to consumer demand. Studies made by Fuhrer, Carroll et al., Bram and Ludvigson have all come to similar conclusions, proving that consumer confidence index is positively correlated with consumer expenditure.[②]

On the other hand, as an application of behavioral economics, consumer confidence index can also be applied to the financial field. Saul and Katona believed that consumer confidence index of consumer durables could well reflect both consumers' perceptions of financial stability and the probability of financial crisis.[③] Since consumer durables are non-liquid assets, when consumers sense a recession or financial instability, they would prefer liquid assets than consumer durables. Consumption economists have been working further on the impact of consumer confidence index on other consumer decisions. For example, Aneta held that consumer confidence had an impact on household financial behaviors, and the index could greatly influence the

---

① K.H. Mclntyre,"Reconciling Consumer Confidence and Permanent Income Consumption,"*Eastern Economic Journal* 2(2007): 257-275.

② J.C.Fuhrer, "On the Information Content of Consumer Surrey Expectations," *Review Economics and Statistics* 1(1988):140-144; C.D.Carroll, J.C.Fuhrer, D.W.Wilcox, "Does Consumer Sentiment Forecast Household Spending? If So, Why?"*The American Economic Review* 84(1994); J.Bram, S.Ludvigson, "Does Consumer Confidence Forecast Household Expenditure?A Sentiment Index Horse Race, "*Economic Policy Review* 4(1998).

③ Saul H. Hymans, "Consumer Durable Spending: Ex Planation and Prediction," *Brookings Papers on Economic Activity* 2(1970):173-199; G.Katona, "Consumer Durable Spending,"*Brookings Papers on Economic Activity* 1(1971):234-239; Frederic S. Mishkin, "Illiquidity, Comumer Durable Expediture and Monetary Policy,"*American Economic Review* 66 (1976):642-654.

stock market and the foreign exchange market.① It is generally believed that a strong consumer confidence index indicates a strong purchase intention, resulting in an expanding economy and a bright future for the stock market. It also means that the central bank may raise interest rates to prevent economic overheating, and that the currency will appreciate in the case of an open economy, just like the appreciation of USD when the Fed raises interest rates.

Scholars in China also agree that consumer confidence index is the leading indicator of consumer demand, which helps predict CPI performance② and affects consumer demand③. Hence, consumer confidence index, as a reflection of the current status and future prospects of economic operation perceived by the consumers, will impact consumer demand through consumer behavior decisions and ultimately affect the operation of the macro economy. Consumer confidence index is subject to regional and individual differences.④ After comparing the consumer confidence of urban and rural residents in Luoyang City, Chu Chunyang held that the increase in consumer confidence and the stronger confidence of rural residents in future consumption and savings resulted from the difference in employment

---

① Aneta Maria Klopcka, "Does Consumer Confidence Forecast Honsehold Saving and Borrowing, Behavior? Evidence for Poland," *Social Indicators Research* 133(2017):693-717.

② Zhang Yingkui, Zhang Shuai, "Correlation Analysis of Consumer Confidence Index and Consumer Price Index Volatility," *Statistical Research* 2014 (12): 66~68; Xu Guoxiang, Liu Lu, "Study on Relationship Between China Consumer Confidence Index and Consumer Price Index," *Statistics & Decision* 23 (2018): 5~10.

③ Zheng Zhangxin, "The Relationship Between the Consumer Confidence Index and the Demand of Consumption: Analysis Based on the Demand of Consumption of Nanjing," *Statistics & Information Forum* 10 (2011): 58~63.

④ Ji Hong, Ren Tao, Ruan Jing, "An Analysis of Consumer Confidence in China: Based on Cross-Strait Consumer Confidence Index," *Economic Perspectives* 1 (2010): 53-55.

and expectation.① In 2009, China UnionPay and Xinhua News Agency co-released the Bankcard Consumer Confidence Index (BCCI) for the first time, and the results showed that although the consumer confidence index oscillated after the international financial crisis, the consumer confidence remained high among urban residents in China.

2.4.1 Regression model

The consumer confidence sub-index (*Confidence*) is the explained variable, and the explanatory variables include: per capita disposable income (*Income*), per capita wealth (*Wealth*), social insurance coverage (*Socialins*), basic medical insurance coverage (*Medicalins*) and unemployment insurance coverage (*Unemploymentins*). The regression equation is as follows:

$$Confidence=\alpha+\beta_1\ Income+\beta_2\ Wealth+\beta_3\ Socialins+\beta_4\ Medicalins$$
$$+\beta_5\ Unemploymentins+\varepsilon$$

The extent and outcome of the impact objective economic environment has on consumer confidence or the subjective / psychological feelings of consumers can be observed with the above equation.

2.4.2 Analysis of variables

The objective data used in the regression equation include per capita disposable income, per capita wealth, social insurance coverage, basic medical insurance coverage and unemployment insurance coverage. These data came from *China City Statistical Yearbook*, *China Economic and Social Development*

① Chu Chunyang, "Consumer Confidence Index Report of Luoyang City," *Marketing Research* 2 (2012): 40-41.

Statistical Yearbook and *China Labor and Social Security Yearbook*. For the convenience of analysis and use, the above data were standardized to obtain the corresponding indices. Table 7 summarizes the values and rankings of the 35 cities in per capita disposable income, per capita wealth, social insurance coverage, basic medical insurance coverage and unemployment insurance coverage in 2019.

The top 5 cities with the highest per capita disposable income are: Shanghai (1.52), Beijing (1.46), Hangzhou (1.36), Ningbo (1.34) and Guangzhou (1.34). The bottom 5 cities are: Guiyang (0.78), Lanzhou (0.78), Chongqing (0.78), Taiyuan (0.75) and Xining (0.72).

The top 5 cities with the highest per capita wealth are: Beijing (2.68), Shanghai (2.54), Hangzhou (2.40), Hangzhou (2.30) and Nanjing (1.58). The bottom 5 cities are: Lanzhou (0.47), Yinchuan (0.46), Nanning (0.45), Xining (0.34) and Kunming (0.32).

The top 5 cities with the best social insurance coverage are: Shenzhen (2.23), Hangzhou (2.10), Shenyang (2.05), Xiamen (1.84) and Beijing (1.77). The bottom 5 cities are: Lanzhou (0.56), Taiyuan (0.48), Nanchang (0.46), Hohhot (0.41) and Harbin (0.39).

The top 5 cities with the highest basic medical insurance coverage are: Hangzhou (2.26), Shenzhen (2.11), Xiamen (2.07), Beijing (1.76) and Dalian (1.71). The bottom 5 cities are: Chongqing (0.51), Nanchang (0.50), Zhengzhou (0.47), Shijiazhuang (0.38) and Xining (0.29).

The top 5 cities with the greatest unemployment insurance coverage are: Shenzhen (3.64), Beijing (2.31), Xiamen (2.30), Hangzhou (1.80) and Guangzhou (1.65). The bottom 5 cities are: Changchun (0.44), Nanning (0.41), Harbin (0.38), Shijiazhuang (0.37) and Xining (0.30).

Table 7 Values and rankings of explanatory variables (2019)

	City	Per capita disposable income		Per capita wealth		Social insurance coverage		Basic medical insurance coverage		Unemployment insurance coverage	
		Value	Ranking	Value	Ranking	Value	Ranking	Value	Ranking	Value	Ranking
1	Beijing	1.46	2	2.68	1	1.77	5	1.76	4	2.31	2
2	Tianjin	0.95	18	1.23	9	1.40	7	1.66	6	0.87	15
3	Shijiazhuang	0.79	28	0.70	21	0.60	28	0.38	34	0.37	34
4	Taiyuan	0.75	34	0.59	26	0.48	32	1.26	11	0.93	13
5	Hohhot	1.04	13	0.58	27	0.41	34	1.03	16	0.78	20
6	Shenyang	0.98	15	0.69	22	2.05	3	0.94	20	0.73	21
7	Changchun	0.79	29	0.64	24	0.73	24	1.59	7	0.44	31
8	Harbin	0.84	25	0.52	30	0.39	35	0.69	24	0.38	33
9	Shanghai	1.52	1	2.54	2	1.67	6	1.46	8	1.49	6
10	Nanjing	1.32	6	1.58	5	0.97	14	1.19	13	1.44	7
11	Hangzhou	1.36	3	2.30	4	2.10	2	2.26	1	1.80	4
12	Hefei	0.93	20	0.98	14	0.78	21	0.58	27	0.83	18
13	Fuzhou	0.99	14	0.86	15	0.80	18	0.51	30	0.67	25
14	Nanchang	0.88	22	0.60	25	0.46	33	0.50	32	0.48	30
15	Jinan	1.12	10	1.13	11	1.15	10	0.75	22	0.89	14
16	Zhengzhou	0.87	24	0.72	20	0.88	15	0.47	33	0.50	29
17	Wuhan	1.06	12	0.98	13	0.77	22	0.96	19	0.87	16
18	Changsha	1.13	9	0.76	18	0.72	25	0.66	25	0.80	19
19	Guangzhou	1.34	5	1.38	7	1.35	8	1.26	10	1.65	5
20	Nanning	0.79	30	0.45	33	0.57	30	1.43	9	0.41	32
21	Haikou	0.81	26	1.21	10	0.64	26	0.55	28	0.68	23
22	Chongqing	0.78	33	0.64	23	0.79	20	0.51	31	0.67	24
23	Chengdu	0.94	19	0.98	12	1.13	11	1.21	12	0.86	17
24	Guiyang	0.78	31	0.82	16	0.82	17	0.70	23	0.59	28
25	Kunming	0.96	17	0.32	35	0.62	27	0.55	29	0.65	26
26	Xi'an	0.88	23	0.81	17	1.09	12	1.11	14	0.72	22
27	Lanzhou	0.78	32	0.47	31	0.56	31	0.61	26	0.64	27
28	Xining	0.72	35	0.34	34	0.58	29	0.29	35	0.30	35
29	Yinchuan	0.79	27	0.46	32	0.88	16	1.00	17	0.98	11
30	Urumqi	0.89	21	0.53	29	0.98	13	0.98	18	1.07	9
31	Dalian	0.97	16	0.56	28	0.80	19	1.71	5	0.96	12
32	Ningbo	1.34	4	1.49	6	1.25	9	1.09	15	1.34	8
33	Xiamen	1.21	7	1.28	8	1.84	4	2.07	3	2.30	3
34	Qingdao	1.13	8	0.76	19	0.75	23	0.91	21	1.00	10
35	Shenzhen	1.09	11	2.40	3	2.23	1	2.11	2	3.64	1

As viewed by the rankings of the 35 cities in the above five variables, Beijing, Shanghai, Guangzhou, Shenzhen, Xiamen and Hangzhou are often among the top of the list, while Lanzhou, Chongqing, Xining, Nanning, Taiyuan and Harbin are among the bottom of the list.

Table 8 shows the variables used in the regression process and their corresponding descriptive statistics.

Table 8　Regression variables and descriptive statistics

Type	Variable	Abbreviation	Mean	Standard deviation	Min	Max
Explained variable	Consumer confidence	*Confidence*	138.61	3.31	129.63	145.35
Explanatory variable	Per capita disposable income	*Income*	1.00	0.22	0.72	1.52
	Per capita wealth	*Wealth*	1.00	0.63	0.32	2.68
	Social insurance coverage	*Socialins*	1.00	0.39	0.51	2.23
	Basic medical insurance coverage	*Medicalins*	1.65	0.53	0.29	2.26
	Unemployment insurance coverage	*Unemploymentins*	1.00	0.68	0.30	3.64

2.4.3　Discussion of results

The variables in Table 7 fall into two categories. Per capita disposable income and per capita wealth are hard budget constraints for consumers. Higher per capita disposable income or per capita wealth equals to stronger purchasing power. Improved coverage of social insurance, basic medical insurance or unemployment insurance, on the other hand, helps to reduce consumption burdens. Thus, the two categories can be regressed first separately then together. Model 1 used the variables of per capita disposable income (*Income*)

and per capita wealth (*Wealth*). Model 2 chose the dependent variables of social insurance coverage (*Socialins*), basic medical insurance coverage (*Meadicalins*) and unemployment insurance coverage (*Unemploymentins*). Model 3 considered the impact of all the independent variables on consumer confidence. Table 9 summarizes the regression results of each equation.

The results of Model 1 indicate that per capita disposable income has a positive impact on consumer confidence. If per capita disposable income increases by 1%, the consumer confidence sub-index may go up by 0.047%. However, per capita wealth changes reversely with the consumer confidence sub-index. When per capita wealth rises by 1%, consumer confidence drops by 0.531%.

The results of Model 2 show that basic medical insurance coverage and unemployment insurance coverage are positively correlated with the consumer confidence sub-index. When basic healthcare coverage improves by 1%, the sub-index goes up by 0.799%; and when unemployment insurance coverage increases by 1%, the sub-index rises by 0.021%. Social insurance coverage is negatively correlated with the sub-index.

The results of Model 3 are basically consistent with the conclusions of Model 1 and 2. That is, per capita disposable income, basic healthcare coverage and unemployment insurance coverage are positively correlated with the consumer confidence sub-index, while per capita wealth and social insurance coverage are negatively correlated with the sub-index. When the two categories are combined, the positive effect of per capita disposable income and unemployment insurance coverage improves, the positive effect of basic healthcare coverage diminishes, and the negative effect of per capita wealth and social insurance coverage weakens.

Table 9 Regression results of Model 1-3

Variable	Model 1		Model 2		Model 3	
	Coefficient	P value	Coefficient	P value	Coefficient	P value
Income	0.047	0.394			0.052	0.689
Wealth	-0.531	0.151			-0.037	0.491
Socialins			-0.418	0.150	-0.386	0.232
Medicalins			0.799	0.263	0.206	0.277
Unemploymentins			0.021	0.490	0.033	0.406
R^2	0.514		0.317		0.321	

All in all, it can be seen from the results of the above three models that consumer confidence is affected by per capita disposable income, per capita wealth, social insurance coverage, basic medical insurance coverage and unemployment insurance coverage. Among them, basic medical insurance coverage and per capita disposable income are of the biggest positive impact, while the influence of per capita wealth and social insurance coverage waits to be improved.

2.5 Conclusions and Enlightenments

2.5.1 Conclusions

The consumer confidence sub-index is designed to measure consumers' subjective perceptions of the objective factors in the economic environment. It is one of the influential factors of consumer motivation, and will therefore affect consumer behaviors. Meanwhile, as consumption and savings together constitute income, consumer financial behaviors will also be affected when the income level is fixed. The more per capita income increases, the more the consumers will be influenced by their own subjective perceptions in consumption and in the selection and allocation of financial assets. In the

context of China's transition to a consumption-driven economy, it is necessary to pay attention to and track changes in consumer confidence. At the same time, as consumer confidence is a precursor to price level, by monitoring the changes in consumer confidence, the fluctuation of the price level can also be predicted to provide a reference for the orientation of macroeconomic policies.

From the perspective of individual consumers, consumer confidence may vary by age, gender and education background. In the 35 cities, the younger or the more educated the consumers, the higher the consumer confidence, and vice versa. The male consumers in the respondents are more confident than the females. The individual differences of the results suggest: the younger consumers are more optimistic about their income expectations and prospects; the males are more rational and optimistic than the females; and the better educated consumers are more confident about their future development.

From regional distribution, the survey shows that consumer confidence has increased at similar rates in all the 35 cities compared with that of 2018. In 2019, consumer confidence is strongest in the central region, but weaker in the eastern region. The Middle Yangtze River economic zone in the central region ranks 1st, and the Great Southwest zone ranked 2nd, outperforming the Middle Yellow River zone by a small margin. This is consistent with the trend of China's economic growth, with the rising of the central region and the slowdown in the eastern region.

As consumer confidence eventually affects consumer behaviors, and the collective will of consumers are reflected in the price level, it can be seen that consumer confidence has an impact on consumption and inflation rates. Through correlation analysis, it is found that except in a few cities, the change

in the consumer confidence sub-index has a positive effect on consumption and inflation rates. That is, the higher the consumer confidence, the higher the consumption rate and the price level.

Consumer confidence is a subjective reflection based on consumers' cognition of the objective economic environment. Existing studies show that its objective influential factors may come from two aspects: 1. hard budget constraints, and 2. social security level. In this report, two variables (per capita disposable income and per capita wealth) are chosen for the former, and three (social insurance coverage, basic medical insurance coverage and unemployment insurance coverage) for the latter. The results of model regression suggest that per capita disposable income, basic medical insurance coverage and unemployment insurance coverage have had a positive effect on the improvement of consumer confidence, but the expected positive impact of per capita wealth and social insurance coverage has not been observed.

2.5.2 Enlightenments

As shown in the analysis of the consumer confidence sub-indices, Chinese consumers constitute a good micro basis for addressing the economic slowdown. Consumer confidence has affected both the actual consumer behaviors and the inflation. Its influential factors have also played their parts. This has to an extent provided theoretical support for the future intervention and management of consumer confidence. The enlightenments obtained are as follows:

First, the current findings show that increasing consumer confidence had better start from stabilizing employment and per capita income. Only with a stable income and a satisfactory expectation for the future, can consumers have higher confidence and the ability to maintain and exceed current

consumption levels.

Second, the coverage of social security might need to be further improved, especially in the less developed areas. As the developed areas can offer higher incomes and better social security systems, social security is not a major constraint on consumption there. In the less developed areas, however, the micro entities are less able to be self-sufficient. As there is a more urgent need for social security, its coverage has a greater impact on the consumer confidence.

Third, as the income level rises, per capita wealth will have a growing influence on the consumer confidence. Therefore, it is necessary to develop and improve the financial market, increase residents' wealth, diversify their ways of wealth management, reduce related financial risks, and encourage the flow of wealth in the financial market rather than merely in real estate, so as to enable the positive impact of per capita wealth on consumption.

References

Zhang Lei, "China's Bankcard Consumer Confidence Index Shows Consumption of Urban Residents is Rising Steadily," *Financial View* 5 (2009).

Li Cheng, "Can Consumer Confidence Predict Output Fluctuation: Based on Empirical Data from China," *Economics Perspectives* 12 (2016).

B.Dosroches, M.A.Grosselin, "Evaluating Threshold Effects in Consumer Sentiment," *Southern Economic Journal* 4 (2004).

S.C.Ludvigson, "Consumer Confidence and Consumer Spending," *Journal of Economic Perspectives* 2 (2004).

M.Malgarini, P. Margani, "Psychology, Consumer Sentiment and Household Expenditures: A Disaggregated Analysis," *Applied Economics* 13 (2007).

J.G.Matsusaka, A.M. Sbordone, "Consumer Confidence and Economic Fluctuations," *Economic Inquiry* 2 (1995).

T.Proietti, C.Frale, "New Proposals for the Quantification of Qualitative Survey Data," *J ournal of Forecasting* 4 (2011).

D.Acecmoglu, A.Scott, "Consumer Confidence and Rational Expectations: Are Agents' Beliefs Consistent with the Theory?" *Economic Journal* 104 (1994).

R.Batchelor, P.Dua, "Improving Macro-economic Forecasts: The Role of Consumer Confidence," *International Journal of Forecasting* 1 (1998).

Eva Mueller, "Ten Years of Consumer Attitude Surveys: Their Forecasting Record," *Journal of the American Statistical Association* 58(1963).

F. Thomas Juster, Paul Wachtel, "Inflation and the Consumer," *Brookings Papers on Economic Activity* 3(1972).

F. Thomas Juster, Paul Wachtel, "Anticipatory and Objective Models of Durable Goods Demand," *American Economic Review* 62 (1972).

Frederic Mishkin, "What Depressed the Consumer? The Household Balance Sheet and the 1973-75 Recession," *Brookings Papers on Economic Activity* 1(1977).

F. Thomas Juster, Paul Wachtel, "Uncertainty Expectations, and Durable Goods Demand Models," in Burkhard Strumpel, Lames N. Morgan, and Ernest Zahn, eds., *Human Behavior in Economic Affairs: Essays in Honor of George Katona* (1972).

Saul Hymans, "Consumer Durables Spending: Explaration and Prediction," *Brookings Papers on Economic Activity* 2(1970).

B.3

Report on the Education Quality Sub-indices of the 35 Cities

Zhang Ziran[*]

Abstract: Since the foundation of the People's Republic of China, the CPC and the government have attached great importance to the development of education. According to the statistical findings, education quality has always been the hottest topic of people's living standards among Chinese residents. The team conducted a questionnaire survey on residents' satisfaction with education quality in the 35 cities. It is observed that in 2019, the weighted mean of the education quality sub-indices of the 35 cities is 67.02, between "acceptable" (50) and "good" (75), and slightly lower than that of 2018 (69.37). However, the indicators of student workloads (26.17) and extracurricular education expenses (24.92) are perceived "unacceptable" or "poor", and both lower than that of last year (29.94 and 28.77, respectively). Based on the analysis of the influential factors of education quality satisfaction, it is found that the capacity of education

* Zhang Ziran, research fellow of the Institute of Economics and director of the Research Office on Economic Growth Theories of CASS, specializes in the study of urbanization, technological progress and economic growth.

provision (No. of schools / 10,000 residents and No. of teachers / 10,000 residents), the per capita disposable income and the ratio of education, culture & entertainment expenditures have positive effects on improving the satisfaction with education quality. Therefore, it is suggested that the government might need to keep holding on to "the strategic priority of education development", while maintaining and stabilizing the public spending on education, and optimizing related investment structure. At the same time, it might also need to further build the teaching team, reinforce and accelerate the reform of the education system, and promote the equitable allocation of educational resources, especially the proper use of quality educational resources.

Keywords: Satisfaction with Education Quality; Student Workloads; Extracurricular Education Expenses; Supply of Quality Educational Resources

3.1 Introduction

Education is the foundation of China's One-Hundred Year Strategy. At the 18th CPC National Congress, the CPC Central Committee clearly stated that China needed to prioritize the development of education, which was of great strategic significance in the new era. President Xi said: "Education is an important way to improve the comprehensive quality and promote the all-round development of the people, an important cornerstone of national

rejuvenation and social progress, and a cause of decisive significance for the great rejuvenation of the Chinese nation. We will speed up the modernization of education and run a satisfactory education for the people."[①] To achieve the great rejuvenation of the Chinese nation and the "Two Centenary Goals", it is of great strategic significance to give priority to the development of education. In order to build a well-off society in an all-round way and run a satisfactory education for the people, in the light of the real situation of China and the major domestic social contradictions in the primary stage of socialism, the report of the 19th CPC National Congress made important arrangements on how to run a satisfactory education for the people. Since then, the government has implemented a series of educational measures to benefit the people, and pointed out that a standard of building a well-off society that could stand the test of history was to see whether China's education was of better architecture and quality, of better teachers and systems, and whether the Chinese people were more satisfied with it.

Since the founding of the People's Republic of China 70 years ago, the Party and the government have always attached great importance to the investment in and the vigorous development of education. At a press conference celebrating the 70th anniversary of the founding of PRC, Chen Baosheng, Minister of Education, said, "Over the 70 years, after generations of unremitting efforts and hard work, China's education has undergone earth-shaking changes. Looking back on our journey in the past 70 years, the course of education development has been truly magnificent. All these

---

① "To Thoroughly Study and Implement the Spirit of the 19th CPC National Congress and Open up a New Era for Educational Reform and Development", people.cn, Mar 15 2018, http://theory.people.com.cn/n1/2018/0315/c40531-29869921.html.

achievements are so closely related to the life of every household and to the growth of each one of us."① In recent years, the Ministry of Finance (MOF) has prioritized education in public expenditure. The government spending on education has accounted for 4% of the GDP for seven consecutive years since 2012. China already has the largest education system in the world, with 519,000 educational institutions, up to 276 million enrolled students and 16.7 million full-time teachers. Education in China is of upper-middle quality compared with the rest of the world, and is properly structured with complete functions, continuously providing all kinds of professional talents for China's economic construction and human capital accumulation. At present, the average length of education for the incoming labor force has reached 13.6 years.

Since 1978, China's economic structure has changed significantly after a period of rapid economic growth, especially in the demographic structure. With increasing per capita income, the birth and mortality rates have both declined. The growth rate of the total population has slowed down. Trends of population aging and low fertility have appeared in the age structure. To address such trends, the government has fully liberalized and started to encourage the birth of two children for each household. Since the two-child policy did not bring a birth peak, scholars believe that the fertility will of each family is closely related to their satisfaction with life, and under the influence of public education.

This report takes the subjective data collected from the survey as the explained variable, and the objective data of education development as the

---

① "Second Press Conference of the Press Center for the Celebration of the 70th Anniversary of the Founding of PRC", people.cn, Sep 26 2019, http://live01.people.com.cn/zhibo/Myapp/Html/Member/html/201909/100738_968_5d8b077702119_quan.html.

explanatory variables. The influential factors of education quality satisfaction are identified through the study of the quantitative relationships. Then suggestions are made based on the results of the quantitative analysis, to improve people's satisfaction with education and the sense of gain in public education services.

The so-called education quality is essentially an evaluation of the level and effect of education, and a measure of education outcomes. To schools at all levels, education quality means whether they have achieved the training goals or educational purpose for their educational objects with qualified outcomes. From the perspective of endogenous evaluation, education quality is often affected by the education itself, including related systems, means, plans and methods, as well as the quality of teachers and students. To the public, however, education quality involves household education expenses and subjective feelings such as the fairness of education, the energy burden on parents, and the breadth and depth of the educational content. Considering that education includes both basic education and higher education, separate surveys are usually conducted when investigating residents' satisfaction with education quality. This survey mainly focuses on the satisfaction with basic education, as it is the compulsory education provided by the Chinese government.

3.2 Analysis of education quality sub-indices

The design of the survey questions is based on the five indices proposed by Department II of Basic Education, Ministry of Education in J.J.E. [2013] No.2 of the "Opinions of the Ministry of Education on Promoting the Reform of Education Quality Evaluation in Primary and Secondary Schools"

for the purpose of "setting up and improving the comprehensive evaluation system of education quality in primary and secondary schools". The questions are as follows:

7. Is your child currently receiving ordinary primary / secondary education (primary / middle school or ordinary high school)? (If you have more than one child, please choose the oldest)

8. In your opinion, do ordinary primary / secondary schools (or the one your child is in) pay attention to moral education (e.g., proper behaviors, citizenship and civility, personal virtues, ideals and beliefs)?

9. In your opinion, do ordinary primary / secondary schools (or the one your child is in) pay attention to the comprehensive development of both physical and mental qualities (e.g., physique and body functions, healthy lifestyle, aesthetic accomplishment, emotion management, interpersonal communication)?

10. In your opinion, do ordinary primary / secondary schools (or the one your child is in) pay attention to the development of hobbies and talents (e.g., initiative and curiosity in learning, personal hobbies, potential development)?

The education quality (degree of attention) sub-index of each city was obtained by calculating the weighted mean of the answers to Q8-10. The value range is 0-100.

3.2.1 Descriptive statistics

As shown in Table 1, in 2019, the minimum value of the education quality sub-index is 61.70, the maximum value is 73.02, and the mean is 67.02. Overall, the sub-index is above the threshold (50), and the mean of 67.02 is between the threshold and "good" (75). In 2018, the minimum value was

64.20, the maximum value was 74.60, and the mean was 69.37. It can be seen that the residents as a whole are less satisfied with the education quality this year, as the index has dropped by 3.5%. In 2019, the variance is 6.36, and the standard deviation 2.52; while in 2018 the variance was 6.43, and the standard deviation 2.53. It can be observed that the dispersion of the education quality sub-indices has slightly narrowed this year.

Table 1 Descriptive statistics on education quality sub-indices (2018-2019)

Year	Min	Max	Mean	Variance	Standard deviation	Skewness	Kurtosis
2018	64.20	74.60	69.37	6.43	2.53	-0.046	-0.279
2019	61.70	73.02	67.02	6.36	2.52	-0.097	-0.278

Figure 1 presents the distribution histogram of the education quality sub-indices in 2018 and 2019. The kurtosis values in both years are negative, indicating a generally flat distribution, but the absolute kurtosis in 2019 is slightly lower than that in 2018. That is, residents' satisfaction with education quality in 2019 is closer to the mean, while that of 2018 is more dispersed. From the perspective of distribution, the sub-indices in both years are slightly left-skewed, which suggests that the values are mostly below the mean.

3.2.2 Comparison among different cities and regions

Figure 2 summarizes the changes in the education quality sub-indices of the 35 cities in 2018 and 2019. It can be seen that the trends of change are not consistent among different cities, and the satisfaction has dropped in most of them. The cities with marked increases include Hangzhou (+7.18%),

Guangzhou (+1.17%), Ningbo (+0.56%), Xiamen (+2.02%), Qingdao (+6.33%), Haikou (+8.17%) and Zhengzhou (+2.22%). The sub-indices of Changsha (+0.11%) and Hefei (+0.26%) have remained stable with slight rises. From the extent of change, Haikou (+8.17%) and Hangzhou (+7.18%) have seen the greatest improvements, while Chengdu (-11.63%) and Tianjin (-10.61%) have experienced the quickest drops.

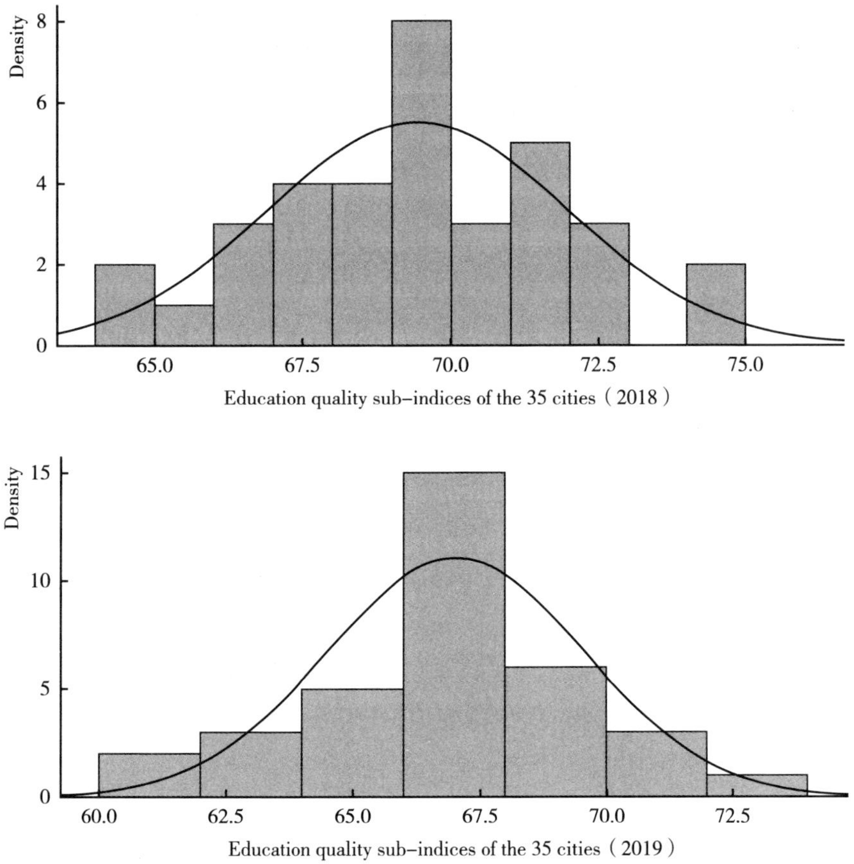

Figure 1　Histogram of education quality sub-indices (2018-2019)

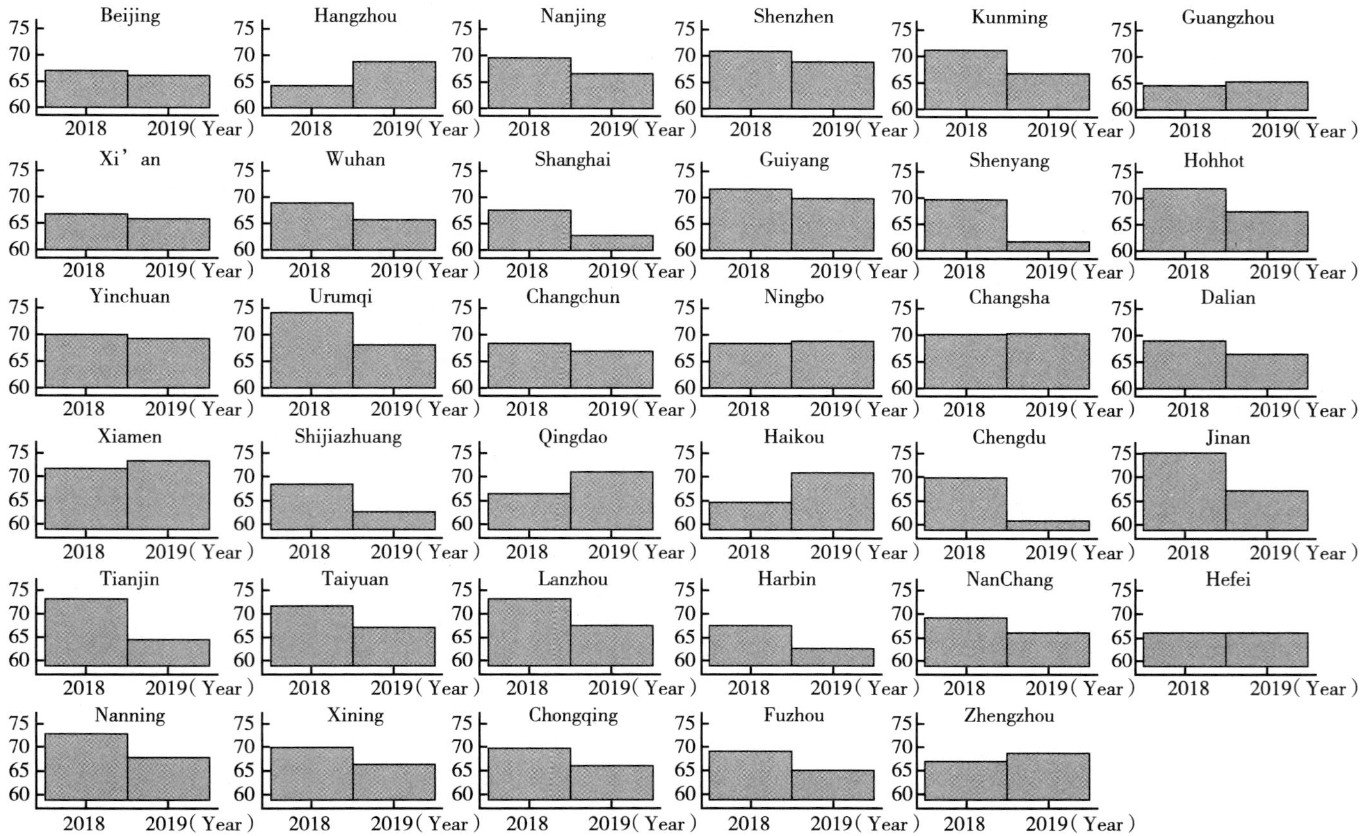

Figure 2 Changes in education quality sub-index by city (2018-2019)

Of the four regions, as shown in Table 2, the western region (71.0) was of the highest education quality sub-index in 2018, followed by the central (68.9), the northeastern (68.8) and the eastern regions (68.7). In 2019 however, the central region (67.6) comes 1st, and the eastern (67.4), the western (67.1) and the northeastern regions (64.6) take the 2nd, 3rd and 4th places respectively. Since 75 stands for "good" on the value scale, only the 2018 sub-index of the western region was close to the "good" interval. Residents in the less developed regions are more satisfied with the education quality, while those in the better developed regions are less satisfied due to higher expectations.

Table 2　Mean education quality sub-indices of the four regions

Ranking in 2018	Region	Mean	Ranking in 2019	Region	Mean
1	Western	71.0	1	Central	67.6
2	Central	68.9	2	Eastern	67.4
3	Northeastern	68.8	3	Western	67.1
4	Eastern	68.7	4	Northeastern	64.6

The Center also designed in-depth questions to further analyze the causes of the low satisfaction:

11. What do you think of the current student workloads of ordinary primary / secondary school students (or your child in school) (e.g., study time, quality and difficulty of schoolwork, stress of study)?

○ Very heavy ○ Heavy ○ Acceptable ○ Light ○ Very light

12. In your opinion, what is the major obstacle that prevents ordinary primary / secondary school students (or your child) from entering prestigious or key schools currently?

○ Domicile of household register ○ School district ○ School-selection fee ○ Academic performance ○ Other factors

13. In your opinion, the current expenses on extracurricular education for ordinary primary / secondary school students (or your child) are:

○ Very high ○ High ○ Acceptable ○ Low ○ Very low

The survey statistics reveal that the student workloads of the northeastern region (23.6) are perceived the heaviest, followed by that of the central (25.9) and the eastern regions (26.5). The western region (26.9) has the lightest workloads. The northeastern region (20.0) is also of the highest extracurricular education expenses, followed by the eastern (25.2) and the central regions (25.6). The western region (26.0) is again of the lightest burden. It can be seen that residents' satisfaction with education quality is highly related to student workloads and extracurricular education expenses. Heavy student workloads and high extracurricular expenses are the main causes of residents' dissatisfaction with the quality of education. Besides, in response to the question about the major obstacle that prevents primary / secondary school students from entering prestigious or key schools, "school district" is regarded by 20%-48% of the urban residents as the primary factor, and "school-selection fee" is another major factor chosen by about 14%-35% of the respondents.

The values of student workloads (26.17) and extracurricular education expenses (24.92) are in the "unacceptable" or the "poor" interval - both lower than that of last year (29.94 and 28.77, respectively) – which indicates that there is still a long way to go in the reform of China's education system.

Overall, urban residents of the four regions are less satisfied with the quality of education this year, as shown in Figure 3. The northeastern region has seen the greatest drop, followed by the western region. The central and the eastern regions have generally stayed where they were.

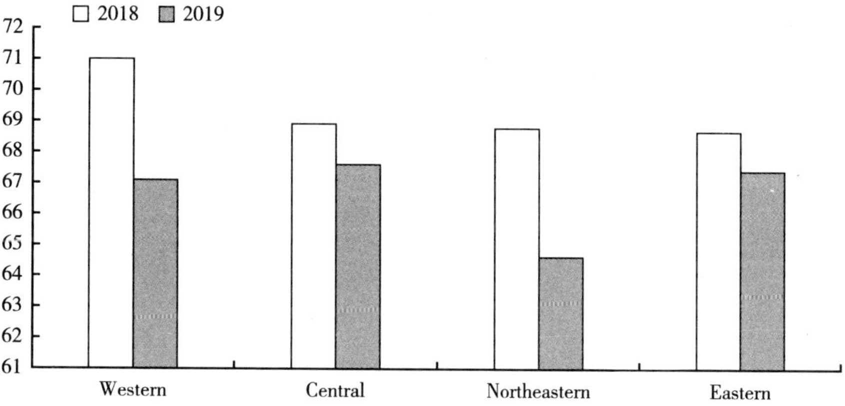

Figure 3 Changes in education quality sub-index by region (2018-2019)

Table 3 summarizes the comparison of the resident satisfaction with education quality in the eight economic zones. In 2018, the Great Northwest zone (71.7) was of the highest resident satisfaction, followed by the Great Southwest (71.0), the Northern Coastal (70.0), the Middle Yellow River (69.4), the Northeast China (68.8), the Middle Yangtze River (68.7) and the Southern Coastal zones (68.3). Residents of the Eastern Coastal zone (67.4) were the least satisfied. In 2019, the Southern Coastal zone (68.7) takes over first place, followed by the Great Northwest (67.9), the Middle Yellow River (67.4), the Middle Yangtze River (67.3), the Eastern Coastal (66.7), the Northern Coastal (66.7) and the Great Southwest zones (66.6). Residents of Northeast China (64.6) are of the lowest satisfaction.

In terms of ranking change, the Southern Coastal and the Eastern Coastal zones have seen the greatest improvements, which may be related to the increase of governmental investment in education and the introduction of outstanding talents to improve teaching excellence. Meanwhile, Northeast China has experienced the quickest drop, probably as a result of the continuous brain drain from the zone.

Table 3 Comparison of mean education quality sub-indices of the eight integrated economic zones (2018-2019)

Ranking in 2018	Economic zone	Mean	Ranking in 2019	Economic zone	Mean
1	Great Northwest	71.7	1	Southern Coastal	68.7
2	Great Southwest	71.0	2	Great Northwest	67.9
3	Northern Coastal	70.0	3	Middle Yellow River	67.4
4	Middle Yellow River	69.4	4	Middle Yangtze River	67.3
5	Northeast China	68.8	5	Eastern Coastal	66.7
6	Middle Yangtze River	68.7	6	Northern Coastal	66.7
7	Southern Coastal	68.3	7	Great Southwest	66.6
8	Eastern Coastal	67.4	8	Northeast China	64.6

As shown in Figure 4, except for the Southern Coastal zone (+0.6%), resident satisfaction with education quality has dropped in all the rest seven zones in 2019, with the largest decline in Northeast China (-6%).

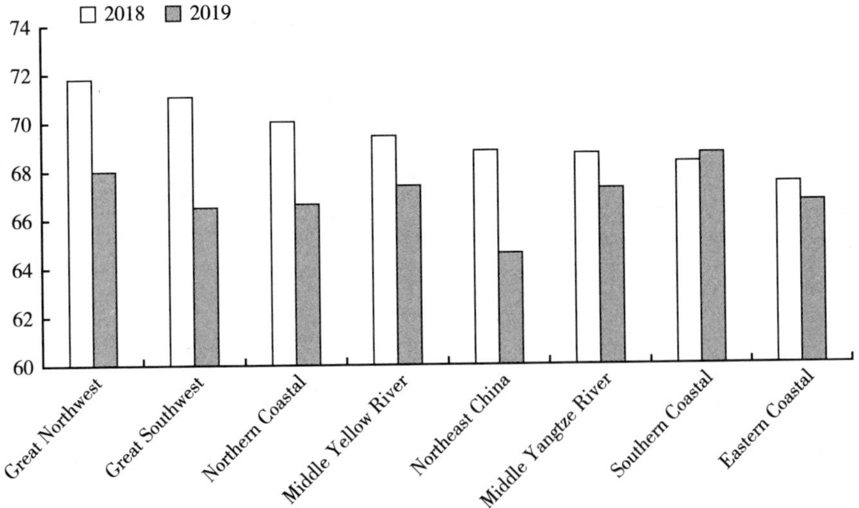

Figure 4 Changes in education quality sub-index by economic zone (2018-2019)

In the future stage of further urbanization, the competition for talents will become more intense. Under the condition of increasing population mobility, resident satisfaction with education quality may lead to the net inflow or outflow of the population. It will also directly and in longer term affect the potential of local economic development.

3.3 Analysis of influential factors

To further analyze the determinants of residents' satisfaction with education quality, the following quantitative analysis was conducted with relation to the influential factors.

Compulsory education has always been a focus of social and public attention. As early as 2012, the National Academy of Economic Strategy, CASS pointed out in its *China Public Finance Development Report 2007-2012* that out of the nine public services (municipal construction, public infrastructure, public services in the government sector, compulsory education, environmental protection, public order & justice, higher education & scientific research, social security and healthcare), compulsory education was of the greatest public concern and had been of the highest satisfaction for five consecutive years. Li Zhifeng and Zhao Chengfu believed that compulsory education as a kind of public goods tended to be non-profit and socially beneficial. They also stated that parents and students were the primary consumers of education, and that the assessment of education quality should be consumer-satisfaction-oriented.① They used the Structural

---

① Li Zhifeng, Zhao Chengfu, "Research on Satisfaction with Compulsory Education Based on SEM: A Case Study of Shandong Province," *Education Journal of Renmin University of China* 1 (2013): 102~111.

Equation Modeling (SEM) approach to construct the evaluation system, and evaluated the questionnaire of compulsory education in Shandong Province. Hu Ping and Qin Huimin investigated and analyzed the compulsory education in Beijing, and found that parents' satisfaction with compulsory education was mainly affected by their income and education. Better educated parents with higher incomes were less satisfied, and vice versa.① In the latest studies, Zheng Fanghui and Hu Xiaoyue conducted a sample survey in Guangdong Province. According to their findings, the public pays more attention to ten issues of people's living standards, among which education is of high satisfaction. Through interactive analysis, it is found that the difference in economic development has little effect on the satisfaction with education, but residents with relatively lower incomes or without local household register are less satisfied.② Cui Ziyun, Qi Wen'e and Lin Xiaoxuan studied the satisfaction of migrant workers in Guangzhou with their children's education. The questionnaire was mainly about the parents' and the students' satisfaction with the process-based and the outcome-based education quality. It was found that the overall satisfaction was positively related to both of them, and that the migrant workers in Guangzhou were generally satisfied with the basic education their children received.③ Based on the data of Chinese General Social Survey (CGSS) 2015, Wei Wei et al. analyzed the extent to

---

① Hu Ping, Qin Huimin, "The Study on the Government Performance of Compulsory Education Services: Based on the Parents' Satisfaction Survey of Compulsory Education in Beijing," *Education Journal of Renmin University of China* 12 (2011): 90~100.

② Zheng Fanghui, Hu Xiaoyue, "Active Fiscal Education Policy Should Focus on Improving Public Education Satisfaction," *Chinese Public Administration* 6 (2019): 111~116.

③ Cui Ziyun, Qi Wen'e, Lin Xiaoxuan, "Study on Perceived Education Quality and Student Satisfaction among Children of Urban Migrant Workers," *Wenjiao Ziliao* 9 (2019): 166~168.

which residents were affected by the subjective well-being and the satisfaction with public education when deciding to have a second child. According to their findings, both factors had a significant positive impact on the birth of a second child, and that the satisfaction with education could increase the willingness among rural families.①

The object of education is students. To ensure education quality, the primary objective of education is to keep improving students' satisfaction, especially in the stage of higher education. The National Institute of Education Sciences (NIES) conducted a special survey on students' satisfaction with higher education in 31 provinces around China in 2016-2018. Zhang Nanxing et al. used PLS-SEM to analyze the survey results. It was found that the satisfaction with undergraduate education was improving with a rising index and a relatively stable structure, and that the influential factors of student satisfaction mainly included student effort, and teachers' / students' awareness of the satisfaction with their college / university.②

According to the above findings, it can be seen that improving residents' satisfaction with education is a very important living-standard project of great governmental and social concern. While existing studies all target better-developed cities, such as Beijing and Guangzhou, this report covers the resident satisfaction of 35 cities across China, and puts forward suggestions

---

① Wei Wei et al., "Influence of Subjective Well-being and Satisfaction with Public Education on the Fertility Desire of Residents to Bear a Second Child: An Empirical Analysis Based on CGSS Data," *Journal of Social Development* 12 (2019): 120~134.

② Zhang Nanxing et al., "Multidimensional Evaluation of Undergraduate Education from the Perspective of University Teachers and Students: Empirical Analysis Based on National Higher Education Satisfaction Survey," *China Higher Education Research* 7 (2019): 70~103.

based on the analysis of the influencing factors.

Considering that the influential factors of residents' perceptions of education quality include parents' income level, the team selected per capita disposable income as the independent variable, and the ratio of education, culture & entertainment expenditures and the education provision index (No. of schools / 10,000 residents and No. of teachers / 10,000 residents) as the independent variables, and studied the influential factors through regression analysis.

3.3.1 Regression model

The education quality sub-index is the explained variable (*Edusatisfaction*), and the explanatory variables include: per capita disposable income (*Income*), ratio of education, culture & entertainment expenditures (*Educonsumption*) and education provision index (*Edusupply*). The regression equation is as follows:

$$Edusatisfaction = \alpha + \beta_1\ Income + \beta_2\ Educonsumption + \beta_3\ Edsupply + \varepsilon$$

The impacts of per capita disposable income, education capacity and the level of educational consumption can be analyzed with the above equation.

3.3.2 Analysis of variables

The objective data used in the regression equation include per capita disposable income, No. of schools / 10,000 residents, No. of teachers / 10,000 residents and the ratio of education, culture & entertainment expenditures. These data came from *China City Statistical Yearbook* and the CEIE database. For the convenience of analysis and use, the above data were standardized to obtain

the corresponding indices for comparison. The education provision index was obtained by calculating the number of schools / 10,000 residents and the number of teachers / 10,000 residents (of equal weighting).

Table 4 summarizes the values of the independent variables and the rankings of the 35 cities in 2019. The top 5 cities with the greatest education capacity are: Kunming (1.77), Lanzhou (1.58), Nanning (1.49), Guiyang (1.34) and Changchun (1.32). The bottom 5 cities are: Beijing (0.76), Urumqi (0.71), Shenyang (0.68), Shanghai (0.63) and Shenzhen (0.53). The cities ranked 6th - 30th are: Nanchang (1.27), Xi'an (1.25), Haikou (1.20), Changsha (1.19), Taiyuan (1.10), Jinan (1.07), Fuzhou (1.06), Guangzhou (1.05), Zhengzhou (1.04), Shijiazhuang (1.02), Harbin (1.01), Qingdao (0.97), Xining (0.93), Chongqing (0.90), Hohhot (0.87), Nanjing (0.87), Dalian (0.85), Tianjin (0.85), Wuhan (0.85), Yinchuan (0.85), Hefei (0.84), Hangzhou (0.81), Xiamen (0.80), Chengdu (0.78) and Ningbo (0.77).

Table 4 Values and rankings of explanatory variables (2019)

	City	Per capita disposable income		Education provision index		Ratio of education, culture & entertainment expenditures	
		Value	Ranking	Value	Ranking	Value	Ranking
1	Beijing	1.46	2	0.76	31	1.42	4
2	Tianjin	0.95	18	0.85	23	0.87	20
3	Shijiazhuang	0.79	28	1.02	15	1.29	6
4	Taiyuan	0.75	34	1.10	10	1.20	11
5	Hohhot	1.04	13	0.87	20	1.05	15
6	Shenyang	0.98	15	0.68	33	0.99	16
7	Changchun	0.79	29	1.32	5	1.07	14
8	Harbin	0.84	25	1.01	16	0.78	25
9	Shanghai	1.52	1	0.63	34	1.28	8

Continued

	City	Per capita disposable income		Education provision index		Ratio of education, culture & entertainment expenditures	
		Value	Ranking	Value	Ranking	Value	Ranking
10	Nanjing	1.32	6	0.87	21	1.88	2
11	Hangzhou	1.36	3	0.81	27	1.31	5
12	Hefei	0.93	20	0.84	26	0.88	19
13	Fuzhou	0.99	14	1.06	12	0.84	21
14	Nanchang	0.88	22	1.27	6	0.73	28
15	Jinan	1.12	10	1.07	11	0.92	18
16	Zhengzhou	0.87	24	1.04	14	0.66	30
17	Wuhan	1.06	12	0.85	24	1.82	3
18	Changsha	1.13	9	1.19	9	0.78	24
19	Guangzhou	1.34	5	1.05	13	1.22	10
20	Nanning	0.79	30	1.49	3	0.80	22
21	Haikou	0.81	26	1.20	8	0.60	31
22	Chongqing	0.78	33	0.90	19	0.50	33
23	Chengdu	0.94	19	0.78	29	0.78	26
24	Guiyang	0.78	31	1.34	4	1.89	1
25	Kunming	0.96	17	1.77	1	1.26	9
26	Xi’an	0.88	23	1.25	7	1.29	7
27	Lanzhou	0.78	32	1.58	2	0.53	32
28	Xining	0.72	35	0.93	18	0.39	35
29	Yinchuan	0.79	27	0.85	25	1.12	12
30	Urumqi	0.89	21	0.71	32	0.77	27
31	Dalian	0.97	16	0.85	22	1.11	13
32	Ningbo	1.34	4	0.77	30	0.80	23
33	Xiamen	1.21	7	0.80	28	0.46	34
34	Qingdao	1.13	8	0.97	17	0.73	29
35	Shenzhen	1.09	11	0.53	35	0.97	17

The top 5 cities with the highest ratio of education, culture & entertainment expenditures are: Guiyang (1.89), Nanjing (1.88), Wuhan (1.82), Beijing (1.42) and Hangzhou (1.31). The bottom 5 cities are: Haikou (0.60), Lanzhou (0.53), Chongqing (0.50), Xiamen (0.46) and Xining (0.39). The cities ranked 6th - 30th are: Shijiazhuang (1.29), Xi'an (1.29), Shanghai (1.28), Kunming (1.26), Guangzhou (1.22), Taiyuan (1.20), Yinchuan (1.12), Dalian (1.11), Changchun (1.07), Hohhot (1.05), Shenyang (0.99), Shenzhen (0.97), Jinan (0.92), Hefei (0.88), Tianjin (0.87), Fuzhou (0.84), Nanning (0.80), Ningbo (0.80), Changsha (0.78), Harbin (0.78), Chengdu (0.78), Urumqi (0.77), Nanchang (0.73), Qingdao (0.73) and Zhengzhou (0.66).

The above comparison of education capacity and educational purchasing power shows that the provinces of better economic development have tighter educational resources due to the large population, while the less developed areas are of relatively abundant resources. Education, culture & entertainment expenditures on the other hand, are mainly affected by economic development and cultural background. Table 5 summarizes the descriptive statistical analysis of the above variables.

Table 5 Regression variables and descriptive statistics

Type	Variable	Abbreviation	Mean	Standard deviation	Min	Max
Explained variable	Satisfaction with education quality	*Edusatisfaction*	67.02	2.52	61.70	73.02
Explanatory variable	Per capita disposable income	*Income*	1.00	0.22	0.72	1.52
	Education provision	*Edusupply*	1.00	0.27	0.53	1.77
	Ratio of education, culture & entertainment expenditures	*Educonsumption*	1.00	0.38	0.39	1.89

3.3.3 Discussion of results

The variables in Table 5 mainly involve the education expenses of the residents and the education capacity of the city. As Model 1 only consider the per capita disposable income and the education capacity, per capita disposable income (*Income*) and education capacity (*Edusupply*) are chosen as the independent variables. On this basis, the ratio of education, culture & entertainment expenditures is introduced in Model 2 as the expenditure structure data, and another independent variable - the ratio of education, culture & entertainment expenditures (*Socialins*) - is chosen in addition to the above two variables. The regression results of Model 1 and 2 are shown in Table 6.

The regression results of Model 1 indicate that residents' satisfaction with education quality is positively correlated to per capita disposable income and education capacity. If per capita disposable income increases by 1%, the education quality sub-index will increase by 0.214%. If education capacity goes up by 1%, the satisfaction with education quality will improve by 0.551%. It can be seen that education capacity is significantly correlated to the sub-index.

The results of Model 2 show that per capita income, education capacity and the ratio of education, culture & entertainment expenditures are positively correlated to the satisfaction with education quality. Among them, the last two are of significant positive correlation with the sub-index. After adding the third variable, the effect of per capita disposable income decreases significantly. If per capita disposable income increases by 1%, residents' satisfaction with education quality will climb by 0.097%. If education capacity rises by 1%, residents' satisfaction will improve by 0.505%. If the ratio of

education, culture & entertainment expenditures goes up by 1%, the sub-index will grow by 0.313%.

Table 6 Regression results of Model 1 & 2

Variable	Model 1		Model 2	
	Coefficient	P value	Coefficient	P value
Income	0.214	0.223	0.097	0.584
Edusupply	0.551	0.03	0.505	0.005
Educonsumpton			0.313	0.054
R^2	0.492		0.573	

The above regression results show that although increase in per capita income or the ratio of education, culture & entertainment expenditures is important to the improvement of education quality, governmental investment in education is still of greater significance. Only when education capacity continues to expand can the quality of education be truly improved.

3.4 Conclusions

Education quality is an important issue of general concern to the CPC, the government and the people. With the continuous development of China's economy and the steady improvement of people's living standards, education quality has become more and more important. Through the above analysis, it can be seen that the most important thing to improving education quality is to raise the capacity and level of education provision. Therefore, the government might need to guarantee related financial support, constantly implement the system reform, and continue to improve the quality and decrease the unequal

distribution of educational resources.

First, the government might need to hold on to "the strategic priority of education development", while maintaining and stabilizing the public spending on education and optimizing related investment structure. Since the founding of PRC, the public spending on education has been increasing in absolute terms, from CYN 1.162 billion in 1952 to CYN 3244.6 billion in 2018. At constant prices in 1952, the spending of 2018 was 329.1 times that of 1952. Nevertheless, China still falls behind the developed countries in terms of per capita education investment. Even in the BRICS club, China's per capita education investment is just slightly higher than that of India. Yang Rong and Liu Tingting pointed out that public finance was the primary source of educational funds in China, and non-government funding constituted only a small portion of it. They also found that in the use of education funds, preschool and senior high school education were of relatively low proportions, while personnel costs remained high, although still lower than the OECD countries.① The study of Liu Qian and Huang Jiaqi also showed that China's investment in preschool education was insufficient compared with that of the OECD countries.② Wang Peishi stated that the public spending on basic education had the greatest impact on increasing residents' income, and that the high proportion of per student expenditure would lower the output efficiency of the economy.③

Since 2012, the public spending on education has entered the "4% Era".

---

① 杨蓉、刘婷婷:《中国教育经费配置结构分析——基于历史趋势和国际视野的双重探讨》,《全球教育展望》2019 年第 6 期。

② 柳倩、黄嘉琪:《中国与 OECD 国家学前教育投入水平的比较研究》,《教育经济评论》2019 年第 3 期。

③ 王培石:《政府教育投入对民众可支配收入提升的关系研究——基于我国 1999 至 2017 年的省际实证分析》,《国家教育行政学院学报》2019 年第 4 期。

Even with the increasing pressure brought by the economic slowdown, it is still necessary to stabilize the government spending in this field. However, the local governments sometimes may find it difficult to maintain the stability or growth of such spending in absolute terms. In poorer areas, improving education quality is a key driver to local economic development. Therefore, it is important that policy makers prioritize such spending, ensure the investment in and the development of public educational resources, avoid the uneven investment caused by local heterogeneity preferences, continue to improve the education capacity of the less developed areas, and address the imbalanced allocation of educational resources among regions. Besides, it is also of particular importance to ensure the adequacy of compulsory education funds in rural areas and improve the level of education equalization.

Second, the government might need to keep building the teaching team and improving the quality of education. Teachers are the practitioners of education. A stable and qualified teaching team is the guarantee of education quality. Especially in rural primary / secondary schools, the stability of the teaching team is the basis of ensuring the quality of compulsory education. In addition to hardware investment in rural basic education, the government might need to constantly improve the remuneration of country teachers, and encourage urban teachers to volunteer for teaching in rural areas. Besides, it is also necessary to strengthen teachers' professional ethics. Teachers are the primary practitioner of school education. A school is supposed to have a team of teachers with noble ethics, profound knowledge and professional competence, of which professional ethics is a basic and essential requirement.

Third, the government might need to reinforce and accelerate the reform of the education system, and promote the equitable allocation of educational resources. President Xi has pointed out in the report of the 19th CPC National

Congress: China needs to promote education equity, and make more efforts to ensure fair and quality education for every child. With the development of China's economy and the increase of the per capita income, a primary social contradiction will be that of the supply and demand of quality educational resources. Therefore, for a long time in the future, the government might need to address the shortage and the unequal allocation of quality educational resources. It is thus necessary to further the reform and innovate the mechanism, improve the design of the top-level system, promote social participation, encourage social capital investment, and broaden the channels for running schools. Meanwhile, the academic pressure on students also needs to be reduced to change the focus of school education from mere exam performance to all-round development.

B.4

Report on the Health Conditions Sub-indices of the 35 Cities

Zhang Ziran[*]

Abstract: The health of the people is an indicator of national power and social progress. Only when physical health is achieved as a nation, can people enjoy a happy life and the country have development potential in the longer term. The team conducted a questionnaire survey on health conditions satisfaction among the residents of 35 Chinese cities. It is observed that the 2019 weighted mean of the health conditions sub-indices is 57.26, between "good" (50) and "very good" (75), but lower than that of last year (64.48). The findings of physical and mental health show that on a monthly average basis, the residents of the 35 cities have been unhealthy more often in 2019 (8.14 days) than in 2018 (5.5 days). The number of mentally unhealthy days has gone up from 3.01 to 5.14, while the number of physically unhealthy days has increased from 2.53 to 2.87. The number of days of limited daily activities due to health problems has increased

* Zhang Ziran, research fellow of the Institute of Economics and director of the Research Office on Economic Growth Theories of CASS, specializes in the study of urbanization, technological progress and economic growth.

from 2.19 to 3.22. There could be a variety of reasons for the decline. The regression results show that the positive influential factors include per capita disposable income, per capita green area and air quality, and the factors of negative impact are the Gini coefficient, house prices, house-price-to-income ratio and transport capacity. Considering all this, it is suggested that the government might need to keep raising the per capita disposable income, improving urban greening and traffic conditions, stabilizing house prices, and exploring the modes of housing provision for the urban residents.

Keywords: Satisfaction with Health Conditions; Physical Health; Mental Health; Adaptability

4.1 Introduction

With the rapid development of China's economy, the pressure of work and life has overtaken economic pressure and become the primary cause of the general concern about health. In the process of marketization and market-oriented reform, competition has also brought greater pressure on the people. Medical research indicates that increasing pressure of study, work, life or family may lead to higher incidence of cardiovascular and cerebrovascular diseases or depression. On the other hand, enjoyment of study, life or work is good to physical health. In 2007-2009, the *Insight China* joined hands with related experts and organizations such as Sina.com.cn to conduct a survey on the Xiaokang Index of Chinese Life. One of the sub-indices was the

satisfaction index of health conditions. From 2007 to 2009, the values of the sub-index were 56.7, 56.9 and 59.8 respectively, improving year by year.

In actuality, health involves medicine, public health, demographics, sociology, economics and a number of other fields, each having a slightly different understanding of health.

The medical community has long regarded health as a systematic view① and believed that health itself is the coordination with the natural system and the ecological environment. Health is the physical, emotional, psychological and social adaptability of individuals to the environment over time. From the medical perspective, people have to constantly exchange materials and information with the outside world (nature and society) during their lifetime. Health is essentially the dynamic balance of such exchanges. If the dynamic balance is lost, people will be physically, psychologically or mentally ill.

The World Health Organization (WHO) believes that a healthy person should be of physical health, mental health, social adaptability and moral health.② Among them, physical health means whether body function and vital activities are normal or how normal they are. Mental health involves the following three criteria: One is to have a complete personality and a stable mood, to feel good about oneself, to be able to control and manage one's own emotions and achieve psychological balance, and to have more or greater positive emotions than negative ones, thus being of self-love, self-esteem, self-confidence and self-knowledge. Two is to have sufficient sense of security in the surrounding environment, normal interpersonal relationships

---

① Du Zhizheng, "Aspects of the Definition of Health," *Medicine & Philosophy* 7 (1990): 19~22.

② What is the WHO Definition of Health, World Health Organization, http://www.who.int/about/who-we-are/frequently-asked-questions.

and the ability to win the trust and love of others. Three is to have a clear goal for one's own future, to be enterprising and to fight for one's own ideals or beliefs in life or career. Social adaptability is that one's psychology and behavior can adapt to the change of the environment, and such behavior can be understood and accepted by others. Moral health means that one does not harm the interests of others when seeking one's own interests, is able to tell the difference between right and wrong, true and false, beauty and ugliness, honor and disgrace according to the universal norms of the society, and can restrain and dominate one's own behavior and actions based on social codes. In this sense, health is not simply a state of no physical illness or defect, but also a state of good mentality and social interaction. Therefore, health is actually a state of physical, mental and social satisfaction.

Dong Xiwang and Wang Dihai believed that health in the modern sense should be understood based on the following four points: First, the content of health involved physical health, mental health, social adaptability and moral health. Second, the four aspects of health should achieve internal balance and be balanced with the external environment. Third, health was the state in which one felt good about oneself at present and in the future. Fourth, such a good state was also a resource with which one could achieve the goals of one's life and work. In this sense, since health was the guarantee and foundation of achieving one's dreams and goals, the pursuit of health itself also became one's goal of life.①

From the perspective of economics, health can be measured at either the macro or the micro level. Health in the macro sense refers to the overall health conditions of a certain group or the national population, and is usually

---

① Dong Xiwang, Wang Dihai, "Health in Economics: Definition and Measurement," *Fujian Tribune (The Humanities & Social Sciences Monthly)* 12 (2014): 19~26.

measured with the public health examination index or the overall population health index. In reference to the metrics of mortality, morbidity and disability rates generally adopted in medicine or epidemiology, macroeconomics often uses indicators such as infant mortality rate (IMR), under-five mortality rate (U5MR) and life expectancy at birth (LEAB) to describe the overall health conditions of the population. In the micro sense, to understand the health conditions of micro individuals, it is necessary to obtain data through health surveys. Strauss and Thomas introduced micro metrics of individual health conditions, including Disease-oriented Definitions of Health Statue, General Health Status (GHS) index, Physical Functioning and Nutrition-based indicators.① Generally, assessment of health conditions are supposed to be made on the basis of medical diagnosis. For example, the National Health and Nutrition Examination Survey (NHANES) of the United States uses the GHS index. Although NHANES also includes a self-assessment based on respondents' subjective feelings, the questionnaire designed is professional in the medical sense. However, its cost of operation is also considerable. For this reason, survey metrics in practice are usually based on respondents' subjective perceptions of their own health conditions. The health conditions of the respondents can be determined by asking how difficult it is for them to engage in specific activities such as moving heavy objects or climbing stairs (easy / possible / difficult), as is done in the Activities of Daily Living (ADL) survey.

To sum up, in the field of economic research, existing studies at home and abroad have clearly pointed out the importance of health from the macro and micro perspectives. To individual residents, health undoubtedly

---

① J. Strauss, D. Thomas, "Health, Nutrition and Economic Development," *Journal of Economic Literature* 36 (1998): 766-817.

affects their survival and quality of life. Health is an important resource not only for individuals to achieve their own economic goals, but also for socio-economic development in the macro sense. Therefore, it is necessary to track and measure the self-assessed health conditions of Chinese urban residents, and conduct in-depth analysis of the corresponding influential factors in the process of China's urbanization. In the following passages, data of the survey on health conditions will be used to analyze the changes and heterogeneity of residents' satisfaction with their own health conditions in different cities and regions, and the related influential factors.

4.2 Analysis of health conditions sub-indices

The questionnaire (Q14-17) is designed based on the health self-assessment theories of micro entities. The value range of Q14 is 0-100. The higher the value, the better the satisfaction. The answers to Q15-17 are the numbers of days. The higher the number, the worse the health conditions.

14. In general, how is your health?

15. During the past 30 days, how much of the time were you physically sick or wounded (physically unhealthy)?

16. In the past 30 days, how much of the time did you feel anxious, depressed or out of control (mentally unhealthy)?

17. In the past 30 days, how much of the time did your physical or mental health problem limit you in daily activities (e.g., self-care, work or entertainment)?

The self-assessed health index, or the health conditions (satisfaction) index comes from the weighted means of the answers to the above four questions.

4.2.1 Descriptive statistics

As shown in Table 1, the mean health conditions sub-index of the 35 cities is 57.26 in 2019 and 64.48 in 2018. Overall, the self-assessed health of the residents has declined by 12.6%. The 2019 minimum (50.94) and maximum (61.50) values of the sub-index are both lower than that of 2018 (57.36 and 70.58, respectively). In terms of statistical distribution, the variance of the 2019 sub-index is 7.07, and the standard deviation 2.66; while in 2018, the variance was 9.05, and the standard deviation 3.01. It can be seen that the dispersion of the health conditions sub-indices has narrowed among the 35 cities, and the consistency has improved.

Table 1 Descriptive statistics on health conditions sub-indices (2018-2019)

Year	Min	Max	Mean	Variance	Standard deviation	Skewness	Kurtosis
2018	57.36	70.58	64.48	9.05	3.01	-0.46	0.29
2019	50.94	61.50	57.26	7.07	2.66	-0.54	-0.19

Figure 1 presents the distribution histogram of the health conditions sub-indices in 2018 and 2019. It can be seen from the skewness of the distribution that although the value distributions in both years are left-skewed, the tailing to the left is longer in the 2019 data, indicating that the sub-indices of more cities are below the mean this year. The kurtosis of the distribution suggests that more cities were of a high sub-index in 2018, and the distribution in 2019 is flatter. It further proves that none of the 35 cities is of high satisfaction this year compared to that of 2018.

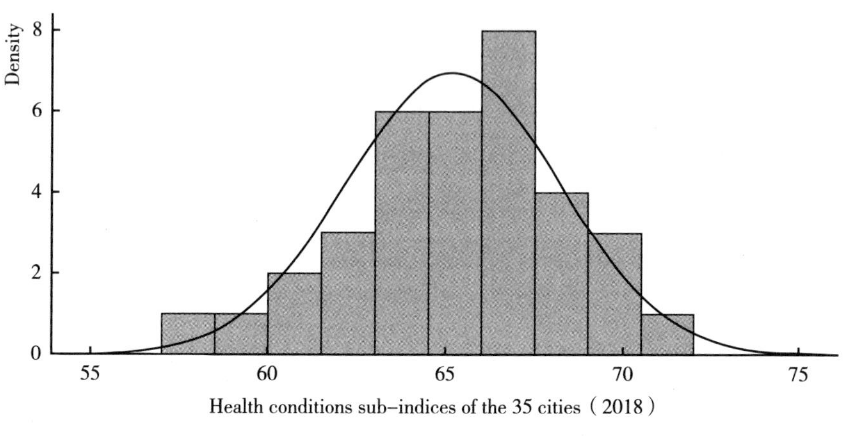

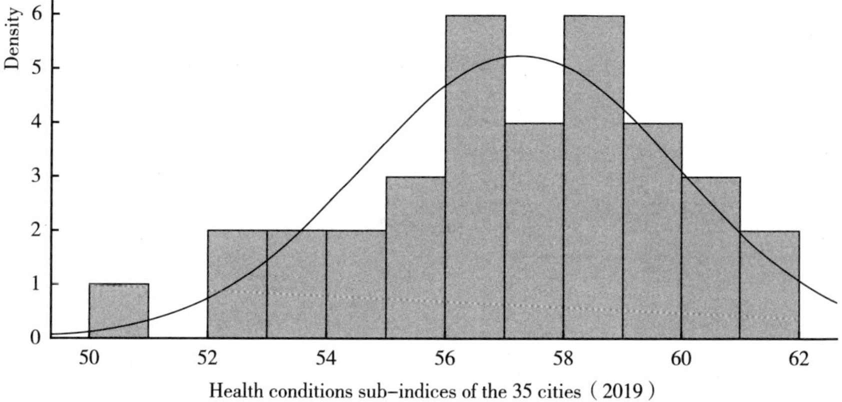

Figure 1 Histogram of health conditions sub-indices (2018-2019)

Table 2 summarizes the descriptive statistics on the number of physically unhealthy days within the past 30 days. In 2019, the minimum, maximum and mean of physically unhealthy days are 2.25, 4.44 and 2.87 days respectively, all higher than that of 2018. It can be seen that the data distributions in both years are right-skewed, which indicates that in actuality, the number of physically unhealthy days is above the mean for most people.

Table 2 Descriptive statistics on physically unhealthy days (2018-2019) (Q14)

Year	Min	Max	Mean	Variance	Standard deviation	Skewness	Kurtosis
2018	1.55	4.43	2.53	0.53	0.73	0.77	-0.07
2019	2.25	4.44	2.87	0.24	0.49	0.99	1.44

Table 3 presents the statistics on the number of mentally unhealthy days within the past 30 days. In 2019, the minimum, maximum and mean of physically unhealthy days are 4.14, 6.86 and 5.14 days, slightly higher than that of 2018 (1.83, 5.25 and 3.01 days, respectively). It can be seen that the value distribution is right-skewed with sharper kurtosis, indicating that the number of mentally unhealthy days is above the mean for most residents.

Table 3 Descriptive statistics on mentally unhealthy days (2018-2019) (Q15)

Year	Min	Max	Mean	Variance	Standard deviation	Skewness	Kurtosis
2018	1.83	5.25	3.01	0.78	0.88	0.84	0.11
2019	4.14	6.86	5.14	0.32	0.56	0.66	1.16

Table 4 shows the statistics on the number of days of limited daily activities due to physical or mental distress (in the past 30 days). In 2019, the minimum, maximum and mean values are 2.24, 5.78 and 3.22 days, while in 2018 the corresponding values were 1.25, 4.74 and 2.19 days, respectively. The variances and standard deviations of the two years are about the same. It can be seen that compared to that of 2018, the number of days when the residents' daily life and work are restricted by their health problems has increased this year, but the individual difference has remained roughly unchanged.

Table 4 Descriptive statistics on days of limited daily activities (2018-2019) (Q16)

Year	Min	Max	Mean	Variance	Standard deviation	Skewness	Kurtosis
2018	1.25	4.74	2.19	0.59	0.77	1.66	3.05
2019	2.24	5.78	3.22	0.52	0.72	1.32	3.62

Overall, in 2019, the value of the perceived health indicator (57.26) is between "good" (50) and "very good" (75), and lower than that of last year (64.48). The findings of physical and mental health show that on a monthly average basis, the residents of the 35 cities have been unhealthy more often in 2019 (8.14 days) than in 2018 (5.5 days). The number of mentally unhealthy days has gone up from 3.01 to 5.14, while the number of physically unhealthy days has increased from 2.53 to 2.87. The number of days of limited daily activities due to health problems has risen from 2.19 to 3.22. It can thus be concluded that, as a whole, the self-assessed physical and mental health has both declined this year.

4.2.2 Comparison among different cities and regions

Figure 2 summarizes the changes in the health conditions sub-indices of the 35 cities in 2018 and 2019. Except for Haikou, residents of all the other cities are less satisfied with their health conditions this year, and the sub-index of Urumqi has experienced the greatest drop (-21.7%).

Of the four regions, as shown in Table 5, the central region (58.0) is of the highest health conditions sub-index in 2019, followed by the northeastern (57.9), the eastern (57.6) and the western regions (56.1). In 2018, the northeastern region (65.5) came 1st, and the eastern (65.4), the central (65.1)

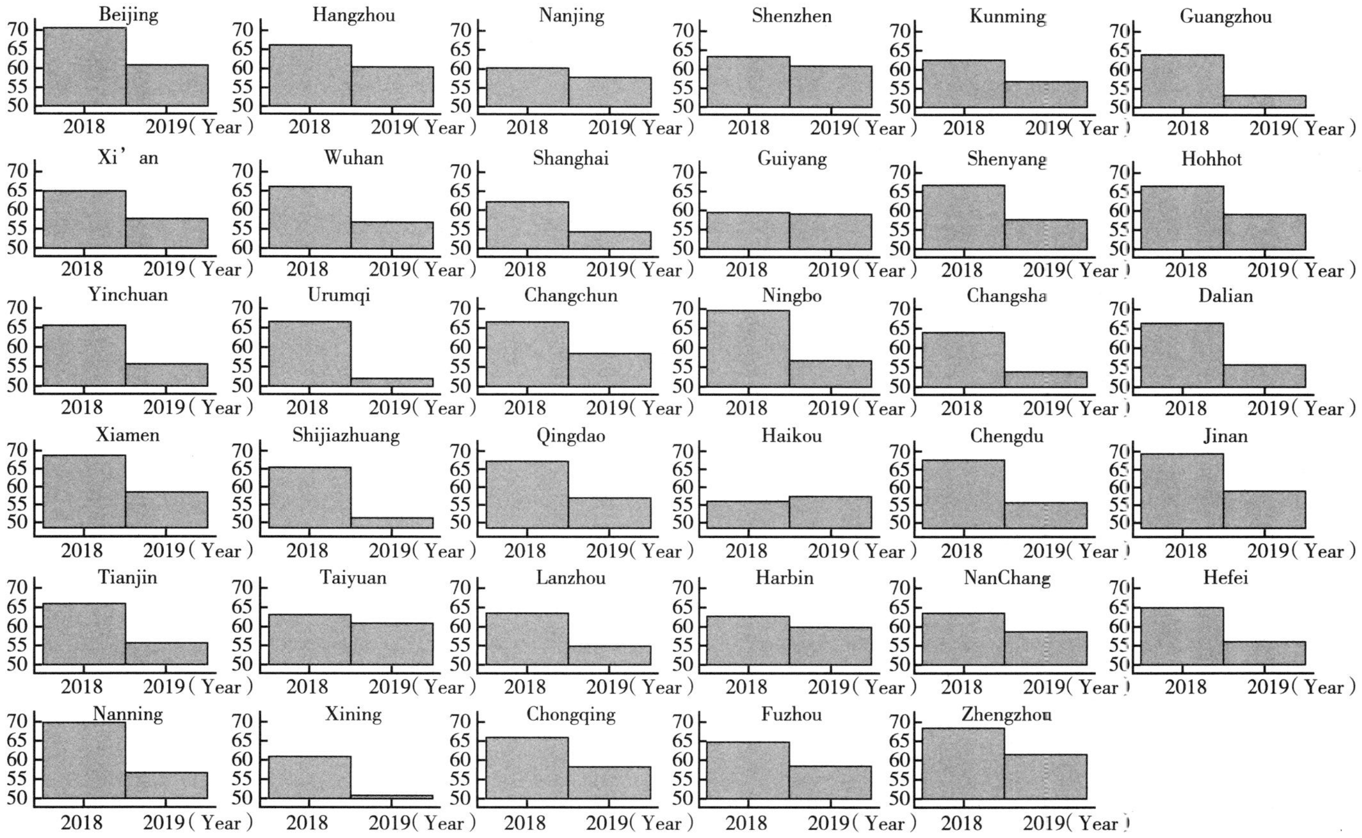

Figure 2　Changes in health conditions sub-index by city (2018-2019)

and the western regions (64.9) took the 2nd, 3rd and 4th places respectively. There is no obvious regional difference in both years.

Table 5 Mean health conditions sub-indices of the four regions (2018-2019)

Ranking in 2018	Region	Mean	Ranking in 2019	Region	Mean
1	Northeastern	65.5	1	Central	58.0
2	Eastern	65.4	2	Northeastern	57.9
3	Central	65.1	3	Eastern	57.6
4	Western	64.9	4	Western	56.1

As shown in Figure 3, the sub-indices of all the four regions have dropped in 2019. The western region has seen the greatest decline (-13.6%) and ranked last. The resident satisfaction of the rest three regions has fallen at similar rates.

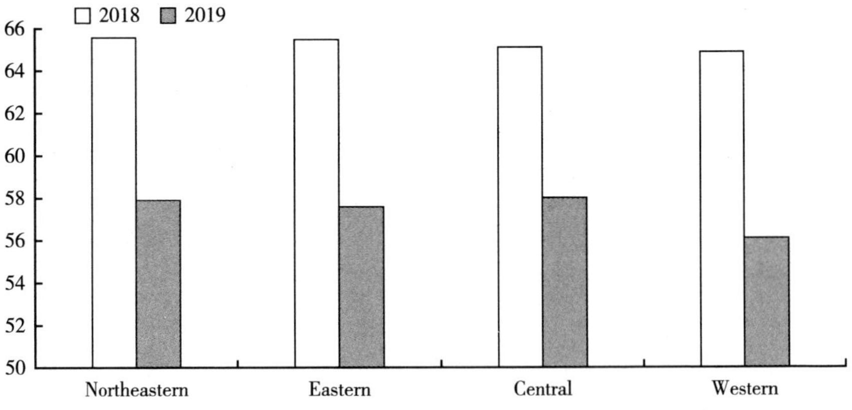

Figure 3 Changes in health conditions sub-index by region (2018-2019)

Of the eight economic zones, as shown in Table 6, residents of the Middle Yellow River zone (59.8) are the most satisfied in 2019, followed by those of

the Southern Coastal (58.1), the Northeast China (57.9), the Great Southwest (57.5), the Northern Coastal (57.4), the Eastern Coastal (57.3), the Middle Yangtze River (56.4) and the Great Northwest zones (53.4). In 2018, the Northern Coastal zone (67.9) was of the highest satisfaction, followed by the Middle Yellow River (65.8), the Northeast China (65.5), the Great Southwest (65.1), the Middle Yangtze River (64.7), the Eastern Coastal (64.5), the Great Northwest (64.1) and the Southern Coastal zones (63.7). In terms of ranking change, the Southern Coastal zone has seen the greatest improvement from the 8th to the 2nd place, while the Northern Coastal zone has experienced the quickest drop from the 1st to the 5th place. Rankings of the other regions have roughly remained the same.

Table 6　Comparison of mean health conditions sub-indices of the eight integrated economic zones (2018-2019)

Ranking in 2018	Economic zone	Mean	Ranking in 2019	Economic zone	Mean
1	Northern Coastal	67.9	1	Middle Yellow River	59.8
2	Middle Yellow River	65.8	2	Southern Coastal	58.1
3	Northeast China	65.5	3	Northeast China	57.9
4	Great Southwest	65.1	4	Great Southwest	57.5
5	Middle Yangtze River	64.7	5	Northern Coastal	57.4
6	Eastern Coastal	64.5	6	Eastern Coastal	57.3
7	Great Northwest	64.1	7	Middle Yangtze River	56.4
8	Southern Coastal	63.7	8	Great Northwest	53.4

As shown in Figure 4, the health conditions sub-indices of all the eight zones have dropped this year. The Great Northwest and the Middle Yellow River zones have seen the greatest and the smallest declines (-16.7% and -8.8%, respectively).

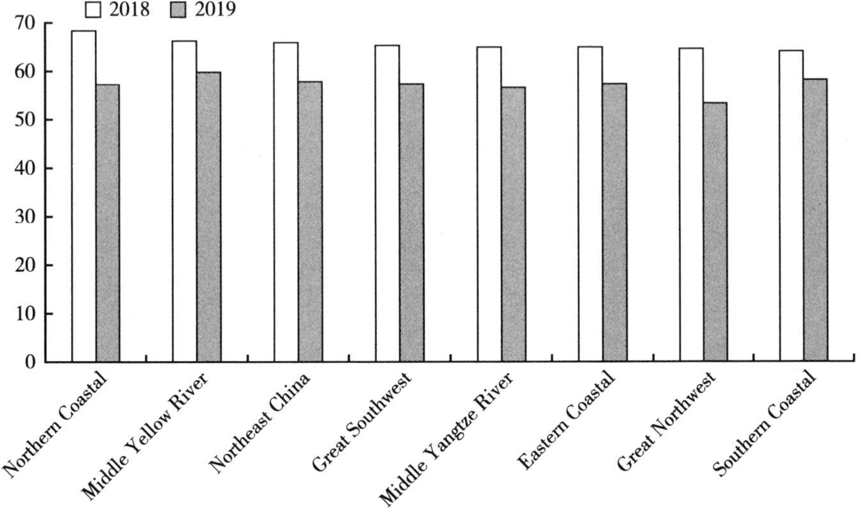

Figure 4 Changes in health conditions sub-index by economic zone (2018-2019)

4.3 Analysis of influential factors

To analyze the influential factors, the team selected relevant variables based on existing studies and found the key factors through empirical regression. Suggestions were also made for the stabilization and improvement of residents' satisfaction with health conditions.

Residents' perceptions of their own health conditions will, on the one hand, affect their sense of well-being. Studies have shown that residents' subjective well-being is mainly and positively affected by their satisfaction with income and health conditions.① On the other hand, residents' health self-assessment will also affect or even change the social mentality. Health satisfaction is an

① Zhou Chunping, "Influencing Factors of Residents' Subjective Well-being: Income Satisfaction and Health Status - An Empirical Analysis from Jiangsu Province," *Journal of Management* 4 (2012): 27~32.

intermediary variable of social participation and social mentality. Chen Bin et al. used the CGSS 2015 data to prove its importance to the stability of social mentality.①

With the continued economic growth, the self-assessment of health becomes increasingly important for economic development and social stability, and has drawn extensive attention in the academic in recent years. Huang Yun et al. used the CGSS 2015 data and the ordered logit model to analyze the influential factors of rural residents' physical and mental health. It was found that individual / group income inequality had a negative impact on the physical and mental health of rural residents, and that the impact of group income was in U-shape.② Hou Jianghong and Liu Wenjing also used the CGSS 2015 data to study the effects of social capital on residents' health perceptions and sense of well-being. It was found that Chinese residents were generally in good physical and mental health conditions, and that social trust and neighborhood interactions had a positive impact on residents' health and well-being.③ Zhang Shuyi et al. conducted in-depth analysis of the influence of neighborhood environment on residents' health self-assessment, and observed that the perception of sports and leisure facilities and the sense of belonging and security had a significant and independent impact on residents'

---

① Chen Bin, Zhang Renpeng, Chen Jisheng, "Study of Relationship among Social Participation, Subjective Wellbeing and Social Mentality - A Study Based on CGSS2015," *Journal of Jinggangshan University (Social Sciences)* 5 (2019): 79~84.

② Huang Yun, Ren Guoqiang, Zhou Yunbo, "The Impact of Income Inequality on the Physical and Mental Health of the Rural Residents: Empirical Analysis Based on CGSS2015," *Journal of Agrotechnical Economics* 3 (2019): 25~37.

③ Hou Jianghong, Liu Wenjing, "Moderating Effect of Social Capital on Residents' Health and Subjective Well-being: Analysis on a Comprehensive Survey of Chinese Social Conditions," *Journal of Wuhan University of Technology (Social Science Edition)* 2 (2019): 105~112.

health self-assessment.① Ouyang Wenjing believed that housing and health were indispensable to the improvement and development of people's living standards. Based on the 2010-2014 China Family Panel Studies (CFPS) data, she carried out a study on the impact of house prices on the physical and mental health of urban residents. It was found that house prices generally had no significant impact on residents' physical / mental health, but further heterogeneity study showed that rising house prices significantly undermined the physical and mental health of young people, since it was beyond their affordability.② Li Xiaotian et al. looked into the influence of physical exercise, medical expenses and individual characteristics on residents' health self-assessment. It was observed that physical exercise had drawn increasing attention among residents and had a continued and significant positive effect on residents' satisfaction with health conditions, and that residents' ideas of health improvement were changing from medical treatment to non-medical approaches.③ Zhang Wenhong and Yu Yimin analyzed the social factors of residents' health self-assessment based on a random questionnaire survey of 10 Chinese cities, and found that residents' socio-economic status and the quality of social capital were both of positive impacts.④

---

① Zhang Shuyi et al., "Influence of Neighborhood Environmental Perception on Self-rated Health of Residents in Cities of China: A Case Study of Wuhan," *Human Geography* 2 (2019): 32~40.

② Ouyang Wenjing, "Housing Prices and Urban Residents' Physical and Mental Health: Empirical Evidence from CFPS," *Journal of Finance and Economics* 9 (2019): 141~153.

③ Li Xiaotian et al., "Physical Exercise, Medical Consumption and Health Satisfaction: Based on Investigation on Residents' Participation in Sports in Jingjinji Metropolitan Region," *Journal of Wuhan Institute of Physical Education* 7 (2019): 34~42.

④ Zhang Wenhong, Yu Yimin, "Study on Social Influencing Factors of Residents' Self-rated Health," *Dongyue Tribune* 9 (2019): 31~41.

4.3.1 Regression model

There could be a variety of reasons for the decline in the health conditions sub-index in 2019. Combining the survey findings with existing studies, the reasons beyond individual factors can be grouped into three categorics: first, income factors, including income level and income gap; second, housing factors; and third, community environment factors, include living convenience and eco-environment. In reference to the Grossman Health Production Function (HPF) in model building[①], per capita disposable income, the Gini coefficient, house prices, house-price-to-income ratio, transport capacity, per capita green area and air quality are chosen as the independent variables. The health conditions sub-index is the explained variable (*Health*), and the explanatory variables include: per capita disposable income (*Income*), the Gini coefficient (*Gini*), house prices (*Houseprice*), house-price-to-income ratio (*Houseincomeratio*), transport capacity (*Trafficsupply*), per capita green area (*Greenspace*) and air quality (*Airquality*). The model built is as follows:

$$Health = a + \beta 1\ Income + \beta 2\ Gini + \beta 3 Houseprice + \beta 4 Houseincomeratio + \beta 5\ Trafficsupply + \beta 6\ Greenspace + \beta 7\ Airquality + \varepsilon$$

Through the regression results, analysis can be made as to the objective influential factors of residents' health self-assessment, and whether residents' physical and mental health are primarily influenced by economic factors or living conditions and living environment factors, in order to provide effective suggestions for the improvement of residents' satisfaction with health conditions.

---

① Michael Grossman, "The Demand for Health: A Theoritical and Empirical Investigation," NBER Press, 1972.

4.3.2 Analysis of variables

The variables used in the equation include per capita disposable income, the Gini coefficient, house prices, house-price-to-income ratio, transport capacity, per capita green area and air quality. These data came from *China City Statistical Yearbook* and the CEIE database. The above data were standardized to facilitate comparison, as shown in Table 7.

Table 7 summarizes the values of the independent variables and the rankings of the 35 cities in 2019 (per capita disposable income is no longer listed). The top 5 cities with the greatest Gini coefficient are: Xi'an (1.32), Changsha (1.28), Beijing (1.27), Shanghai (1.26) and Guangzhou (1.25). The bottom 5 cities are: Harbin (0.81), Yinchuan (0.80), Chengdu (0.80), Haikou (0.80) and Wuhan (0.79). The cities ranked 6th – 30th are: Lanzhou (1.21), Shijiazhuang (1.19), Hangzhou (1.19), Xiamen (1.14), Chongqing (1.13), Ningbo (1.09), Kunming (1.07), Dalian (1.07), Nanchang (1.02), Fuzhou (1.01), Hefei (0.99), Shenyang (0.98), Nanning (0.97), Tianjin (0.97), Jinan (0.93), Zhengzhou (0.91), Changchun (0.91), Qingdao (0.90), Hohhot (0.87), Taiyuan (0.86), Nanjing (0.85), Shenzhen (0.84), Urumqi (0.84), Xining (0.84) and Guiyang (0.82).

The top 5 cities with the highest house prices are: Xiamen (1.10), Shenzhen (1.10), Shanghai (1.09), Nanjing (1.09) and Tianjin (1.08). The bottom 5 cities are: Kunming (0.94), Guiyang (0.93), Hohhot (0.91), Haikou (0.90) and Xi'an (0.90). The cities ranked 6th – 30th are: Beijing (1.07), Hefei (1.06), Hangzhou (1.04), Ningbo (1.04), Urumqi (1.03), Guangzhou (1.02), Fuzhou (1.01), Nanning (1.01), Yinchuan (1.01), Nanchang (1.01), Zhengzhou (1.00), Wuhan (0.99), Lanzhou (0.99), Changsha (0.99), Taiyuan (0.99), Chongqing (0.99), Changchun (0.98), Xining (0.98), Shenyang (0.98),

Chengdu (0.98), Qingdao (0.97), Harbin (0.96), Dalian (0.96), Shijiazhuang (0.96) and Jinan (0.95). It can be observed from the rankings that house prices are higher in the better developed areas and lower in the less developed areas.

Table 7 Values and rankings of explanatory variables (2019)

	City	*Gini*		*Houseprice*		*Houseincomeratio*		*Trafficsupply*		*Greenspace*		*Airquality*	
		Value	Ranking	Value	Ranking	Value	Ranking	Value	Ranking	Value	Ranking	Value	Ranking
1	Beijing	1.27	3	1.07	6	0.42	34	0.87	23	1.32	8	0.72	32
2	Tianjin	0.97	19	1.08	5	0.63	29	0.92	21	0.82	20	0.82	29
3	Shijiazhuang	1.19	7	0.96	29	1.03	15	1.57	1	0.60	30	0.57	35
4	Taiyuan	0.86	25	0.99	20	0.66	28	1.14	12	1.29	9	0.61	34
5	Hohhot	0.87	24	0.91	33	1.83	2	1.20	10	1.48	5	1.02	17
6	Shenyang	0.98	17	0.98	24	1.28	8	0.93	20	1.51	4	1.03	16
7	Changchun	0.91	22	0.98	22	1.08	13	1.21	9	1.08	14	1.05	15
8	Harbin	0.81	31	0.96	27	0.95	21	1.14	11	0.70	23	1.12	10
9	Shanghai	1.26	4	1.09	3	0.50	32	0.74	31	1.15	10	1.00	18
10	Nanjing	0.85	26	1.09	4	0.73	24	0.91	22	1.67	3	0.95	22
11	Hangzhou	1.19	8	1.04	8	0.47	33	0.84	27	1.01	15	0.94	23
12	Hefei	0.99	16	1.06	7	0.73	25	1.05	15	0.70	24	0.97	20
13	Fuzhou	1.01	15	1.01	12	0.74	23	0.99	18	0.60	31	1.22	7
14	Nanchang	1.02	14	1.01	15	1.31	7	1.36	6	0.62	29	1.15	8
15	Jinan	0.93	20	0.95	30	0.94	22	0.75	30	0.42	34	0.73	30
16	Zhengzhou	0.91	21	1.00	16	0.96	19	0.26	34	0.62	28	0.73	31
17	Wuhan	0.79	35	0.99	17	1.00	18	1.24	8	0.95	18	0.89	26
18	Changsha	1.28	2	0.99	19	1.52	6	0.53	33	0.64	26	0.97	21
19	Guangzhou	1.25	5	1.02	11	0.61	30	1.06	14	2.07	2	1.12	11
20	Nanning	0.97	18	1.01	13	0.95	20	0.84	26	0.81	21	1.26	6
21	Haikou	0.80	34	0.90	34	0.52	31	1.54	2	1.14	11	1.31	1
22	Chongqing	1.13	10	0.99	21	1.10	12	0.20	35	1.13	12	1.09	13
23	Chengdu	0.80	33	0.98	25	1.02	17	0.87	25	0.69	25	0.91	25
24	Guiyang	0.82	30	0.93	32	1.02	16	0.73	32	0.96	16	1.27	5
25	Kunming	1.07	12	0.94	31	2.16	1	0.99	19	0.82	19	1.31	3

Continued

	City	*Gini*		*Houseprice*		*Houseincomeratio*		*Trafficsupply*		*Greenspace*		*Airquality*	
		Value	Ranking	Value	Ranking	Value	Ranking	Value	Ranking	Value	Ranking	Value	Ranking
26	Xi'an	1.32	1	0.90	35	1.10	11	1.03	16	0.63	27	0.68	33
27	Lanzhou	1.21	6	0.99	18	1.23	9	0.80	29	0.57	33	0.98	19
28	Xining	0.84	29	0.98	23	1.60	3	0.87	24	0.77	22	0.83	28
29	Yinchuan	0.80	32	1.01	14	1.57	5	1.25	7	1.12	13	0.93	24
30	Urumqi	0.84	28	1.03	10	1.59	4	1.09	13	1.42	6	0.89	27
31	Dalian	1.07	13	0.96	28	1.04	14	1.01	17	0.96	17	1.15	9
32	Ningbo	1.09	11	1.04	9	0.71	26	0.81	28	0.36	35	1.12	12
33	Xiamen	1.14	9	1.10	1	0.66	27	1.44	3	1.35	7	1.31	2
34	Qingdao	0.90	23	0.97	26	1.13	10	1.42	5	0.59	32	1.08	14
35	Shenzhen	0.84	27	1.10	2	0.21	35	1.42	4	2.42	1	1.28	4

The top 5 cities with the highest house-price-to-income ratio are: Kunming (2.16), Hohhot (1.83), Xining (1.60), Urumqi (1.59) and Yinchuan (1.57). The bottom 5 cities are: Haikou (0.52), Shanghai (0.50), Hangzhou (0.47), Beijing (0.42) and Shenzhen (0.21). The cities ranked 6th – 30th are: Changsha (1.52), Nanchang (1.31), Shenyang (1.28), Lanzhou (1.23), Qingdao (1.13), Xi'an (1.10), Chongqing (1.10), Changchun (1.08), Dalian (1.04), Shijiazhuang (1.03), Guiyang (1.02), Chengdu (1.02), Wuhan (1.00), Zhengzhou (0.96), Nanning (0.95), Harbin (0.95), Jinan (0.94), Fuzhou (0.74), Nanjing (0.73), Hefei (0.73), Ningbo (0.71), Xiamen (0.66), Taiyuan (0.66), Tianjin (0.63) and Guangzhou (0.61). By comparing the rankings of house-price-to-income ratio and house prices, it can be seen that the better developed areas are of higher house prices and incomes but relatively low ratios, and the less developed areas are of higher ratios.

The top 5 cities with the greatest transport capacity are: Shijiazhuang (1.57), Haikou (1.54), Xiamen (1.44), Shenzhen (1.42) and Qingdao (1.42). The bottom 5 cities are: Shanghai (0.74), Guiyang (0.73), Changsha (0.53),

Zhengzhou (0.26) and Chongqing (0.20). The cities ranked 6th – 30th are: Nanchang (1.36), Yinchuan (1.25), Wuhan (1.24), Changchun (1.21), Hohhot (1.20), Harbin (1.14), Taiyuan (1.14), Urumqi (1.09), Guangzhou (1.06), Hefei (1.05), Xi'an (1.03), Dalian (1.01), Fuzhou (0.99), Kunming (0.99), Shenyang (0.93), Tianjin (0.92), Nanjing (0.91), Beijing (0.87), Xining (0.87), Chengdu (0.87), Nanning (0.84), Hangzhou (0.84), Ningbo (0.81), Lanzhou (0.80) and Jinan (0.75). In terms of ranking, coastal cities as a whole have better transport capacity than inland cities.

The top 5 cities with the biggest per capita green area are: Shenzhen (2.42), Guangzhou (2.07), Nanjing (1.67), Shenyang (1.51) and Hohhot (1.48). The bottom 5 cities are: Fuzhou (0.60), Qingdao (0.59), Lanzhou (0.57), Jinan (0.42) and Ningbo (0.36). The cities ranked 6th – 30th are: Urumqi (1.42), Xiamen (1.35), Beijing (1.32), Taiyuan (1.29), Shanghai (1.15), Haikou (1.14), Chongqing (1.13), Yinchuan (1.12), Changchun (1.08), Hangzhou (1.01), Guiyang (0.96), Dalian (0.96), Wuhan (0.95), Kunming (0.82), Tianjin (0.82), Nanning (0.81), Xining (0.77), Harbin (0.70), Hefei (0.70), Chengdu (0.69), Changsha (0.64), Xi'an (0.63), Zhengzhou (0.62), Nanchang (0.62) and Shijiazhuang (0.60).

The top 5 cities with the best air quality are: Haikou (1.31), Xiamen (1.31), Kunming (1.31), Shenzhen (1.28) and Guiyang (1.27). The bottom 5 cities are: Zhengzhou (0.73), Beijing (0.72), Xi'an (0.68), Taiyuan (0.61) and Shijiazhuang (0.57). The cities ranked 6th – 30th are: Nanning (1.26), Fuzhou (1.22), Nanchang (1.15), Dalian (1.15), Harbin (1.12), Guangzhou (1.12), Ningbo (1.12), Chongqing (1.09), Qingdao (1.08), Changchun (1.05), Shenyang (1.03), Hohhot (1.02), Shanghai (1.00), Lanzhou (0.98), Hefei (0.97), Changsha (0.97), Nanjing (0.95), Hangzhou (0.94), Yinchuan (0.93), Chengdu (0.91), Wuhan (0.89), Urumqi (0.89), Xining (0.83), Tianjin (0.82)

and Jinan (0.73).

Table 8 shows the descriptive statistics of the explained variable and the explanatory variables in the model, and all the data are standardized.

Table 8 Regression variables and descriptive statistics

Type	Variable	Abbreviation	Mean	Standard deviation	Min	Max
Explained variable	Satisfaction with health conditions	*Health*	57.26	2.66	50.94	61.50
Explanatory variable	Per capita disposable income	*Income*	1.00	0.22	0.72	1.52
	Gini coefficient	*Gini*	1.00	0.17	0.79	1.32
	House price	*Houseprice*	1.00	0.06	0.90	1.10
	House-price-to-income ratio	*Houseincomeratio*	1.00	0.43	0.21	2.16
	Transport capacity	*Trafficsupply*	1.00	0.31	0.20	1.57
	Per capita green area	*Greenspace*	1.00	0.46	0.36	2.42
	Air quality	*Airquality*	1.00	0.21	0.57	1.31

4.3.3 Discussion of results

Based on the above analysis, the variables in Table 8 are divided into three categories, corresponding to the three models: Model 1 - per capita disposable income (*Income*) and the Gini coefficient (*Gini*); Model 2 - house price (*Houseprice*) and house-price-to-income ratio (*Houseincomeratio*), in addition to the variables of Model 1; and Model 3 – the variable of Model 2 and living environment factors, namely transport capacity (*Trafficsupply*), per capita green area (*Greenspace*) and air quality (*Airquality*).

The regression results of the three models are consistent, as shown in Table 9. According to the survey findings, per capita disposable income has a positive effect on residents' satisfaction with health conditions. It

can be seen from the comprehensive results of Model 3 that if per capita disposable income rises by 1%, residents' satisfaction will go up by 1.89%. The Gini coefficient has a negative correlation with the sub-index. As shown by the results of Model 3, if the Gini coefficient increases by 1%, residents' satisfaction will drop by 4.8%. House-price-to-income ratio is also negatively correlated to the sub-index. If house prices climb by 1%, residents' satisfaction will decrease by 16.70%; and if house-price-to-income ratio is up by 1%, residents' satisfaction will decline by 3.38%. Of the living environment factors, per capita green area and air quality both have a positive impact on residents' satisfaction with health conditions. If per capita green area increases by 1%, residents' satisfaction will go up by 0.06%; and if air quality improves by 1%, residents' satisfaction will rise by 0.26%. It can be seen from the regression results that per capita income is the primary positive influential factor of residents' satisfaction with health conditions, while house price is the most important negative factor. Improvement in per capita green area or air quality is of relatively insignificant impact. Income distribution inequality and the increase of house-price-to-income ratio will create psychological pressure on urban residents. They are also important factors, though not as impactful as house prices. Continuous improvement of transport capacity is supposed to make residents' life easier. However, probably due to the fact that the cities surveyed are all provincial capitals or developed cities where an overcrowded traffic system may lead to traffic jams and other problems, going out is often a stressful rather than pleasant experience despite the improvement in traffic capacity.

Table 9 Regression results of Model 1-3

Variable	Model 1		Model 2		Model 3	
	Coefficient	P value	Coefficient	P value	Coefficient	P value
Income	2.67	0.25	2.04	0.42	1.89	0.48
Gini	-4.56	0.14	-4.47	0.12	-4.80	0.12
Houseprice			-15.54	0.12	-16.70	0.12
Houseincomeratio			-3.22	0.10	-3.38	0.10
Trafficsupply					-4.43	0.36
Greenspace					0.06	0.91
Airquality					0.26	0.58
R^2	0.28		0.52		0.55	

4.4 Conclusions and suggestions

Based on the analysis of the sub-indices of the 35 cities in 2019 and the comparison of the changes in different regions and zones, the team made quantitative study on the influential factors of residents' satisfaction with health conditions.

4.4.1 Conclusions

The modern understanding of health has expanded beyond mere physical and mental health, and included good socio-economic adaptability and proper moral standards. As shown by the questionnaire survey, the mean health conditions sub-index has dropped to 57.26 in 2019, slightly above the threshold of the "good" interval (50). By region, the western region has seen the greatest decline and ranked last. Residents' satisfaction of the rest three regions has fallen at similar rates. Of the eight economic zones, the Southern

Coastal zone has seen the greatest improvement from the 8th to the 2nd place, while the Northern Coastal zone has experienced the quickest drop from the 1st to the 5th place. Rankings of the other zones have roughly remained the same.

It can be seen from the empirical analysis of the influential factors that, at present, house price has the greatest negative impact on residents' satisfaction, followed by the Gini coefficient, transport capacity and house-price-to-income ratio. The positive factors include per capita disposable income, per capita green area and air quality, of which per capita disposable income is the most important, and then air quality and per capita green area.

4.4.2 Suggestions

Based on the above analysis, it can be concluded that residents' satisfaction with health conditions can be improved by:

First, constantly increasing per capita disposable income. Since the reform and opening up, the per capita disposable income has been greatly improved, and the country has been on the fast track toward a well-off society. All this has laid a solid foundation for China to become a moderately developed country in the mid-21st century. To further increase the income of residents, the government might need to reinforce the reform, expand the opening up, eliminate the obstacles of the systems and mechanisms, and most importantly, stimulate the vitality of related elements through the structural reform on the supply side, in addition to the construction of the social security system. The report of the 19th CPC National Congress stated that to reinforce the construction of the social security system, it was necessary to develop a social security system that covered the entire population in both urban and rural areas, with clearly defined rights and responsibilities, and support that hits the

right level. In the report, President Xi stressed that the original aspiration and the mission of Chinese Communists was to seek happiness for the Chinese people and rejuvenation for the Chinese nation. This founding aspiration, this mission, was what inspired Chinese Communists to advance, to further improve the social security system and to constantly enhance people's sense of gain, in accordance with the general requirements of "ensuring people's access to childcare (maternity protection, including child welfare), education (education guarantee), employment (employment security, including wage income), housing (housing security), medical services (medical security), elderly care (old age security) and social assistance (poverty relief) ".

Second, improving urban greening and traffic conditions. As the per capita income increases, residents come to have higher requirements of the living environment and urban greening. The development and improvement of urban ecological environment helps to conserve moisture and soil, maintain ecological balance, absorb carbon dioxide and harmful gases, purify and improve the quality of air and regulate temperature and climate. It also provides a beautiful and tranquil leisure environment for residents to go back to nature, relieve stresses and uplift their mind and spirit. All this is of great help to the improvement of urban residents' satisfaction with health conditions. Moreover, with the development of the economy, the household car ownership is increasing as well, resulting in the urban problems of insufficient parking spaces and overcrowded traffic. It is therefore necessary to formulate long-term comprehensive traffic development plans for the cities, and promote multi-dimensional transport and parking garages, while rectifying traffic offences and raising the public awareness of traffic rules.

Third, stabilizing house prices and providing housing support through multiple channels. The government had better continue to firmly restrict

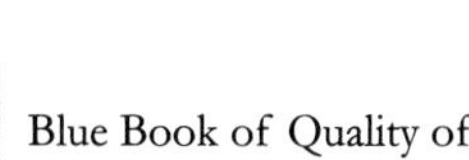

housing speculation to curb surging house prices. In the 2016 Central Economic Work Meeting, it was pointed out that housing was for accommodation rather than speculation. Since then, to curb excessive house prices and return housing to its original attributes, the government has even adopted administrative measures to effectively control the surging in house prices. At the 19th CPC National Congress, the State Council once again stressed this concept, and began to take measures to "ensure housing supply through multiple sources, provide housing support through multiple channels, and encourage both housing purchase and renting". In many places, attempts have been made in the effort to build a long-term development mechanism in the real estate market. Stable house prices can not only improve the living conditions of residents, but also are conducive to the development of the real economy and the realization of economic transformation in a higher sense.

To sum up, people's satisfaction with health conditions in essence depends on how happy they are with their own life and work. It is one of the goals of living-condition improvement. To seek happiness and physical / mental health for the Chinese people has always been a mission of the CPC and the government.

B.5

Report on the Medical Services Sub-indices of the 35 Cities

*Wang Yu**

Abstract: Improving medical services and the health conditions of the Chinese people has become a national strategy. Quality and efficient medical services are the guarantee and pathway to ensure that all the people get all-round and full-cycle healthcare. According to the questionnaire survey on medical service satisfaction, the 2019 weighted mean of the medical services sub-indies of the 35 cities is 63.04, between "acceptable" (50) and "good" (75), but slightly lower than that of 2018 (65.31). Based on the analysis of the four categories of related influential factors, the regression results show that the positive factors include per capita disposable income, medical care capacity and basic medical insurance coverage, while the negative factors are the Gini coefficient and the number of physically / mentally unhealthy days in the past 30 days. It is therefore suggested that the government might need to improve the medical care capacity steadily and expand the utilization of quality medical

* Prof. Wang Yu, PhD, from School of Economics of CUEB, specializes in the study of economic growth and economic cycle.

service resources, while increasing and stabilizing the coverage of basic medical insurance, and doing a good job in the use and management of insurance funds.

Keywords: Satisfaction with Medical Services; Medical Care Capacity; Basic Medical Insurance Coverage; Allocation of Quality Healthcare Resources to Small Towns and Rural Areas

5.1 Introduction

At the 2016 National Health Conference, President Xi introduced the concept of "comprehensive health".① In the report of the 19th CPC National Congress, the State Council presented the road map of "Healthy China", and further specified that the core of comprehensive health was to "provide all-round and full-cycle healthcare services for the people", and that the health and longevity of the Chinese people were important indicators of national prosperity. To ensure the realization of the comprehensive health strategy, the General Office of the State Council (GOSC) released the "Key Tasks for Deepening the Reform of the Healthcare System (2017)" on May 5 2017, and listed 70 tasks of building a basic healthcare system with Chinese characteristics. The report of the 19th CPC National Congress also further pointed out the need to develop and improve four major healthcare systems - public healthcare system, medical service system, medical security system and drug supply system - so as to ensure

① "President Xi's Speech at the National Health Conference Sparks Heated Discussion," XINHUANET.com, Aug 21 2016, http://www.xinhuanet.com/politics/2016-08/21/c_1119428119.htm?from=singlemessage&isappinstalled=0.

that the healthcare system with Chinese characteristics provided "quality and efficient medical services". It can be seen that improving medical services and the health conditions of the Chinese people has become a national strategy.

To study the satisfaction with medical services, the team needs to first get to know how satisfied people are. Using data from different sources and multiple research methods, scholars have conducted extensive research on the medical service satisfaction of patients at different levels, in different regions and of different stages in the patient journey as well as the related influential factors. According to their findings, residents' satisfaction with medical services varies between relatively "unsatisfied" to relatively "satisfied". It can be observed that great differences exist in the medical service satisfaction among different population groups or regions, and between urban and rural areas. The influential factors may also vary, but all the scholars agreed that there was room for improvement. Therefore, it is necessary to further track residents' satisfaction with medical services and its influential factors.

5.2 Analysis of medical services sub-indices

The micro data of residents' assessment of medical services were obtained based on the answers to Q18-20 in the survey questionnaire. The value range of Q19-20 is 0~100. The higher the value, the better the satisfaction.

18. In the past year, have you visited hospital(s) or clinic(s) because of your own health problems or accompanying your relative(s) / friend(s) (please choose the latest experience)?

19. Considering your latest medical experience (your own or when accompanying your relative(s) / friend(s)), were you satisfied with the service of the healthcare provider (including diagnosis & treatment, service attitude

and medical environment)?

20. In general, are you satisfied with the non-reimbursable part of the medical insurance?

The medical services sub-indices of the 35 cities in 2019 can be obtained by calculating the weighted mean of the answers to the above questions designed on the basis of the 5-point Likert scale.

5.2.1 Descriptive statistics

Table 1 summarizes the descriptive statistics on the 2019 medical services sub-indices. In 2019, the sub-indices range from 59.16 to 66.79, and the mean is 63.04, while in 2018, the values ranged from 53.91 to 70.58, and the mean was 65.31. Compared to that of last year, the minimum value has increased, while the maximum and the mean values have decreased, indicating a decline in residents' overall satisfaction. From statistical distribution, the variance of the 2019 sub-index is 3.93, and the standard deviation 1.98, while in 2018, the variance was 13.95, and the standard deviation 3.73. It can be observed that the dispersion of the sub-indices has narrowed among the 35 cities. As shown in Figure 1, in terms of skewness and kurtosis values, the skewness is below zero (left-skewed) in both years, indicating that the sub-indices of most cities are above the mean value. The fact that the distribution kurtosis of the 2018 sub-indices is steeper than that of 2019 shows that less respondents are satisfied with medical services this year.

Table 1 Descriptive statistics on medical services sub-indices (2018-2019)

Year	Min	Max	Mean	Variance	Standard deviation	Skewness	Kurtosis
2018	53.91	70.58	65.31	13.95	3.73	-0.65	0.61
2019	59.16	66.79	63.04	3.93	1.98	-0.04	-0.80

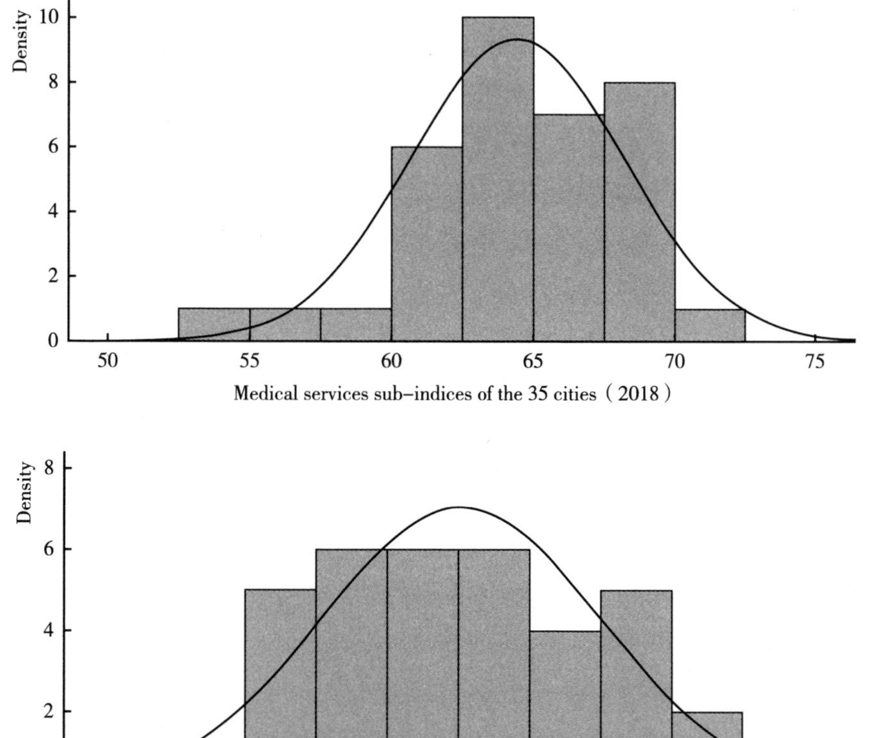

Figure 1 Histogram of medical services sub-indices (2018-2019)

5.2.2 Comparison among different cities and regions

Figure 2 summarizes the changes of the medical services sub-indices of the 35 cities in 2018-2019. Overall, the directions of change are not consistent among all the cities. Residents' satisfaction has dropped in Kunming (-13.06%), Harbin (-11.61%), Taiyuan (-11.11%), Shenzhen (-10.94%), Guiyang (-10.14%), Qingdao (-9.98%), Dalian (-9.57%), Changchun (-9.20%), Hefei (-6.07%), Tianjin (-5.18%), Fuzhou (-4.94%), Chengdu (-4.54%), Hohhot

(-4.45%), Xi'an (-3.78%), Jinan (-3.72%), Changsha (-3.11%), Shanghai (-2.56%), Zhengzhou (-1.47%), Xiamen (-1.42%), Beijing (-1.35%), Nanning (-1.20%), Wuhan (-0.12%) and Xining (-0.09%); while improved in Hangzhou (+22.29%), Guangzhou (+8.51%), Yinchuan (+8.40%), Shijiazhuang (+6.05%), Nanjing (+4.88%), Nanchang (+4.43%), Ningbo (+4.14%), Shenyang (+3.39%), Haikou (+1.77%), Urumqi (+1.59%), Chongqing (+1.19%) and Lanzhou (+0.69%). As the satisfaction has decreased in most cities, the sub-index of medical services has declined as a whole.

Of the four regions, as shown in Table 2, the eastern region (63.8) is of the highest satisfaction with medical services in 2019, followed by the central (63.4), the western (62.5) and the northeastern regions (61.0). In 2018, the northeastern region (65.5) came 1st, and the eastern region (63.8) came last. Compared to that of 2018, the eastern and the northeastern regions have swapped places, while the central and the western regions have stayed where they were. The reason for this is that the sub-index of the northeastern region has dropped greatly this year, and that of the eastern region has remained the same.

Table 2 Mean medical services sub-indices of the four regions

Ranking in 2018	Region	Mean	Ranking in 2019	Region	Mean
1	Northeastern	65.5	1	Eastern	63.8
2	Central	65.4	2	Central	63.4
3	Western	64.2	3	Western	62.5
4	Eastern	63.8	4	Northeastern	61.0

As shown in Figure 3, except in the eastern region, residents' satisfaction with medical services has significantly declined in all the other three regions, especially in the northeastern region (-6.9%). The sub-indices of the central and the western regions have decreased by 3.1% and 2.6%, respectively.

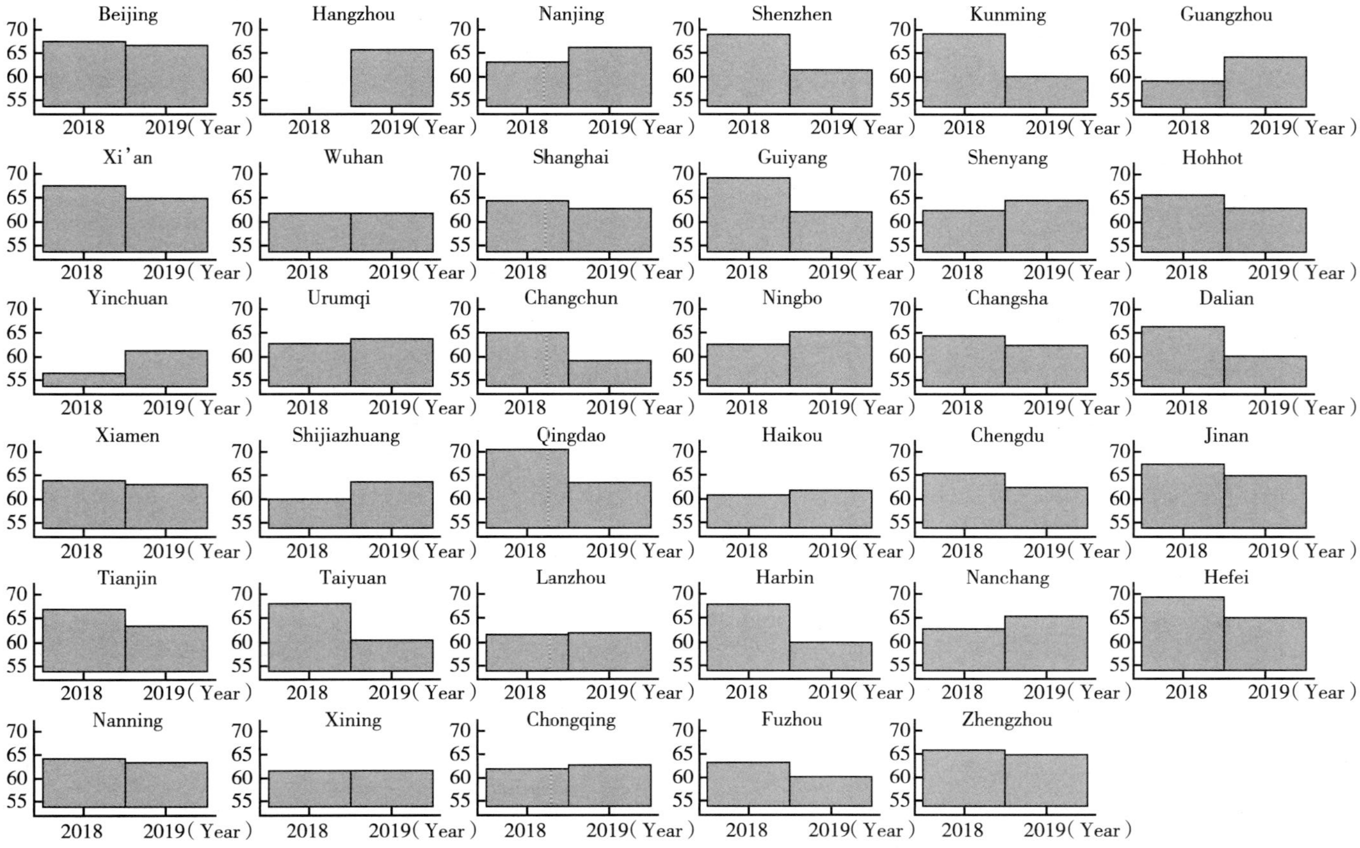

Beijing | Hangzhou | Nanjing | Shenzhen | Kunming | Guangzhou

Xi'an | Wuhan | Shanghai | Guiyang | Shenyang | Hohhot

Yinchuan | Urumqi | Changchun | Ningbo | Changsha | Dalian

Xiamen | Shijiazhuang | Qingdao | Haikou | Chengdu | Jinan

Tianjin | Taiyuan | Lanzhou | Harbin | Nanchang | Hefei

Nanning | Xining | Chongqing | Fuzhou | Zhengzhou

(Axes: 55, 60, 65, 70; 2018, 2019(Year))

Figure 2　Changes in medical services sub-index by city (2018-2019)

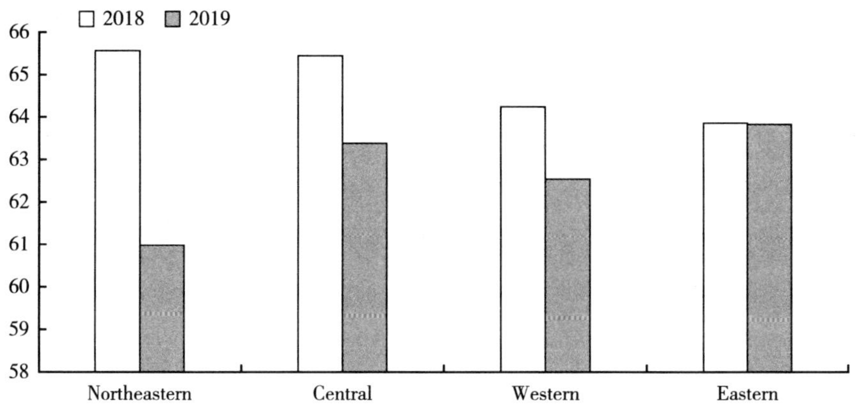

Figure 3 Changes in medical services sub-index by region (2018-2019)

Of the eight economic zones, as shown in Table 3, residents of the Eastern Coastal zone (65.1) are the most satisfied in 2019, followed by those in the Northern Coastal (64.5), the Middle Yangtze River (63.7), the Middle Yellow River (63.4), the Great Northwest (62.2), the Great Southwest (62.2), the Southern Coastal (62.2) and the Northeast China zones (61.0). The Great Northwest, the Great Southwest and the Southern Coastal zones are of equal index values.

Table 3 Comparison of mean medical services sub-indices of the eight integrated economic zones (2018-2019)

Ranking in 2018	Economic zone	Mean	Ranking in 2019	Economic zone	Mean
1	Middle Yellow River	66.9	1	Eastern Coastal	65.1
2	Northern Coastal	66.6	2	Northern Coastal	64.5
3	Great Southwest	66.0	3	Middle Yangtze River	63.7
4	Northeast China	65.5	4	Middle Yellow River	63.4
5	Middle Yangtze River	64.6	5	Great Northwest	62.2
6	Southern Coastal	63.3	6	Great Southwest	62.2
7	Eastern Coastal	61.1	7	Southern Coastal	62.2
8	Great Northwest	60.7	8	Northeast China	61.0

Compared to that of 2018, as shown in Figure 4, the medical services sub-indices of the Eastern Coastal (+6.5%) and the Great Northwest (+2.5%) zones have gone up this year. Of all the other zones, the Northeast China zone has experienced the greatest decline, followed by the Great Southwest (-5.76%), the Middle Yellow River (-5.23%), the Northern Coastal (-3.15%), the Southern Coastal (-1.74%) and the Middle Yangtze River zones (-1.39%).

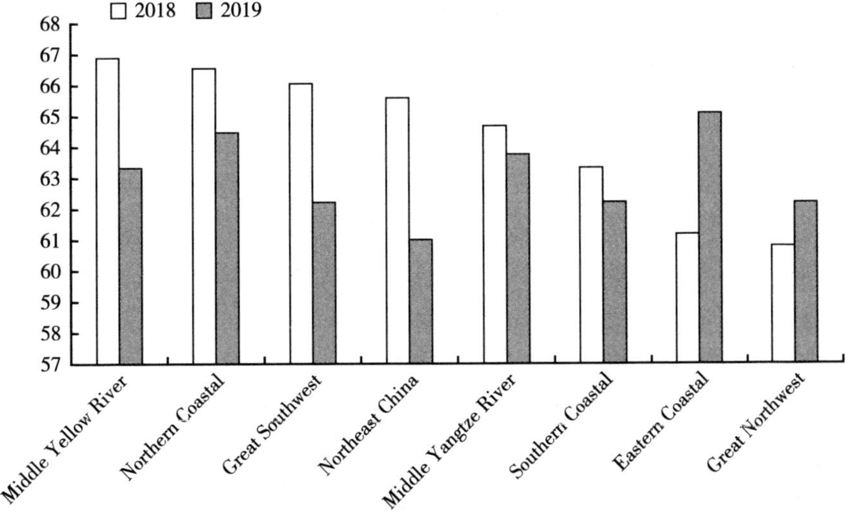

Figure 4 Changes in medical services sub-index by economic zone (2018-2019)

It can be seen from the above comparison that by city, the satisfaction with medical services has dropped in most cities; by region, the sub-indices of the four regions have generally declined; and by economic zone, the satisfaction has decreased in all but two zones. As a whole, the sub-indices range from 60 to 70, that is, in the "satisfied" interval. Obviously, there is still room for improvement in this aspect.

5.3 Analysis of influential factors

To explain the low and declining satisfaction among residents and make corresponding suggestions, further empirical analysis was conducted on the influential factors of the sub-index.

Zhao Dahai studied the trust of the Chinese people in the healthcare system and its influential factors. It was found that only 25.12% of the respondents trusted the healthcare system, and that the influential factors included the satisfaction with medical services and the trust in the government. It was also observed that the Chinese public was of high government trust and low medical service satisfaction. The former had a positive impact on the trust in the healthcare system, and the latter was an important factor that dragged down the trust.① Zhai Yufei et al. investigated the medical service satisfaction in Haikou with the stratified sampling telephone survey approach. Of the 872 respondents, the overall satisfaction was 76.37%. The urban residents were most satisfied than the rural ones, and the satisfaction of residents in different administrative districts varied greatly.②

Residents' satisfaction with medical services are in fact affected by many factors. Extensive empirical studies have been conducted in this regard. Xu Guanglu and Shen Huizhang studied the effects of basic medical insurance on basic medical services and social conflicts with the CGSS (2008) data. The results showed that the three basic medical insurances had positive effects on improving residents' satisfaction with medical services and eliminating social

---

① Zhao Dahai, "Determinants of Public Trust in Health Care System in China," *Journal of Zhejiang University* 1 (2019): 67~79.

② Zhai Yufei et al, "Investigation of Residents Awareness Rate and Satisfaction on Basic Public Health Services in Haikou," *Chinese Journal of Public Health Management* 2 (2019): 153~156.

conflicts, especially the New Cooperative Medical System (NCMS). The Basic Medical Insurance for Urban Employees was of the second greatest impact, and the one for urban residents was of the most insignificant impact.① Wang Xiaoyan and Hang Dan looked into the effect of the tripartite (medical insurance, medical treatment and medicine) system on medical service satisfaction under the background of the new healthcare reform. It was found that in the tripartite system, medical treatment was the primary influential factor of medical service satisfaction, while the other two factors had positive effects as well.② Fan Jingbo used the SEM to study the perceptual structure of medical services, and concluded that there was still a lot of room for improvement in residents' satisfaction with medical services as a whole.③ Lei Xiansheng used the CGSS 2015 data to compare the influential factors of medical service satisfaction in urban and rural areas, and found that the primary factor of urban residents' satisfaction was the adequacy of healthcare resources, while the most important factor to rural residents was the easy access to medical services. The reason for the difference lied not in the disparity of healthcare resource allocation between urban and rural areas, but in the influence of policies. The coverage of basic medical insurance was the primary factor, especially for urban residents. The fairness of policy

---

① Xu Guanglu, Shen Huizhang, "The Basic Medical Insurance System's Effects on Satisfaction to the Basic Health Service and Sense of Social Conflict," *Insurance Studies* 2 (2015): 117~127.

② Wang Xiaoyan, Hang Dan, "An Analysis on Factors Influencing Health Reform Medical Service Satisfaction Based on the Structural Equation Model," *Mathematics in Practice and Theory* 11 (2016): 83-89.

③ Fan Jingbo, "Research on the Perceptual Structure of Current Resident Satisfaction with Public Healthcare Services," *Journal of East China Normal University (Philosophy and Social Sciences)* 6 (2018): 163~177.

was involved.[①] Xu Ning et al. analyzed the factors that affected residents' satisfaction with medical services, based on the data in the "public medical services" section of the CGSS 2013 Questionnaire A. It was concluded that Chinese residents in urban and rural areas perceived the medical services to be "acceptable", and the related influential factors included income, education, endowment insurance and mental health in four weeks.[②]

Wang Baoqian and Li Ziwei studied rural residents' satisfaction with medical services based on the CGSS 2015 data. It was observed that income, self-assessed health, social insurance coverage and Internet use had positive impacts on the satisfaction, and that in terms of regional distribution, residents of the eastern region were more satisfied than those of the central region.[③]

Studies have also been made on the medical service satisfaction in healthcare providers of different levels (e.g., hospitals, community healthcare centers) and in different regions. Dai Shiyuan et al. used the sixth health service survey data of Jiangsu Province to investigate the medical service satisfaction of inpatients. The overall satisfaction rate was 76%, and the influencing factors included household income, reimbursement rate, and quality of diagnosis & treatment.[④] Wang Mengyuan et al. measured patients'

---

① Lei Xiansheng, "Study on the Satisfaction of Medical Services between Urban and Rural Residents," *Journal of Agrotechnical Economics* 4 (2019): 16~28.

② Xu Ning et al., "Satisfaction of Urban and Rural Residents with Medical and Health Services in China Based on a Social Survey," *China Medical Administration Sciences* 3 (2019): 61~66.

③ Wang Baoqian, Li Ziwei, "Study on the Influencing Factors of Rural Residents' Satisfaction with Healthcare Services," *Medicine and Society* 7 (2019): 28~31.

④ Dai Shiyuan, Gu Xinyue, Xu Aijun, "Analysis of the Service Satisfaction of Inpatient and Its Influencing Factors - Based on the Sixth Health Service Survey Data of Jiangsu Province," *Health Economics Research* 11 (2019): 41~43.

non-medical service satisfaction of 3A hospitals in Nanjing City, and found that the 820 respondents were generally satisfied in this regard.① Shao Hongyan and Wang Xi conducted a questionnaire survey on residents' satisfaction with medical services in the Hebei neighborhood healthcare center of Jiangchuan Road block association, Minhang District, Shanghai. Based on a sample of 540 cases, it was concluded that the patients as a whole were quite satisfied, but there was still room for improvement.②

4.2.1 Regression model

Combining the survey finding with existing studies, the reasons for the overall decline in medical service satisfaction (*Medicalsatisfaction*) in 2019 can be grouped into four categories: first, economic factors (income level and income gap); second, medical care capacity (No. of medical practitioners / 10,000 residents, No. of hospital beds / 10,000 residents and No. of hospitals / 10,000 residents); third, social security (basic medical insurance coverage); and fourth, individual difference in health conditions (recent self-assessment of physical and mental health). The independent variables chosen for the regression model include: per capita disposable income growth (*Incomegrowth*), the Gini coefficient (*Gini*), medical care capacity (*Medicalsupply*), basic medical insurance coverage (*Medicains*), the number of physically unhealthy days in the past 30 days (*Physicalhealth*) and the number of mentally unhealthy days in the past 30 days (*Mentalhealth*). The regression model built is as follows:

---

① Wang Mengyuan et al., "Factor Analysis of Out-Patient's Satisfaction on Non-Technical Service of Third-Grade Class-A Hospitals in Nanjing City," *Medicine and Society* 3 (2019): 95~111.

② Shao Hongyan, Wang Xi, "Research on Resident Satisfaction with Medical Services in a Neighborhood Center in Shanghai," *Chongqing Medicine* 6 (2019): 2133~2135.

$$Medicalsatisfaction = a + \beta_1\ Incomegrowth + \beta_2\ Gini + \beta_3 Medicalsupply + \beta_4 Medicalins + \beta_5\ Physicalhealth + \beta_6 Mentalhealth + \varepsilon$$

Based on the regression results, the team was able to analyze the influence of the above factors and provide effective suggestions accordingly.

5.3.2 Analysis of variables

The data used in the regression model came from the official website of the National Bureau of Statistics, *China City Statistical Yearbook*, *China Health and Family Planning Statistics Yearbook* and the CNKI China Statistical Yearbooks Database (CSYD). To facilitate analysis and comparison, all the data were standardized to obtain the corresponding indices. Table 4 summarizes the values of the independent variables in the equation and the rankings of the 35 cities in 2019 (the Gini coefficient and basic medical insurance coverage are no longer listed).

In 2019, the top 5 cities with the highest per capita disposable income growth are: Tianjin (1.44), Shenyang (1.28), Urumqi (1.22), Hefei (1.10) and Wuhan (1.09). The bottom 5 cities are: Nanchang (0.84), Shenzhen (0.82), Xi'an (0.69), Dalian (0.65) and Chengdu (0.56). The cities ranked 6th – 30th are: Guiyang (1.09), Xiamen (1.07), Nanjing (1.07), Hangzhou (1.06), Shanghai (1.06), Fuzhou (1.05), Haikou (1.05), Chongqing (1.04), Zhengzhou (1.04), Lanzhou (1.04), Guangzhou (1.04), Changsha (1.03), Xining (1.03), Ningbo (1.02), Kunming (1.02), Shijiazhuang (1.02), Yinchuan (1.02), Qingdao (1.01), Jinan (0.99), Hohhot (0.96), Taiyuan (0.96), Changchun (0.93), Harbin (0.93), Nanning (0.91) and Beijing (0.84).

The top 5 cities with the greatest medical care capacity are: Xining (2.17),

Chengdu (1.79), Kunming (1.44), Hefei (1.35) and Urumqi (1.33). The bottom 5 cities are: Nanjing (0.68), Xiamen (0.61), Shanghai (0.58), Ningbo (0.58) and Shenzhen (0.40). The cities ranked 6th – 30th are: Guiyang (1.26), Nanchang (1.24), Lanzhou (1.19), Taiyuan (1.19), Yinchuan (1.17), Changsha (1.09), Shenyang (1.05), Xi'an (1.04), Chongqing (1.02), Changchun (1.00), Qingdao (0.97), Hangzhou (0.96), Harbin (0.90), Jinan (0.89), Nanning (0.88), Fuzhou (0.87), Beijing (0.87), Haikou (0.86), Wuhan (0.84), Dalian (0.84), Tianjin (0.82), Guangzhou (0.82), Shijiazhuang (0.80), Hohhot (0.76) and Zhengzhou (0.75). It can be seen from the rankings that densely-populated cities are of lower capacity and limited resources, in terms of medical care capacity as measured by per capita healthcare resources, and vice versa.

The top 5 cities with the most physically unhealthy days are: Xining (4.44), Urumqi (3.71), Hohhot (3.51), Dalian (3.44) and Changchun (3.40). The bottom 5 cities are: Xiamen (2.32), Chengdu (2.30), Nanjing (2.27), Ningbo (2.25) and Shenzhen (2.25). The cities ranked 6th – 30th are: Yinchuan (3.34), Shenyang (3.31), Haikou (3.31), Lanzhou (3.30), Taiyuan (3.07), Changsha (3.05), Kunming (3.05), Nanning (3.03), Harbin (3.01), Shijiazhuang (2.92), Beijing (2.85), Guiyang (2.84), Shanghai (2.79), Qingdao (2.76), Guangzhou (2.75), Tianjin (2.72), Chongqing (2.70), Xi'an (2.63), Zhengzhou (2.55), Hangzhou (2.52), Jinan (2.49), Wuhan (2.47), Fuzhou (2.43), Hefei (2.39) and Nanchang (2.36). In general, residents in the less developed areas feel physically unwell more often than those in the better developed areas.

The top 5 cities with the most mentally unhealthy days are: Urumqi (6.86), Shijiazhuang (5.95), Hohhot (5.91), Harbin (5.88) and Yinchuan (5.73). The bottom 5 cities are: Guangzhou (4.52), Ningbo (4.46), Fuzhou (4.31), Xiamen (4.26) and Wuhan (4.14). The cities ranked 6th – 30th are: Xining

(5.67), Changchun (5.63), Guiyang (5.56), Kunming (5.45), Beijing (5.43), Tianjin (5.43), Lanzhou (5.37), Shenyang (5.29), Taiyuan (5.24), Dalian (5.22), Chengdu (5.21), Nanning (5.14), Xi'an (5.14), Zhengzhou (5.04), Qingdao (5.03), Nanchang (5.01), Haikou (4.95), Chongqing (4.93), Hefei (4.85), Hangzhou (4.83), Changsha (4.76), Shenzhen (4.72), Nanjing (4.69), Shanghai (4.63) and Jinan (4.61). It can be observed that urban residents in the developed areas have better mental health than those in the less developed areas.

Table 5 presents the descriptive statistics of the variables. The minimum value of per capita disposable income growth is 0.56. The maximum value is 1.44. The standard deviation is 0.16. And the kurtosis is of a positive and relatively large value. All this indicates that the values of different cities vary greatly. As for medical care capacity, the mean value is 1.00. The minimum is 0.40. The maximum value is 2.17. The standard deviation is 0.34. In terms of value distribution, there is a significant difference between the two ends.

Table 4 Values and rankings of explanatory variables (2019)

	City	Perc capita disposable income growth		Medical care capacity		No. of physically unhealthy days in the past 30 days		No. of mentally healthy days in the past 30 days	
		Value	Ranking	Value	Ranking	Value	Ranking	Value	Ranking
1	Beijing	0.84	30	0.87	22	2.85	16	5.43	10
2	Tianjin	1.44	1	0.82	26	2.72	21	5.43	11
3	Shijiazhuang	1.02	21	0.80	28	2.92	15	5.95	2
4	Taiyuan	0.96	26	1.19	9	3.07	10	5.24	14
5	Hohhot	0.96	25	0.76	29	3.51	3	5.91	3
6	Shenyang	1.28	2	1.05	12	3.31	7	5.29	13
7	Changchun	0.93	27	1.00	15	3.40	5	5.63	7

Continued

	City	Perc capita disposable income growth		Medical care capacity		No. of physically unhealthy days in the past 30 days		No. of mentally healthy days in the past 30 days	
		Value	Ranking	Value	Ranking	Value	Ranking	Value	Ranking
8	Harbin	0.93	28	0.90	18	3.01	14	5.88	4
9	Shanghai	1.06	10	0.58	33	2.79	18	4.63	29
10	Nanjing	1.07	8	0.68	31	2.27	33	4.69	28
11	Hangzhou	1.06	9	0.96	17	2.52	25	4.83	25
12	Hefei	1.10	4	1.35	4	2.39	29	4.85	24
13	Fuzhou	1.05	11	0.87	21	2.43	28	4.31	33
14	Nanchang	0.84	31	1.24	7	2.36	30	5.01	21
15	Jinan	0.99	24	0.89	19	2.49	26	4.61	30
16	Zhengzhou	1.04	14	0.75	30	2.55	24	5.04	19
17	Wuhan	1.09	5	0.84	24	2.47	27	4.14	35
18	Changsha	1.03	17	1.09	11	3.05	11	4.76	26
19	Guangzhou	1.04	16	0.82	27	2.75	20	4.52	31
20	Nanning	0.91	29	0.88	20	3.03	13	5.14	17
21	Haikou	1.05	12	0.86	23	3.31	8	4.95	22
22	Chongqing	1.04	13	1.02	14	2.70	22	4.93	23
23	Chengdu	0.56	35	1.79	2	2.30	32	5.21	16
24	Guiyang	1.09	6	1.26	6	2.84	17	5.56	8
25	Kunming	1.02	20	1.44	3	3.05	12	5.45	9
26	Xi'an	0.69	33	1.04	13	2.63	23	5.14	18
27	Lanzhou	1.04	15	1.19	8	3.30	9	5.37	12
28	Xining	1.03	18	2.17	1	4.44	1	5.67	6
29	Yinchuan	1.02	22	1.17	10	3.34	6	5.73	5
30	Urumqi	1.22	3	1.33	5	3.71	2	6.86	1
31	Dalian	0.65	34	0.84	25	3.44	4	5.22	15
32	Ningbo	1.02	19	0.58	34	2.25	34	4.46	32
33	Xiamen	1.07	7	0.61	32	2.32	31	4.26	34
34	Qingdao	1.01	23	0.97	16	2.76	19	5.03	20
35	Shenzhen	0.82	32	0.40	35	2.25	35	4.72	27

Table 5 shows the standardized data of the explanatory variable and the explanatory variables used in the model.

Table 5 Regression variables and descriptive statistics

Type	Variable	Abbreviation	Mean	Standard deviation	Min	Max
Explained variable	Satisfaction with medical services	*Medicalsatisfaction*	63.01	1.98	59.16	66.79
Explanatory variable	Per capita disposable income growth	*Incomegrowth*	1.00	0.16	0.56	1.44
	Gini coefficient	*Gini*	1.00	0.17	0.79	1.32
	Medical care capacity	*Medicalsupply*	1.00	0.34	0.40	2.17
	Basic medical insurance coverage	*Medicalins*	1.05	0.53	0.29	2.26
	No. of physically unhealthy days in the past 30 days	*Physicalhealth*	2.87	0.49	2.25	4.44
	No. of mentally unhealthy days in the past 30 days	*Mentalhealth*	5.14	0.56	4.14	6.86

5.3.3 Discussion of results

Based on the above analysis, the variables in Table 5 fall into four categories, corresponding to the four models: Model 1 (economic factors) - per capita disposable income growth (*Incomegrowth*) and the Gini coefficient (*Gini*); Model 2 (medical supply) - medical care capacity (*Medicalsupply*); Model 3 (social security) - basic medical insurance coverage (*Medicalins*); and Model 4 (individual difference in health conditions) - the number of physically unhealthy days in the past 30 days (*Physicalhealth*) and the number of mentally unhealthy days in the past 30 days (*Mentalhealth*).

Table 6 presents the regression results of the models. The qualitative

conclusions of the four models are basically consistent. That is, per capita disposable income growth, medical care capacity and basic medical insurance coverage play a positive role in the improvement of medical service satisfaction, while the Gini coefficient and the number of physically / mentally unhealthy days have a negative correlation with it. According to the regression results of Model 4, income factors are of the greatest impact, followed by self-assessed health, per capita healthcare resources and basic medical insurance coverage. If per capita disposable income rises by 1%, medical service satisfaction will go up by 2.930%. If the Gini coefficient increases by 1%, residents' satisfaction will drop by 4.003%. Obviously, the latter has a greater impact than the former. In terms of medical supply and security, if medical care capacity improves by 1%, residents' satisfaction will climb by 0.655%. If basic medical insurance coverage increases by 1%, residents' satisfaction will rise by 0.146%. The former is a more important influential factor than the latter. As for self-assessed health, if the number of physically unhealthy days increases by 1%, the satisfaction will decrease by 2.430%, and if the number of mentally unhealthy days rises by 1%, the satisfaction will drop by 0.964%. It can be seen that the self-assessment of physical health is of greater impact than that of mental health.

Table 6　Regression results of Model 1-4

Variable	Model 1		Model 2		Model 3		Model 4	
	Coefficient	P value	Coefficient	P value	Coefficient	P value	Coefficient	P value
Incomegrowth	1.990	0.330	1.858	0.3672	1.948	0.368	2.930	0.154
Gini	-4.084	0.044	-3.843	0.07	-3.820	0.730	-4.003	0.047
Medicalsupply			0.507	0.06	0.408	0.720	0.655	0.577
Medicalins					0.143	0.845	0.146	0.829
Physicalhealth							-2.430	0.012
Mentalhealth							-0.964	0.215
R^2	0.371		0.381		0.382		0.571	

5.4 Conclusions and Enlightenments

China has long faced a shortage of healthcare resources, especially in cities with a large population where the problems of medical accessibility and affordability become even more prominent. Medical services have been of great concern to the CPC and the state leaders, as the level and quality of medical services are the fundamental guarantee for the health and longevity of the people, and an important content of the equalization of social public services. In July 2019, the State Council issued the "Healthy China 2030" blueprint, and called for the strengthening of the public health services covering the entire population. Specific measures included the prevention and control of major infectious and chronic diseases, and the equalization of basic public services. It was also pointed out that to provide quality and efficient medical services, it was necessary to upgrade the medical service system. The healthcare system around China has been fully committed to the strategic deployment of the CPC Central Committee and the State Council, and to the upgrading of medical care capacity and disease prevention capability. As a result, the health conditions of infants and the elderly have been effectively improved, as well as the ability of disease prevention and control. All this has helped to boost residents' health. According to *China Health Development Statistics Bulletin* (2018), the life expectancy of Chinese residents was 76.7 in 2017, and increased to 77.0 in 2018, while the infant mortality decreased from 6.8‰ to 6.1‰. The maternal mortality also declined significantly at the same time. It proves that China's medical services have played an important role in the healthy development of the population.

5.4.1 Conclusions

As shown in the 2019 questionnaire survey on medical service satisfaction, residents' satisfaction has declined compared to the results of 2018. The maximum value of the sub-index has dropped, but the minimum value has risen significantly from 53.91 in 2018 to 59.16 in 2019. It can thus be concluded that despite the decrease in residents' average satisfaction, the minimum satisfaction level has gone up, which indicates that urban medical services in China have improved to a certain extent.

As to individual difference, in terms of age, the sub-index values of the 20-29, the 30-39 and the ≥40 age groups are 65.16, 63.08 and 59.95, respectively. It can be observed that the older residents are less satisfied with the medical services. The reason for this may be that the older residents get sick and go to hospital more often than the younger ones, and are thus more intensely affected by the objective factors such as long waiting time, medical burden and limited access to drugs per visit. In terms of gender, the value of the females is 63.53, and that of the males is 64.32. That is, the female residents have lower satisfaction than the males. In terms of education, the value of the residents without a bachelor's degree is 61.93, while the values of the group with a bachelor's degree and the group with at least a master's degree are 63.94 and 65.68, respectively. It can be seen that the better educated residents are more satisfied with the medical services.

Of the 35 cities, residents of most cities have lower satisfaction with the medical services this year. Of the four regions, except in the eastern region where residents' satisfaction has remained the same, the satisfaction has declined in all the rest three regions, especially in the northeastern region. Of the eight integrated economic zones, the sub-indices of the Eastern

Coastal and the Great Northwest zones have improved this year. The former has seen a quicker rise of 6.55%. The sub-indices of all the rest six zones have declined. Northeast China (-6.87%) has experienced the greatest drop, followed by that of the Great Southwest (-5.76%).

To explain the decline in medical service satisfaction in 2019, it is necessary to determine and further analyze the factors of positive or negative impacts. Based on the above literature review, per capita disposable income growth and the Gini coefficient are chosen as the income factors to represent the aspects of income level and income gap. Medical care capacity is selected as the medical supply factor, consisting of three indicators that reflect the amount of per capita healthcare resources - the number of medical practitioners / 10,000 residents, the number of hospital beds / 10,000 residents and the number of hospitals / 10,000 residents. Basic medical insurance coverage is the factor used to illustrate the cost burden of residents receiving medical services. Finally, the numbers of physically / mentally unhealthy days in the past 30 days are adopted to reflect individual conditions. It can be seen from the regression results that the economic factors are of the greatest impacts, followed by the self-assessed health factors (No. of physically / mentally unhealthy days in the past 30 days). The worse the self-assessed health, the higher the expectation of health improvement after medical services, and the lower the satisfaction. Medical care capacity and basic medical insurance coverage are of less influence.

5.4.2 Enlightenments

According to the above regression results, the positive influential factors include per capita disposable income growth, medical care capacity and basic medical insurance coverage. Among them, per capita disposable

income growth is an economic factor and can only be achieved at the macroeconomic level. Therefore, to the healthcare industry itself, the most important action to raise the resident satisfaction is to improve the level and capacity of medical services. It is also necessary to increase and stabilize basic medical insurance coverage from within the state-run social security system, and to do a good job in the use and management of medical insurance funds.

Firstly, the government might need to expand the medical care capacity steadily. In October 2016, the State Council issued the "Healthy China 2030" blueprint, and called for the strengthening of the public health services covering the entire population. Specific measures included the prevention and control of major infectious and chronic diseases, and the equalization of basic public services. Meanwhile, to provide quality and efficient medical services, it was also necessary to upgrade the medical service system. According to *China Health Development Statistics Bulletin* (2018), there were 33,009 hospitals in China in 2018, along with 943,639 primary care units and 18,033 professional public health agencies. Compared with that of the previous year, the number of hospitals and primary care units increased by 1,953 and 10,615 respectively, while the number of public health agencies decreased by 1,862. Of the primary care units, there were 34,997 neighborhood healthcare centers, 36,461 township health centers, 228,019 clinics and infirmaries, and 622,001 village clinics. 121,918 of these units were run by the government. Figure 5 shows the composition and number of healthcare providers across the country in 2014-2018. It can be observed that the number of providers had been increasing during the period.

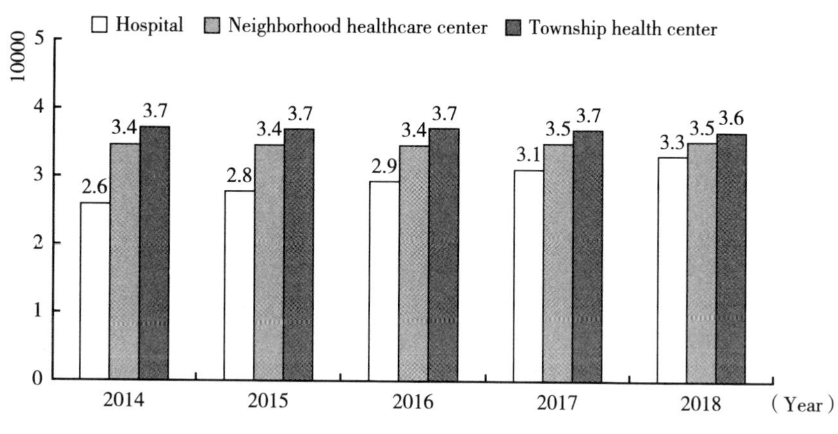

Figure 5 Number of healthcare providers nationwide (2014-2018)

Source: *China Health Development Statistics Bulletin* (2018).

As healthcare providers increase, the number of beds provided also continued to rise in 2014-2018. As shown in Figure 6, there were a total of 8.404 million beds in 2018 – an YoY growth of 464,000 beds (+5.8%), and the number of beds / 1,000 persons also went up from 5.72 to 6.03.

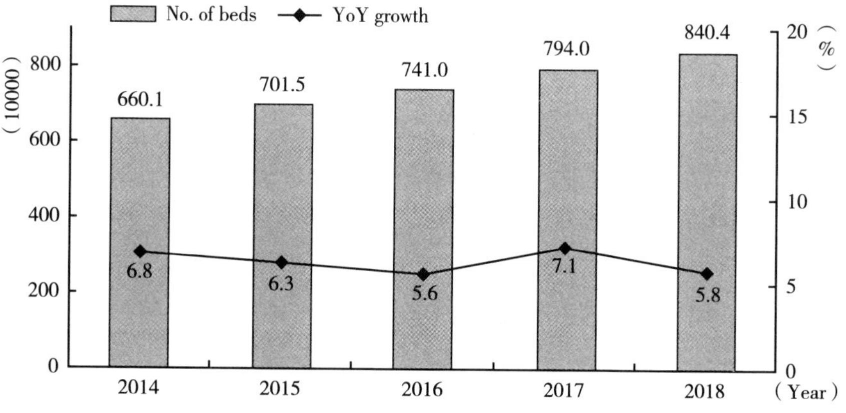

Figure 6 Number of hospital beds nationwide (2014-2018)

Source: *China Health Development Statistics Bulletin* (2018).

As shown in Table 7, in 2018, the national workload of medical services increased to 8.31 billion patients. The number of inpatients also increased from 244.36 million in 2017 to 254.53 million.

To reduce the waiting and queuing time of patients, by the end of 2018, 45.4% of the public hospitals of class-2 or above launched the medical appointment system, along with telemedical and quality care services, to ensure and improve the quality of healthcare.

It can be observed that to enhance the overall health of the Chinese people, and to improve and upgrade the quality of medical services, the CPC and the government have continuously invested in the hardware and fundamentally changed the conditions of healthcare provision. The total numbers of healthcare professionals (HCPs) and hospital beds both increased in 2017-2018. The number of HCPs per 10,000 residents increased from 6.28 to 6.34, and the number of beds per 1,000 residents went up from 5.72 to 6.03. Besides, as the total visits rose significantly, the daily visits per doctor started to decline slightly in 2018.

Table 7 National workload of medical services

Type of provider	Visits (100M)		Inpatients (10,000)	
	2017	2018	2017	2018
Total	81.8	83.1	24436	25453
Hospital	34.4	35.8	18915	20017
Public	29.5	30.5	15595	16351
Private	4.9	5.3	3321	3666
Class: Class 3	17.3	18.5	8396	9292
Class 2	12.7	12.8	8006	8177
Class 1	2.2	2.2	1169	1209
Primary care unit	44.3	44.1	4450	4375
Others	3.1	3.2	1071	1061
Non-pubic providers within the total	18.4	18.9	3401	3737

Source: *China Health Development Statistics Bulletin* (2018).

In addition to building the hardware, the government might also need to further improve the supply of quality healthcare resources. To urban residents, especially those living in big cities, the so-called quality healthcare resources such as prestigious doctors, departments or hospitals are often difficult to access. With the development of the economy and the improvement of the per capita income, residents come to have higher requirements of the quality of medical services. Therefore, it is not enough to merely improve the hardware, but to develop a large number of trusted doctors and medical teams with high ethics and skills. To this end, the governments at all levels might need to keep building medical capabilities so as to produce more famous doctors, hospitals and departments, and increase the visiting rate of these quality healthcare resources. To expand the access to quality resources, developed countries generally advocate the allocation of these resources to small towns and rural areas. To China, it means to create mechanisms, opportunities and conditions that enable doctors or medical teams with exceptional expertise in 3A hospitals to assist primary care providers in diagnosis, treatment or surgery remotely, or to pay short-term visits to grassroots medical units. All this may help expand the residents' access to quality healthcare resources, improve the quality of diagnosis and treatment, and enhance patients' satisfaction with medical services.

Secondly, the government might need to increase and stabilize the basic medical insurance coverage, and do a good job in the use and management of medical insurance funds. According to the *National Statistical Bulletin on the Development of Basic Medical Security* (2018) released by the National Healthcare Security Administration (NHSA), 1.34459 billion people had participated in the National Basic Medical Insurance by 2018. With a participation rate of

over 95%, it already covered nearly the entire population. In 2018, the total income of the National Basic Medical Insurance Fund was CYN 2138.4 billion. The total expenditure was CYN 1782.2 billion, and the accumulated balance was CYN 2344 billion. Compared with that of 2017, both the income (+19.3%) and the expenditure (+23.6%) of the Fund increased, accounting for 2.4% and 2.0% respectively of the total GDP. The number of participants was increasing, so was the number of beneficiaries. Take the Basic Medical Insurance for Urban Employees as an example. There were up to 316.81 million participants in 2018 (+4.5%), while the number of reimbursements reached 1.98 billion (+9.0%). Meanwhile, to reduce the likelihood of disease-induced poverty, MOF has granted another CNY 8 billion for medical aid in areas of deep poverty over the past two years, and has achieved remarkable results.

Moreover, to ensure the safety of the Medical Insurance Fund, a special campaign against fraud on the Fund was carried out in 2018, and the illegal acquisition of the Fund was investigated and dealt with.

With the aging of the Chinese population, the Medical Insurance Fund may face the risk of deficit in the future. In 2018, CPIC Allianz Health Insurance and Ernst & Young issued the *White Paper on China's Commercial Health Insurance* and pointed out the risk. To reduce the pressure on the Fund, it is necessary to develop commercial health insurances, in line with the actual development needs of China.

Finally, the government might need to pay more attention to the management and improvement of residents' mental health, so as to further enhance the satisfaction with medical services. The tense and competitive urban life of our times brings great mental pressure on the residents. Feeling physically and psychologically drained, the residents are often in a sub-healthy

state. It is therefore necessary to provide the environment for entertainment and leisure, promote the public education on stress-reduction and sub-health rehab, and improve residents' perception and awareness of health from the perspective of humanistic care. All this will also help to increase residents' satisfaction with medical services.